Indelible Inequalities in Latin America

Indelible Inequalities in Latin America

Insights from History, Politics, and Culture

EDITED BY PAUL GOOTENBERG
AND LUIS REYGADAS

FOREWORD BY ERIC HERSHBERG

Duke University Press

Durham and London

2010

© 2010 Duke University Press
All rights reserved.
Printed in the United States of
America on acid-free paper ∞
Designed by Amy Ruth Buchanan
Typeset in Quadraat by
Keystone Typesetting, Inc.
Library of Congress Cataloging-
in-Publication Data appear on the
last printed page of this book.

CONTENTS

This book grew out of an exploratory project called Durable Inequalities in Latin America, funded by the Rockefeller Foundation and hosted at the Latin American and Caribbean Studies (LACS) Center at Stony Brook University between 2003–2006. The original idea was to take an urgent social problem—inequality in the Americas—one with a strong presence in the "social sciences," and revisit it with emerging humanistic, cultural, and historical perspectives. Stony Brook became a bustling interdisciplinary site, with six residential visiting fellows, most of them from Latin American universities, who sparked a wide dialogue with our faculty, graduate students, and other new inequality study groups. For if there was one thing we discovered during these years of debate, it was that inequality is now an issue with a deep resonance among scholars, activists, and communities across the hemisphere. The recent election of Barack Obama to the presidency of the United States, in 2008, presaged by the democratic turn to the Left in much of Latin America and by the Bush-era global economic collapse, should lend further momentum to anti-inequality movements. The moment to confront inequality is here, but we need new intellectual tools and mobilizing strategies to do it. This book is a modest attempt at this retooling.

In terms of resources, we need to thank the generosity of the Rockefeller Foundation's (now redefined) Program in Creativity and Culture, especially the vision of the program officers Tomás Ybarra-Frausto and Scott Mac-Dougall, who took a personal interest in the Stony Brook initiative, though it lay slightly off their usual map of concerns. Domenica Tafuro, our remarkable LACS administrative assistant, was active at all stages of the project—from helping to polish Gootenberg's first proposal as then LACS director, to welcoming the fellows at Stony Brook, to aiding in the final editing of this book. Other offices of the university also supported the project: especially the College of Arts and Sciences (under the deans Bob Liebermann and James Staros), Office of the Provost, Graduate School, Linda Merians in University Advancement, the Humanities Institute (HISB), and the Departments of History, Sociology, and Hispanic Languages and Literature. The most crucial individuals, besides our fellows, were an interdisciplinary team of "Latin Americanista" faculty who served on the selection committee and participated in seminars and a series of symposiums convened at Stony Brook's Manhattan site. Most notable were Javier Auyero (formerly of sociology, who first suggested inequality as our topic and who contributes to this volume), Katy Vernon (Hispanic languages), Fred Moehn (music), and Eduardo Mendieta (philosophy), as well as Tim Moran (sociology), Tracey Walters (Africana studies), Tom Klubock and Brooke Larson (history), and the anthropologists Pamela Block and Karen Kramer. Said Arjoman and E. Ann Kaplan served as program advisors. We are also indebted to Eric Hershberg, then at the Social Science Research Council (SSRC), who took an immediate interest in the initiative, served as the external member of the selection committee, participated in our events, linked us to other inequality study groups (such as the Princeton project of Jeremy Adelman and Miguel Centeno), and contributed the foreword to this collection. At one point, the legendary Columbia University sociologist Charles Tilly, who first lit this theme, played interlocutor to a memorable discussion at the SSRC around the "relational" and proactive nature of inequalities. Sadly, Tilly passed away in April 2008, as we were putting the final touches on this volume so influenced by his ideas. A string of graduate students in history worked as research assistants to the fellows: Gabriel Hernández, Consuelo Figueroa, Greg Jackson, Alberto Harambour, and Alexis Stern. Celina Bragagnolo, a graduate student in philosophy, helped with two of the book's translations. Martín Monsalve, a historian now doctored and teaching in Lima, did a savvy job of organizing the multilingual publicity and applications process for the Durable Inequalities program, which garnered scores of fascinating applicants from across the globe.

At the center of this collective learning experience were six interdisciplinary visiting scholars: Jeanine Anderson (Pontificia Universidad Católica del Perú), Luis Reygadas (Universidad Autónoma Metropolitana [UAM], Iztapalapa, Mexico), Lucio Renno (Universidade de Brasilia, Brazil), Odette Casamayor (Cuba, and now University of Connecticut, Storrs), Christina Ewig (University of Wisconsin, Madison), and Margaret Gray (Adelphi University), all represented in this volume. What a stimulating and committed team of colleagues! It is they who brought questions of inequality and now this book to life, born from papers presented at a fellows symposium held in May 2006.

Paul Gootenberg wants to especially thank his coeditor Luis Reygadas for his intellectual vision as well as his patience, insight, and skills in navigating the shared tasks of criticism and editing. Mexico City and New York are now linked by an anthropologist and a historian from different academic cultures, even if our home universities share the same "statist" architecture. In 2005 the Mexican anthropological journal *Alteridades* published some of this volume's essays in embryonic form in a special Spanish-language issue, "La desigualdad en América Latina" (14, no. 28 2004).

Luis Reygadas, in particular, wants to express his gratitude to the Universidad Autónoma Metropolitana, for providing the sabbatical year for his research leave in New York, and Stony Brook–LACS, which hosted him during 2003–2004 with a Rockefeller fellowship in the Durable Inequalities in Latin America program. Eduardo Mendieta made valued comments on the first draft of the essay Reygadas contributed to this volume. Gabriel Hernández, who is a living example of overcoming inequality, worked as Reygadas's research assistant at Stony Brook.

At Duke University Press, we thank Valerie Millholland for her timely nod to the project, as well as Miriam Angress, who was so indispensable in guiding the book through the editorial process. Many thanks to the excellent copy editor, Patricia Mickelberry, and to Amy Chazkel, who prepared the index. We also thank three insightful and sympathetic press readers, including John H. Coatsworth.

The Paradox of

Inequality in Latin America

ERIC HERSHBERG

At first glance there is something paradoxical about the stubborn persistence of inequalities in Latin America, a part of the planet that a recent sociological study labeled "the lopsided continent" (Hoffman and Centeno 2002). Military regimes have given way to civilian rulers almost everywhere in Latin America, but patron-client relationships endure throughout the region. Human rights are central to the rhetorical repertoire of governments, yet large segments of the population are routinely subjected to striking levels of everyday violence and brutality. The restoration of civilian rule over the past quarter century has given rise to new understandings of citizenship, including long-suppressed recognition of indigenous peoples and populations of African origins. Still, the rule of law is upheld unevenly, and discrimination pervades employment, education, and the judiciary. And if the integration of Latin America into global markets has created new opportunities for investment and employment, these opportunities for the most part present themselves unevenly, as evident in Gini coefficients that, as Luis Reygadas makes clear in his contribution to this volume, confirm strikingly unequal income distribution. In short, Latin America is experiencing an era of unprecedented social, political, and economic opening, yet this new environment coincides with—and perhaps even reinforces or exacerbates—longstanding, deeply entrenched dynamics of exclusion and inequality.

Seeking to make sense of current trends, some scholars have been tempted to conclude that underlying structures refined since the Iberian conquest have proven their enduring powers. Indeed, historians and others have often tended to invoke durable inequalities in Latin America as evidence of the intractable power of continuity to explain present conditions. Ironically, this misses what is so important about examining inequality since, in spite of the apparent timelessness of the gap between haves and have-nots, Latin America has also been the region where leaders, intellectuals, and social forces have most explicitly made inequality a matter of public debate and policy initiative.

The present volume thus fits into a long tradition of analytic inquiry and practical intervention. Pushing the boundaries of research on inequalities in Latin America, it encompasses studies that cross traditional disciplines from a variety of complementary perspectives and empirical foci. In so doing, the book identifies promising, intersecting themes that can help to illuminate both the nature of deeply embedded inequalities and the factors that foster their reproduction over time. The title's depiction of inequalities as "indelible" offers an apt metaphor for layered phenomena that endure as if imprinted on the region's DNA. Social scientists and humanists alike will find much to be gained from a reading of the individual chapters and of the volume as a whole. The book is sure to have appeal for teaching as well as for scholarly research.

A crucial recognition of this volume, and of the research fellowship program at Stony Brook University from which it arose, is that inequality has never been limited to simply the economic sphere. Whether conceived in terms of access to information, which Lucio Renno shows in this book to be profoundly unequal, or in terms of the policies of welfare-state regimes, which Christina Ewig reveals in her essay as producing systematic gender bias, inequalities pervade political and social domains as well. Nor is inequality a phenomenon that can be adequately grasped exclusively through quantitative methods. The divides that separate groups into what the late sociologist Charles Tilly (1998) articulated as "bounded categories," which operate through discursive and performative mechanisms, are no less important than the factors rooted in differential control over tangible resources. This is one reason why it is essential to bring insights from the humanities to bear on fields normally reserved for social scientists. Odette Casamayor's analysis of popular culture in contemporary Cuba reinforces this point, as does Jeanine Anderson's textured treatment of everyday life in impoverished neighborhoods of Lima. What is clear throughout is that inequality is more than just a "cause" of moral outrage: when social actors see themselves as historical victims of inequality, they engage in a gamut of distributional and symbolic struggles. In so doing they acquire or change social identities. It is by examining the everyday forms of (re-)making inequality that scholars can reveal the activities of groups as they created, developed, or dismantled collective identities in ways that defined their relationship to other social forces and to the state (Joseph and Nugent 1994). A focus on everyday interactions also illuminates the workings of institutional mechanisms through which groups are set apart from one another, whether inside entities such as the workplace or across organizational space.[1]

Latin America is a wealthy region in which resources are horribly distributed. Contrary to much conventional wisdom, what ails Latin America today is not poverty alone, which remains rampant but which affects a declining portion of the population, nor is it economic stagnation, which is conjunctural, if not infrequent. Rather, the specifically Latin American dilemma is the intractable persistence of inequality and the scarcity of mechanisms for reducing the gulf between haves and have-nots, rich and poor, insiders and outsiders. The unequal distribution of valuable resources, money, information, status, and opportunity permeates politics and social life.

That this appears to be the case in periods of prosperity as well as during the region's recurrent bouts of economic decline undoubtedly has much to do with the revived fortunes of the Latin American Left, which in the first decade of the twenty-first century has experienced a series of electoral victories that challenge longstanding inequalities in the sphere of the polity. The discourse of successful presidential candidates (Lula in Brazil, Evo Morales in Bolivia, Fernando Lugo in Paraguay), as well as that of aspirants who nearly achieved victories at the polls (Ullanta Humala in Peru, Andrés Manuel López Obrador in Mexico), has centered in large measure around the scourge of inequality. Yet as much as they suggest an empowerment of long-excluded constituencies, the inroads achieved by the Latin American Left have failed so far to engender tangible progress toward reversing economic inequalities. In some quarters, this generates pessimistic conclusions about the limitations of civilian-led competitive political systems across the region (Robinson 2006), while for other observers it jeopardizes the consolidation of democracy itself (Smith 2005).

Skepticism as to the prospects for achieving meaningful redistribution through representative government has motivated a growing number of subaltern actors to abandon the preoccupation with liberal citizenship, opting to reimagine questions of rights in radically different ways. Indeed, it could be argued that the expression of frequently suppressed collective identities—most notably nowadays in the central Andes, but evident in the practices of social movements across much of the region—is simply the latest of the countless ways in which inequalities have been framed along ethnic and racial lines throughout centuries of Latin American history (Wade 1997; Yashar 1999). By framing their demands in terms of categorical differences, as exemplified by the confrontation between indigenous and mestizo in Bolivia, subaltern populations may ironically in the end reinforce the very identities that their historic antagonists have drawn on in order to set themselves apart from, and above, those who are by such definition intrinsically different.

A core message of this volume is that inequalities are relational, which suggests that understanding them requires attention to elite behavior as well as to dynamics in the broader society. Drawing effectively on the insightful work of Tilly, the authors in this collection reiterate that inequality does not exist because it is natural; rather, it persists because it is produced and reproduced over time, and this involves relationships within and between groups, as well as institutional mechanisms that reinforce and channel conflicts to produce distributive outcomes. The idea that inequalities are "reinforced" is particularly crucial in Tilly's analysis: interactions shaped within institutions coincide with category divides that cross-cut the domains of social life. Such a dynamic is clearly in play in Christina Ewig's exploration of the ethnic and gendered dimensions of welfare-state regimes.

In turn, the institutionalization of bounded categories has been explicitly contested, enforced, and reshaped over time. Indeed, looking at inequality through the great shifts in the identification of collective actors, under sharply different models of capitalism and various types of political regimes, compels one to see inequality as a multifaceted process rather than as a fixed condition.

Whether expressed in terms of "nations" inserted into the world economy in ways that transfer wealth to rich countries; in terms of classes locked in a struggle for control of the workplace and thus seeking to enforce or redress property relations; or in terms of political subjects with unequal rights who are thus trying to expand or redefine the terms of political membership along gender, ethnic, and regional lines, resistance to inequalities has been a basic catalyst to social mobilization. At times, resistance has undermined democracy; at other times, it has contributed to the restoration and even the strengthening of democracy.

Latin America today is replete with examples of popular mobilizations around emerging categories of identity that reflect experiences of inequality and that have ambiguous implications for democratic development. Consider the widespread protests of public-sector employees, who throughout most of Latin America find their long-fought-for middle-class status to be jeopardized by market-oriented reforms that expose them to extreme degrees of economic risk.[2] Or witness the support that the Venezuelan president Hugo Chávez has received from shantytown dwellers, whose networks have been essential as a bulwark for his regime, but whose precursors and identities go back to the upheavals of the late 1950s, which toppled the dictatorship of General Pérez Jiménez. These shantytown movements must be understood in ways that go beyond the common view of them as spasmodic reactions of basically atomized and marginalized masses to material deprivation. Rather, these movements and the reactions they elicit reflect the acute divisions that separate rich and poor, privileged and excluded, and the particular ways in which these are articulated at specific moments in time. An important insight to be gleaned from Margaret Gray's contribution to this volume is that these divisions, and the identities and movements they spawn, are increasingly transnational in nature, encompassing Latin Americans living as migrants in the north as well as those who live in their countries of origin.

If democracies are to foster the development of more inclusive societies, in which citizenship is more equally distributed than has been the case up to the present, the problem of inequalities will need to rise to the front and center of governmental agendas. Whether this comes to pass will hinge in large measure on the degree to which Latin American societies broadly reject the persistence of vast expanses of discrimination and exclusion. One is reminded here of Albert Hirschman's classic formulation (1973) concerning shifting levels of tolerance for inequalities. Contributors to this volume offer grounds for cautious optimism: inequalities have made it onto the Latin American agenda, and important books such as this one will ensure that the topic remains in the public eye. If fresh perspectives on inequalities open the way to tangible social and political changes, the paradox to which we have alluded may finally be overcome, and inequalities may prove less indelible than they have been thus far.

Notes

This foreword draws on ideas developed in an essay prepared in collaboration with Jeremy Adelman, which gave rise to a project on "paradoxical inequalities" at Princeton University, as well as on ongoing exchanges with participants in the Stony Brook University project from which this volume emerged.

1. This distinction follows Tilly's (1998, chap. 3) consideration of internal and external categories.
2. Of course, as an anonymous reviewer pointed out, public employees may also

monopolize resources that might otherwise be directed toward meeting the needs of the most disadvantaged segments of the population. Interpreted in Tillyian terms (1998, chap. 5), public-sector employees, and indeed formal-sector workers as a whole, engage in "opportunity hoarding" in order to capture rents and thus to maintain their comparatively privileged status.

PART I

New Approaches,

Old Disciplines

Latin American Inequalities

New Perspectives from History, Politics, and Culture

PAUL GOOTENBERG

As an introduction to this volume, this essay broadly paints Latin American inequalities onto their larger canvas of politics and scholarship. Latin America's historically defining inequalities cry out for newer and sustained kinds of historical, political, and cultural analyses, ones to complement the largely social and structural-reformist frameworks common to past understandings of inequality. This introduction then charts the way to a series of bold essays written by a working group of inter-American scholars that, from a variety of disciplinary angles, grapples with the task of thinking anew the many dimensions and legacies of indelible inequalities.

The Weight of Inequalities

Latin America is in fact a critical region for the global study of inequalities. Neither the poorest nor the most culturally divided region of the world, Latin America is by far the most unequal. By standard social indicators (cross-national Gini coefficients), Latin America is much more unequal than Asia, Africa, and of course the post-industrial West (Inter-American Development Bank [IDB] 1999). These measurements derive from wage differentials and thus overlook other material factors (such as wealth or the instability of work) that further skew the region's opportunity structures. In a vivid daily sense, Latin Americans live and see these disparities in how they do politics, build urban spaces, work the land, join new and older social movements, experience crime and environmental stress, and access educational, nutritional, healthcare, legal, cultural, and media resources. The problem lies not simply in the existence of rampant poverty in the region—during the last decade, some 210 million (or 40 percent of) Latin Americans fell in that category of distress—but in the more conveniently ignored other part of the problem: the region's extraordinarily wealthy and politically sheltered upper classes. The wealthiest 5 percent of the population hoards a quarter of total income, making some nations—such as Brazil or Guatemala—among the most unequal places on earth (IDB 1999; Korzeniewicz and Smith 2000). Few exceptions stand out against the typical Latin American pattern. Only Uruguay, Costa Rica, and Trinidad support reasonably egalitarian societies in the region, and even relatively developed economies such as Argentina and Colombia have recently experienced sharp increases in social inequality, which has ignited internecine conflicts and governability crises. Even Cuba, after its flurry of initial revolutionary redistributive programs, has suffered renewed inequality over the last decade (during its post-Soviet crisis), replete with new signs of racial and gender discrimination. Latin America's inequalities are not just or simply a matter of underdevelopment, poverty, or bad policy—they run much deeper.

Since the very birth of European colonialism, Latin America has likely been the zone of the sharpest global inequalities—the veritably eternal land of contrasts—between privilege and destitution. Historical evidence remains impressionistic, though historians have long grasped the larger picture. Caste divisions born from the Spanish Conquest (in Mesoamerica and the Andes) and African slavery (in Brazil and the Caribbean) hardened during centuries of colonialism; through the advent of two dozen independent republics and the liberal export-capitalism of the nineteenth century, such inequalities eventually transformed into class, cultural, and citizenship differentials, but carried forth anew (Burns 1983; Thurner 1997). Twentieth-century modernities (urbanization, mass culture, industrialism), active liberation movements (agrarian-reform, populist, democratic, and revolutionary), and now globalization, neoliberalism, and even emergent reactions to them have done little to change Latin America's historical inequality, despite the high hopes invested in all these ideas and programs (e.g., Eckstein [1977] 1988). In fact, from the 1980s to the 1990s Latin America suffered deepening social gaps, during the so-called lost decade of development, with no clear sign of relief at the start of the twenty-first century. Latin American inequality is a disturbing paradigm for the resilience of oppressive and dysfunctional social systems.

The key words "durable inequality" come from the renowned sociologist Charles Tilly's recent book of that title (1998). Tilly challenges scholars and citizens alike to confront the centrality of inequalities in modern societies: "categorical inequalities," shaped by relational processes, boundary-making, and resilient social bonds. Inequality assumes a bewildering array of concrete forms: of wealth, income, and opportunity; of gender, race, age, region, and ethnicity. Hierarchies of power, education, technology, language, culture, honor, beliefs, and influence pervade individuals, groups, and nations, perhaps more than anytime in history. Tilly's book is part of a new movement to reclaim, in subtle ways, the methodological vitality of the social in cultural and historical analysis, as a foil to the methodological individualism of mainstream North American social science and to some variants of the "cultural turn."[1] However, with his stress on relational structures, Tilly himself tends to downplay the cultural, historical, or global dimensions of inequality.

Latin American inequality is certainly durable in Tilly's sense, as well as being historically, socially, and culturally "constructed," which suggests the unnatural origins of hierarchy and subordination. But we prefer in this volume the guiding term "indelible inequalities," which underscores the human agency and culture at play in their creation and perseverance, their complexity and camouflage beyond stark categorical divides, and their fluid and peopled possibilities of change. Historically, indelible legacies are difficult to erase, but they are not structurally ordained or inevitable. Indelibility also implies that inequality is no longer the sole domain of model-building and data-crunching social scientists. But neither can indelible inequality be wished away, from the other academic shore, simply by a new critical discourse or a postmodern imagination, as useful as these may be for overcoming teleological understandings of poverty, development, or progress (Escobar 1995). In cultural-history terms, recognizing the indelibilty of inequalities may help unveil the larger commonalities behind ephemeral or essentialized fissures of racial, class, or gender discrimination and difference. It is also a move, one hopes, beyond the often non-analytical particularism of academic "identity politics" (Brubaker and Cooper 2000) and its analogous new "ethnic politics." Foucauldian-inspired cultural studies has heightened awareness of culturally construed, power-laden realities, and those insights are useful to grasp why inequalities continue to pervade social, cultural, and political edifices. A focus on inequalities interrogates how diverse societies and cultures have reproduced (tolerated and elided, contested or altered) hierarchy over the long term. Study of indelible inequalities helps center the social, historical, and cultural issues at the heart of Latin American studies, but not as a monolithic paradigm or research agenda.

Inequality is now a global concern. If the twentieth-century world was marked by fundamental struggles over the "color line" (race and colonial-ism) and the conflict between capitalism and socialism, the new century may well be defined by multiple global struggles over inequality. Concerned inter-national organizations such as the Inter-American Development Bank (Igle-sias 1992; IDB 1999) and the World Bank (Stiglitz 2002; de Ferranti et al. 2004), economists and social scientists, agenda-setting foundations, and prescient public thinkers are beginning to trace the new profile of this global dilemma. Inequalities are not fading away with twenty-first-century "global-ization"; in fact, it is quite the opposite, with most observers predicting that disparities will widen along with global informational processes of change, which generally lower labor costs and reward high-tech, capitalized, and edu-cated strata and migrants both within and between nation-states. For exam-ple, intensified global migration, rather than narrowing income and cultural gaps, has tended to create more heterogeneous pools of exploited minorities. Significantly, unlike eighteenth- or nineteenth-century humanism and liber-alism, the current wave of historical globalization barely tries to legitimate itself by making universal equality claims, beyond equal access to markets, regardless of equity outcomes. This agnostic stance is now evoking an intel-lectual and ethical backlash. Such global cultural fragmenting and its ratio-nalizers have not escaped the notice of respected sociocultural analysts (such as Appadurai, Harvey, and Jameson), who read the postmodern global condi-tion precisely in terms of these intensifying and kaleidoscopic inequalities.

Another factor in play is steeply rising inequality (and a growing tolerance for such) in the United States, which already holds the position of an outlier in post-industrial societies. In the so-called New Economy since the 1980s, 47 percent of income gains accrued to the top 1 percent of families (Wolff [1995] 2001; Lardner and Smith 2006). With the erosion of its mid-twentieth-century fiscal policies, industrial base, and blue-collar working class, the United States now has a wealth-distribution profile that approaches those of Latin America, with the upper 5 percent hoarding nearly half of all national assets. Illustrative of the social impact of these developments, average life expectan-cies in the United States, while longer, are now demonstrably more unequal. These shifts have occurred alongside the abandonment of hard-won social-welfare policies, freer hemispheric trade (North American Free Trade Agree-ment and its emulations), and the arrival of a new generation of unskilled immigrant workers, most of whom are refugees from Latin American and Caribbean inequalities and who are forming new classes of categorical in-equalities. The United States's own global cities (Sassen 1991) now exhibit

Third World extremes, with homelessness, hunger, street bazaars, resurgent diseases of poverty, and the specter of terrorism. A flurry of academic critiques of North American inequalities (Jacobs and Skocpol 2005) note the paradox, so familiar to Latin Americanists, that social distances have widened in the same era as the expansion of individual rights (civil rights, multiculturalism, gender equity), and that rising inequalities are, Latin American-style, eroding prospects for political equality and the democratic process in the United States. Inequality has become an open topic of debate in major political campaigns, with those who speak out on the issue being labeled "populists." The Latin American experience governing harsh inequalities may have much to say now to North Americans, and also about the possible linkages between Latin Americans and North Americans.

Finally, there are both scholarly and real-world movements to contest inequalities, driven by the recognition that not all hierarchies are created by material conditions alone, with concerns such as gender, sexual orientation, nature, indigenous and cultural autonomy, and human rights. The contributors to this volume refer not only to the long-vaunted "new" social movements of Latin America (Alvarez and Escobar 1992) or to the developed world's motley antiglobalization forces, long laying low after 9/11. There are multiple voices: a decade-old post-Marxist discussion, rooted in Latin American labor and civic rights, of "open-economy social democracy" (Roxborough 1992; Castañeda 1993); and sociological specialists on inequality who call for the "high road to globalization" for Latin America, including equity, sustainability, and social-capital initiatives (Korzeniewicz and Smith 2000). There are surprising Latin American cases, such as Costa Rica, which have grasped equality-enhancing environmental and upgrading technological niches in the new global order; there are also the recent successes of Chile, a nation traditionally marked by inequality, in combining export dynamism with poverty-alleviation programs. During Mexico's post-2000 democratic transition, a devoted capitalist president, supported by key nongovernmental organizations (NGOs), embraced as a path out of Mexico's persistent inequalities *micro-empresa* experiments reminiscent of those of Peru's neo-capitalist intellectual Fernando da Soto (de Soto 1986), and gaping Mexican class divisions framed the controversies of the country's 2006 presidential election. The Brazilian president Lula de Silva's now second-phase social-democratic experiment is bringing the subject of inequality openly into an expanding public sphere; Bolivia's centuries-silent have-nots have somehow reached the apex of their wobbly state; whereas in Venezuela inequality politics dons a more traditional uniform. Inequalities are fueling the early-twenty-first-century return of Left-leaning and nationalist politics to Latin America, but it is unclear how much these new regimes will be able to do to redress the problems that generated them, given the political and economic constraints of the post-1980s global order (Hershberg and Rosen 2006; Drake and Hershberg 2006). But one cannot approach inequalities in the Americas from the dismal standpoint of the region's apparent stubborn social realities alone, in the spirit of "fracaso-mania"—the political economist Albert O. Hirschman's wise lament of Latin American policy fatalism (Hirschman 1972). One must also seek out and embrace emerging ideas, possibilities, or utopistics (Wallerstein 1998) of hope and change.

Shifting Scholarly Paradigms

Much has been said and written about inequality in the Latin American context. In the academy at large, the issue of inequality has suddenly assumed a central urgency: the 2008 Presidential Address of the American Historical Association was titled "Developing Inequality" (Weinstein 2008), the American Anthropological Association meeting of 2007 focused on inequality and difference, and the Latin American Studies Association adopted the keynote theme "Rethinking Inequalities" for its international congress in 2009. For Latin America, inequality may have been the overriding, if rarely explicit, motif of the region since 1492. Scholarly works also point to major omissions: the construction of inequality over long historical transitions, the nonmaterial bases of inequality, and the seemingly indelible politics and cultures of inequality.

In disciplinary terms, economists and political scientists staked out the most explicit studies of inequality and are among the most methodologically conservative of social-science researchers. During the mid-twentieth century, economics discourse on inequality was dominated by debate of the "Kuznets curve": the notion that developing countries faced a necessary trade-off between accumulation (or growth) and distribution. The policy lesson, taken all too well in Latin America, was that countries should throw themselves into rapid, large-scale development and only later worry about equity. In today's era of waning neoliberalism, paradoxically, an opposing view has emerged; investments in social and human capital or in democratic and micro-institutions are now believed to potentially spur economic growth. In part this reflects better knowledge, since no strong correlations were ever found between growth and inequality. It also reflects the example of East Asia, which with its more equalitarian postwar societies, and even distributional reform, managed to far outperform Latin America, at least until the late 1990s (Haggard and Kaufman 2008; Amsden 2005). Future studies will likely reinforce the idea that distribution is largely neutral to growth prospects, yet inequality still indirectly affects political stability, the sustainability of development, and the efficacy of the state. Among economists, a small group of Latin Americanists always valorized equity concerns. Developmentalists such as Rosemary Thorp, whose economic history of Latin America for the Inter-American Development Bank (IDB) focuses on the quality of growth and on social exclusion, draw from the Latin American structuralist tradition of the Comisión Económica para América Latina y el Caribe (CEPAL). In a provocative classic essay Albert O. Hirschman shifted the dilemma to subjectivities: under what conditions do people long tolerate growing maldistribution? Do aspirations count in economic equations? (Hirschman 1981). There is plenty of new thinking to go around in economics. The Nobel Laureate Amartyra Sen is reconsidering development as qualitative enhancements of human capacities and freedoms (Sen 1999); retired World Bank economists offer sharp critiques of inequality-producing globalization (Stiglitz 2002); United Nations development agencies now routinely employ broad-based "human development" standards that encompass benchmarks for equality.

Latin American political scientists have long concerned themselves with the functioning or stability of political systems under constraints of inequality. A core concept has been clientelism or "populism": vertical urban or rural mobilizations of the poor unthreatening to the status quo. Modernization theorists focused on the nebulous Latin American "middle sectors" in political regimes, eliding the key problem of the region's two extremes of wealth and poverty (Johnson 1958). During the 1970s, the bureaucratic authoritarianism school of Latin Americanist analysis, led by Guillermo O'Donnell, posited a necessary pervasive link between regressive distribution, industrialization, and that era's systematized military repression. A vigorous debate contested much of bureaucratic-authoritarian theory, including its underlying economic determinism (Collier 1979). In the 1990s, and with the return of tenuous and narrow democracies to the region, more scholars turned to the timely dilemma of how to consolidate democratization or governance in conditions of deep inequality (Tulchin 2001). Others looked at movements pitted against regimes of inequality (Rubin 1997), even among so-called marginals and "informal" sectors, including symbolic and unstructured events such as popular subsistence riots. The postwar concept "political culture" has also been resurrected (Jacobsen and Aljovín de Losada 2005), now as a means to critically grasp the historical formation of deeply divided polities in the region.

Sociologists are intimately concerned with inequalities, in part because it was their pioneering task to measure and theorize inequality at multiple social levels—individual, community, national, and international (van den Burghe and Primov 1977). Sociology has also opened to "hermeneutics," that is, how it is that people interpret their own social worlds and predicaments, and act on them collectively, and how subjective notions of class, gender, or race are enacted and performed. A recent line of inquiry harks to the "symbolic interaction" tradition to analyze how equality and inequality are experienced and constructed around people from within and without (Harris 2000, 2006). The "intersectionality" of subordination categories of class, race, and gender has emerged as a new branch of social analysis. The considerable Latin American "social movements" literature, which looks at how poor people come to contest barriers, has a primarily sociological or ethnographic tilt (Edelman 1999; Auyero 2000). Recently, many sociologists have also engaged the powerful theoretical tools of Foucault and Bourdieu: the former helps one to grasp invisible everyday threads of power; the latter, the gamut of distributable inequalities. Bourdieu's chief contribution is in accelerating the shift from strictly material definitions of unequal power to other kinds of allotments and struggles over social, cultural, or political capital. Besides this sociocultural turn, sociologists of Latin America ponder why "grand theories" of society fail to fit or make sense under historical conditions of sharp inequality (see esp. Centeno and López-Alves 2001). There is, as well, Tilly's *Durable Inequalities*, a work analyzed ahead that inspires this book.

An entire essay could be dedicated to surveying how historians, like myself, have placed inequality in Latin American history. It is a tacit theme underlying the majority of historical work on the region. Inequality is often considered as a constant that replicates itself across periodizations (though some historians note eras of social "de-compression" or remote frontier zones with relative social fluidity). Late Pre-Columbian states, Aztecs and Incas, were hierarchically organized yet developed distinctive ideologies to mask their unequal modalities of rule (Katz 1972). The Conquest built on such structures of domination and subordination in the Spanish core colonies; Europeans also imported feudalistic and caste distinctions into their domains, quickly coming to define Indian or African slaves as natural inferiors. In colonial historiography, the concentration of land and labor resources becomes a central motif, as befits a rural society more unequal than early modern Europe itself (Gibson 1964). Catholic and baroque cultural and religious projects reified these colonial hierarchies. The expanding historiography of the nineteenth century follows how such social distances fared under national ruling groups, new states, and export capitalism. A key thesis of research by social historians is that in Latin America market forces and juridical liberalism have worked primarily to reinforce inequality, rather than to attenuate it. Resources and influence accrued to the wealthy and Europeanized, who monopolized emerging individual citizenship claims against subaltern actors, or alternative political projects (Burns 1983; Tutino 1989; Mallon 1995). Positivist and racialist doctrines of progress paved this postcolonial oligarchic path. For the twentieth century, there is mounting research on class, gender, and race in the making of national hegemonies over diverse and divided populations. Historians are also actively exploring how modernity projects—including national and social revolutions—spawned new inclusions and exclusions, often based on the reworking of extant categories of subordination (Ferrer 1999; Joseph and Nugent 1994; Rosemblatt 2000). Others track how regional and racial inequalities become spatially mapped onto national histories (Appelbaum 2003; Weinstein 2008). Eclectic by nature, historians privilege by trade the long term and often "continuity" itself, but they often lack the theoretical tools to grapple with extremely long-range problems (Adelman 1999; Stein and Stein 1970), such as the reproduction of inequality in Latin America. Here, much can be learned from sustained sociological or cultural analysis.

Economic historians of Latin America have been less concerned with equality than they could have been, and the field now finds itself more narrowly defined than during its height in the 1960s and 1970s (Gootenberg 2004). Many generally assume that neoclassical factor endowments (land-intensity, coercive labor rents, mineral resources) left by the Conquest period lie behind the region's long-term inequalities, a structural view that could use a more dynamic sociology of power. Recent institutionalists suggest that weak and imperfect economic institutions, such as credit markets or property rights, distorted Latin American opportunity structures though the nineteenth century, reinforcing monopolies or class privileges, or that historical caste discrimination or slavery was itself a drag on market dynamism or industrialization (Glade 1969; Haber, Razo, and Maurer 2003; Engerman and Sokoloff 1997). From the 1950s to the 1970s, Latin American "structuralists," historical economists such as Brazil's Celso Furtado, openly grappled with maldistribution. It was seen as a major "obstacle" to industrialization, which would, it was hoped, offer greater equity. The structuralists characterized the region as structurally heterogeneous, with inequalities that impeded well-integrated markets, an economic concept resembling the later culturalist idea of "hybrid cultures." Structuralists also subscribed to the Lewis dual-economy models of postwar developmental economists: that Third World agrarian structures possessed pools of low-productivity "traditional" labor that could be tapped in modern urban pursuits or redressed by comprehensive agrarian reform (Griffin 1969; Furtado 1970). However, the region's economic experience since 1950 does not support dual-economy models, much less hopes of costless industrialization or better distribution via migration, given import substitution's bias against agriculture (and the environment) and the mass exodus from the countryside into urban, low-productivity, informal employment. The distributive gains of industrialism, or those of agrarian reform where tried, proved short-lived.

In short, Latin American modernization projects did not alleviate historical inequalities, though some notable advances occurred in public heath (life span) or education (where the regional gender gap has narrowed) (Hirschman 1987). Nor, of course, did the manifold crises of development after 1980 do anything but exacerbate inequality. In the present crisis of neoliberalism, in which many Latin American economies have stagnated under its persistent pro-market prescriptions, economic structuralists are stirring anew about equitable development (Love 2005).

Finally, economic history was famously invoked during the dependency and kindred neo-Marxist mode-of-production debates of the 1970s. André Gunder Frank's *Capitalism and Underdevelopment in Latin America* (1967) assailed liberal dogmas about social dualism and their historical corollary about Latin American "feudalism" (i.e., that Latin American backwardness and social inequalities were retrograde leftovers of feudalistic colonialism). Instead, *dependentistas* implicated "modernization" and market integration itself, arguing that Latin America has been fully capitalist since its incorporation into the world economy in the sixteenth century. Thus, greater modernization would not help; only a full retreat from world capitalism would suffice. Dependentistas situated Latin America's unjust social relations within a decidedly global context. Most of the heated historical debates and research sparked by issues of dependency concerned North-South disparities, but some of them beneficially complicated long-held assertions about internal agrarian social relations on both sides of the feudal-capitalist debate (Frank 1967; Love 1996; Duncan and Routledge 1977). After 1989, such conceptions of underdevelopment (with their own suspect ordering teleology) fell out of favor among the Latin Americanist Left, deservedly or not. Recently, however, a few sober economic historians have begun revisiting older structuralist and dependency debates with a sharper eye on inequality. John Coatsworth (2005), as one prominent example, has observed over the long-term a perverse relationship in Latin America between exports and inequality: the economies of Latin America do profit historically from integration with the world economy, yet almost always with the cost of rising inequality.

Anthropologists also come face-to-face with inequality and were especially long active in fieldwork to unearth the microdynamics of unequal relations in Latin America (Lewis 1961; Murphy and Stepick 1991). Through inventive cross-disciplinary and historical work, anthropologists long ago overcame the culture of poverty or "folk-modern" binaries of mid-twentieth-century social science, a cultural framework analogous to the "dual-economy" thesis once used to explain or justify growing inequality in modernizing nations. By the 1970s, anthropologists had joined Latin American sociologists in their concern with macrosocial questions, such as those advanced by the dependency-inspired internal colonialism thesis, which sought to illustrate how "minorities" such as Indian peasants suffered asymmetric exploitation over extended periods by central elites and nation-states. Paradoxically, ethnicity per se was downplayed in this era of salient class analysis, even among cultural anthropologists. Two recent exemplars of historical anthropology show the dramatic return of race and ethnicity in relation to inequality: Marisol de la Cadena's *Indigenous Mestizos* (2000) and Deborah Poole's *Vision, Race and Modernity* (1997). Both books work on the puzzle of how racial and cultural categories coalesce over the long term. One sees cultural difference, the other visual representation, as paradoxical modern building blocks in changing Andean pyramids of discrimination and domination. Anthropologists thus use inequality as a barometer for critical examination of cultural distinctions. In a notable new anthropological reading, Charles Hale (2006) sees the rise of ethnic cultural politics in parts of Latin America as "neoliberal multiculturalism" and as a cheap means to divert claims from redistributive economic rights. And in a deeply historical vein, anthropologist Claudio Lomnitz questions the scholarly mania for Benedict Anderson's culturalist "imagined communities": in Latin America's long history, vertical, group, and dependent ties, rather than individual fraternal bonds of imagined equality, have been the sinews of the affective as well as the real nation (Lomnitz 2001b; Benedict Anderson [1983] 1995).

Finally, recent years have witnessed an explosion of fresh literary, cultural, and humanistic approaches to Latin America, with the ethics of unequal cultural practice and cultural citizenship becoming a leading concern. This power-sensitive new cultural studies is thus converging with the increasingly interpretive social sciences. Literary specialists trace and critique how changing literary canons divide nations and cultural agency by gender, region, and race (Sommers 1991; Shumway 1991; Moreiras 2001). Silenced subjects outside the regional canon are being heard in testimonial and ethnographic voices; other literary theorists explore how politics and social exclusion construct cultural consumption and the ways that genres and identities perform or transgress cultural authority. Postmodern, postcolonial, and globalization debates are critically read in the light of highly heterogeneous societies that seemingly exist in multiple and divergent times and spaces. Feminist scholars unpack the conundrums of private and public "sameness/difference."[2] A rich essay in Mexican cultural studies, La jaula de la melancolía (Bartra 1987; or Lomnitz 2001a), exemplifies new critical approaches to national mythologies and to the durability of cultural identities across historical change. Whether the excluded of Mexico constitute a deep or silenced country turns on more than semantics. For contemporary Latin Americanists, the dominant paradigm, in play or for general critique, is "hybridity" (García Canclini [1989] 1991; Dussel 1998; Moreiras 2001). The continuing stress on difference, "alterity," or "multiculturalism" contrasts with the official nationalist mestizaje (culture blending) of mid-twentieth-century nation states, as well as with homogenizing narratives of cultural imperialism and globalization.

In sum, these new tools of cultural analysis are crucial for interpreting Latin American inequality, as they enrich the more explicit and elaborated structural or social theories of inequality. In what ways do hybrid cultural fragments and subjects relate to, blend into, or resist relations of inequality?

Recent inequality models from social-scientific camps such as economics and politics are actually becoming *less* deterministic, allowing an opening to further interdisciplinary research and thinking about inequalities.
The "interpretive turn" in such converging human sciences as history, anthropology, and sociology also broadens the common ground between culture, politics, and history. Can these softer tools help us better grasp such
inequality-related categories as factor endowments, social capital, or exter-
nally or internally bounded identities? On the other hand, a more theorized
social or relational sensibility from the social sciences may help illuminate
how identity-based hybridities are made and passed along as constructed
categorical inequalities over the long term. These kinds of Tillyesque durable
inequalities may well characterize the Américas as a cultural and social
whole. Just as "underdevelopment" served as a unifying and mobilizing
paradigm for Latin America during the Cold War developmental decades
after 1950, inequality may be the ethical and political calling of our times. To
paraphrase Brazil's former president (and former dependency theorist) Fernando Henrique Cardoso, "underdeveloped" no longer captures the essence
of Latin American societies; they are, instead, now fundamentally "unjust"
societies. Redressing social injustice requires a broader set of perspectives—
normative, humanistic, interpretive, and historical—to complement the received social-scientific toolbox, and here interdisciplinary Latin Americanists may make a contribution as distinctive as the development thinkers of a
generation before.

What Now

Inequality represents a vast and complex terrain of Latin America's history,
society, and culture, though it is still rarely undertaken as an explicit topic of
study. Latin American scholars can help to shape a new academic discourse
about inequality and power in Latin America and encourage scholarship that
actively contests across civil society the region's many indelible inequalities.
Conventional approaches to inequality persist—more sensitive and broader
indicators, ameliorative public policies (about poverty, governance, or empowerment)—but over the last decades, even in the face of rising inequalities, they have not won the wider audience or the constituencies needed,
though there are encouraging signs in the region's turn to a working Left
politics in Brazil, Argentina, Bolivia, Chile, and elsewhere. Using the social-
science traditions, we will extend social inequality studies and critiques in

new and particularly more historical, political, and cultural directions. Above all, the research agenda beyond durable inequalities poses questions that make explicit and fundamental the long-term construction, cultures, and reproduction of inequalities. The inequalities research represented in this volume pursued, in some from or another, eight key areas of study.

—*The Historical Long-Term*: How and when do invented, fluid, or temporal categories of inequality—constructed on caste, gender, class, race, region—become durable ones? How do such identities or boundaries intersect in making persisting or double inequalities?

—*Hybridity and Difference*: How do hybridity, diversity, and difference, common cultural terms across the Americas, become transformed into markers and hierarchies of inequality? Conversely, how do relational inequalities impinge on cultural difference? Is difference ever neutral or equal? When does sameness mask imbalances of peoples and cultures?

—*Transitions and Metamorphosis*: How do inequalities survive or shift forms during periods of political and social stress or rupture (postcolonial regimes, revolutions, coups and restorations, new global orders?) What are their specific mechanisms, processes, or dialectics of continuity?

—*Agency and Resistance*: How do long-privileged sectors protect, justify, camouflage, and protect bonds of social, political, and cultural inequality? Conversely, how and when do subaltern actors come to recognize and contest such bonds or justification narratives of inequality? Can agency also mark or leave new boundaries of inequality?

—*Transnational Flows of Ideas and Peoples*: How do universalizing ideals of equality, or of naturalized hierarchy, traverse the Americas? How do historical contacts and now accelerating flows of peoples reinforce, or sometimes loosen, constructed inequalities? How do North-South power disparities intersect with locally entrenched inequalities?

—*Inequality as Culture*: What is the location of Latin American inequality? What makes it so seemingly diffuse, stubborn, indelible? What theoretical toolkits or combinations of tools work best for its study? How can abstracted cultural knowledge aid actors and activists?

—*Qualitative Equalities*: How do the novel qualitative social-science norms relate to equalities and to new identity movements and liberation politics in the Americas? How can a cultural stress on differences—of race, gender, creed, position—transform into new thinking on equality?

—*Revolutionizing Inequalities*: How can Latin American civil society—itself rife with difference inequalities—place the need for greater equality onto political agendas? How can equality movements link or relate on equal terms with global forces for change (nongovernmental organizations, movements, institutions)? What can North Americans grasp about their own current predicaments from the long Latin American experience with indelible inequalities?

This new dialogue about inequality between North-South scholars does not simply replicate datasets or policy recommendations, which already exist abundantly in governmental, civic, and academic proposals (see Chalmers et al. 1997; IDB 1999; de Ferranti et al. 2004). An inequalities focus galvanizes a renewed sensibility about the problem, a new urgency, in a rising transnational conversation beyond the confines or interests of policy elites and think-tanks. As a scholarly focus, it can shed light over a number of broadly concurrent debates across the Americas, about civil society, democratization, globalization, economic citizenship, rights, and identities. We hope this volume fosters, among researchers and critical thinkers in both Americas, a richer, sharper sense of the role of inequalities in their subjects and disciplines, in framing how questions are asked about this essential social question, and in how we commit ourselves to intellectual work. Inequalities demand bringing the social back into our scholarly endeavors and communities, in other words, pursuing scholarship with a purpose.

Charles Tilly's *Durable Inequalities* (1998) provides for this volume a starting point for rethinking the problem of Latin American inequalities. Tilly's generalist modeling concerns "categorical" inequalities, those that create, subordinate, and sustain ordered types of human beings beyond their transitory differences and identities, and that likely lie behind current preoccupations with the academic trinity of race-gender-ethnicity. The central problem attacked by Tilly is how and why unequal life possibilities come to distinguish and define categories of personhood. What are the consequences of sustained, systematic inequalities? Unlike the many inequality studies that accent the attributes of individuals, Tilly's work concerns social groups and the power relationships between them (Pérez Saínz and Mora 2007). He insists that "large, significant inequalities of advantages among human beings correspond mainly to categorical differences such as white/black, male/female, citizen/foreigner or Muslim/Jew, more than to individual differences in attributes, propensities, and performances" (Tilly 1998: 7). Yet the mere existence of classes of humans is insufficient to explain inequality: the key is an ensemble of social processes that generate durable inequalities among such groupings.

Tilly isolates four basic social mechanisms that consolidate and spread inequalities: "opportunity hoarding," "exploitation," "emulation," and "adaptation." Classification in itself does not produce deep or lasting inequality. Classification must combine with hierarchy—asymmetrical social ties that link members of two categories and that link to an unequal flow of resources —to fuel their interaction. One way this works is through exploitation, which occurs when powerful persons dispose of resources or surpluses extracted from coordinating the efforts of excluded others. Exploitation is most frequently organized along the lines of categories cut from social distinctions of gender, race, ethnicity, religion, or nationality.

For Tilly, the other key mechanism for inequalities is opportunity hoarding, which emerges when members of one network gain access to or monopolize a valued resource, which in turn bolsters the operation of the network (Tilly 1998: chap. 5). As with exploitation, a boundary separates off beneficiaries in categories that order the unequal relationship and preserve advantages and disadvantages. As the technological and institutional change of modern societies reduces the viability and allure of open exploitation, opportunity hoarding and related exclusions acquire a greater weight in fostering inequality.

Durable inequality depends on institutionalizing categorical pairings. Transactions between people come together in social ties, and these fuse into networks that serve to address some kind of organizational problem. The consolidation and diffusion of categories links to two other Tilly mechanisms: emulation and adaptation. Emulation is the copying of established organizational models or the transplanting of dominant social relations from one place or culture to another. Adaptation holds categorical inequalities in place, through the invention of routine interactions and social relationships across existing divides.

Tilly notes that inequality is reinforced when there is confluence between the internal categories of an organization and those of the larger society. Internal categories pertain to the visible structures of institutions: officers and recruits, professors and students, managers and workers, or doctors and nurses. External categories derive from the outside and are widely deployed in society: man and woman, white and black, citizen and foreigner.

Organizations often seek to harmonize external and internal categories—for example, hospitals with male physicians and female nurses—and systematically define differences in their authority, attributes, pay, and perspectives. Well-drawn internal boundaries facilitate exploitation and opportunity hoarding by providing justifications, explanations, and routines for unequal gains. Harmonizing external and internal categories (such as race) keeps down the costs of policing social boundaries.

Like Bourdieu, Tilly is resolutely *relational*: inequality cannot happen or persist for long without strong working bonds to others. Thus, Tilly's work challenges the standard metrics of social mobility, the empirical centerpiece of traditional inequality studies, built from long-dominant methodological individualism. Much of what observers see as individual differences are in fact social constructs. For example, the performance levels and compensation of workers are organized categorically. The acquisition of their skills is also grounded in unequal and segregated schooling. A relational analysis of social inequality does not deny the existence of individuals or the impact of inequality on people, but fits them into an organizational context. Tilly's model is also dynamic: inequality does not just happen through inertia and time, but must be constantly created and renewed. In recent years, Tilly has also tied the calculus of inequality to overarching political structures such as "Democracy" (Tilly 2007: chap. 5). Modern capitalism undermined many older forms of political organization (strict racial rule or political intermediaries such as feudal lords), yet must constantly insulate and strengthen public politics against the newer forms of categorical inequality.

Yet within Tilly's corpus as a social thinker, his work on inequality is the least historically grounded and the most abstractly structural. Tilly's core categories themselves call for greater historical and cultural interrogation, which can be actively pursued in the Latin American context of long-term inequality. How were dyads of inequality constructed and maintained over centuries of change? Moreover, the fact that many categorical boundaries between Latin American social groups are and have long been highly permeable (such as foundational colonial racial lines like black-white or Indian-mestizo) or fluid and multifarious (like modern "racial democracy") complicates the kinds of categorical divides tagged by Tilly. How they are masked, managed, tolerated, and reproduced as lasting inequalities? Drawing on Tilly, this book explores the diversity of processes that have combined in the construction of inequalities in Latin America, leaving indelible marks on the region's societies. In doing so, it moves beyond Tilly's initial conceptual framework for inequalities, as study of these concrete historical cases reveals other angles and aspects of the problem.

The essays in this book, derived from the projects of six inequalities researchers, develop all of these themes in diverse ways. Rather than attempt to paint a comprehensive or balanced picture of Latin American inequalities, either by an array of national cases or by the gamut of inequalities, each of these studies focuses on a new methodological portal into the problem. Complimenting this chapter, the Mexican political anthropologist Luis Reygadas offers a panoramic and nuanced survey of what Latin American inequality is and what it isn't, anchored in the distinctive privileges that Latin American elites have retained and reproduced over the past five centuries. Reygadas forcefully argues there is no "single-factor" theory to explain Latin America's extremes, refining instead a broad approach based on the region's historically cumulative set of "advantages and disadvantages." Along the way, Reygadas offers five new theses for thinking about the construction and indelibility of Latin American inequalities. Following Tilly's lead, he argues that the crucible is the region's peculiar juxtaposition of ethnic and class categorical differences. These relate to the secular social distance of elites from mass society, the region's polarizing economic structures and impact, the capacity of power-holders to weather shifting economic and political regimes, and Latin America's weak public, political, and governmental capacities to counteract economic and social inequality.

The feminist political scientist Christina Ewig offers an exploration in historical sociology, zeroing in on the early bifurcation of healthcare systems in Peru—which, by the 1930s, was paralleled throughout Latin America—into one for urban male workers (social security), and the other for "colonizing" distantly controlled rural populations (public health). With historical alacrity, Ewig shows how these initial state distinctions ended up actually reinforcing the country's ethnic and gender divisions across a gamut of twentieth-century social transformations and political regimes, although this was surely not the intent of Peru's crusaders for public health. In addition to providing historical lessons for social-policy reform, Ewig's essay exemplifies how social and cultural categories are deployed generally as mechanisms of classification and distinction, and in Peruvian society as a means of organizing unequal access to health services, reinforcing opportunity hoarding.

The Peruvian-based anthropologist Jeanine Anderson bases her study on a uniquely long dataset of ethnographic interviews with the slumdwellers of

Pamplona Alta, which took place over thirty years. Anderson revisits six key microrelationships between abject poverty—a condition most of her informants have never escaped—and struggles for equality and a dignified life. In excavating the agency of the poor, Anderson stresses the poor's own diversely expressed "transcendence" projects—ranging from political involvements to house building and religion—themselves expressions of the social distances of inequality. These deserve greater recognition in anti-poverty and developmental programs. The locally embedded culture of the poor should be embraced in seeking solutions to material deprivation and inequality. The incommensurability of the transcendence projects of the poor and the relation of poverty to anti-poverty programs is also a sign of the categorical inequality studied by Tilly. The poor see and measure themselves as a category of people distinct from the non-poor, yet outsiders consider them mere survivors, without life projects of their own, who need only to be "helped."

The Brazilian political scientist Lucio Renno also bases his study on a uniquely rich dataset: thousands of voters in two contrasting Brazilian cities during the 2002 elections. Brazil has become a more democratic polity in the last decade and has even begun (particularly under President Lula de Silva) to confront some of its longstanding egregious social inequalities. Apart from his quantitative findings, Renno is drawn to the larger qualitative question of the relationship between democratization, participation, and cumulative equality, as analyzed through the differential uses of political information. Despite reforms in Brazilian electoral politics, strong biases persist in how information is absorbed and acted on, most notably by neighborhood, income, and gender. This demonstrates that an asymmetrical distribution of political information is not just a question of individual attributes, but a social construction infused by categorical differences. A better-informed electorate can strengthen Brazil's democratic future, but will that consolidated democracy insulate itself from inequalities, or work against them?

The Cuban literary and cultural scholar Odette Casamayor investigates a spreading aesthetics of inequality in the 1990s, confronting the official myth of a post-1959 socialist Cuba that has banished racial categories. In fact, the evolving artistic movement, infused by hip-hop and other transnational cultural currents, reveled in its blackness, indeed embracing aspects of difference (such as primitivism, gangsterism, sexuality) still officially taboo in Cuba. Casamayor's work is a cultural analysis both of the long-term reproduction of inequality, even under an ostensibly antiracist egalitarian regime, and, in a larger sense, of how an aesthetic of subjective alienation and inequality pervades the region's rich cultural expressions. In this way, she expands Tilly's analysis to aesthetic and cultural dimensions of the processes that construct and contest inequalities.

The North American political scientist Margaret Gray brings the dilemmas of Latin American inequalities north into the United States. Drawing on intensive fieldwork among new immigrant, mainly Mexican farmworkers in upstate New York, Gray finds a compelling case for examining Tilly's "categorical" inequality under actual processal construction. Undocumented farmworkers are now coming together as an identifiable rural underclass, without yet viable means to counteract their political vulnerability and social distress. In several ways, this represents a kind of export-import of Latin American inequality, grafted by stubborn American farm interests onto their own history of categorical exclusion in agriculture. Gray brings home how North American society is becoming trapped locally in a growing web of hemispheric inequalities.

The afterword is provided by Javier Auyero, the pioneer Argentine political ethnographer and a student of Tilly. Auyero invokes Borges's semiotic fable of Funes to underscore the need for analytical categories or tools like those deployed in this volume for making sense of the kaleidoscope of inequalities that afflict Latin America. How do these tools relate back to relational and reflexive social thinkers like Tilly and Bourdieu? Are they coming together in a new toolbox for the study of indelible inequality? What real world impact can be made by this rising scholarly concern?

Notes

I thank the contributors—Jeanine Anderson (Peru), Luis Reygadas (Mexico), Lucio Renno (Brazil), Odette Casamayor (Cuba), Maggie Gray (United States), and Christina Ewig (United States)—who developed these themes during our dialogues at Stony Brook. An incipient version of this essay was read at the Latin American Studies Association (Las Vegas, October 2004) and published in Spanish as "Desigualdades persistentes en América Latina: Historia y cultura" (*Alteridades* 14, no. 28 [2004]: 9–19). Luis Reygadas and Eric Hershberg critiqued reincarnations of this chapter; Reygadas in particular helped focus the analysis of Tilly.

1. For the broader critique in social sciences, see Bourdieu and Wacquant 1992; Douglas and Ney 1998; Eric Wolf 1999; and Jane Jacobs 2000.
2. See *Nepantla* (2000) for a sampling of the Latin American Cultural studies boom.

The Construction of
Latin American Inequality

LUIS REYGADAS

A vast literature exists on the deep social inequalities of Latin America. Thanks to the work of many specialists, diverse angles are known about a phenomenon, inequality, that has left an indelible mark on the region. Nevertheless, the majority of studies that deal with Latin American inequality employ a dramatic and fatalist literary style. Many begin with the affirmation that Latin America is the most "disparate" region in the world, then analyze the causes of inequality, before concluding on a pessimistic note, emphasizing the power of the mechanisms that reproduce these dismal disparities (Portes and Hoffman 2003). Frequently, these studies resort to the image of a vicious cycle, suggesting that the condition is inexorable (Karl 2002; Vuskovic 1996). On occasion, and at worst, they naturalize inequality, claiming that it is an inherent characteristic of Latin American societies and cultures. Following Tilly's inspiration for this book, I argue that inequality is not an immutable essence but a mutable historical construction: the levels and types of inequality change from one country to the next as well as vary through time. They are products of complex and contradictory processes, not of a cultural or economic destiny. The particular characteristics of Latin American inequality must therefore be unraveled. This task even requires a shift in rhetorical style, abandoning the fatalism that naturalizes inequalities for a more sober analysis of the factors that produce them. Thus, I have opted for a constructivist approach (Harris 2000, 2006), which starts from another angle: pointing to factors that make Latin America less unequal than other parts of the world.

For example, in the realm of gender relations, even though vast inequalities remain between men and women, Latin America is not the most disparate region in the world. Taking into account the proportion of women who work for wages or the educational index by gender, Latin American women are better off than sub-Saharan, Middle Eastern, and Southeast Asian women. Their life expectancy is also higher than those in other Third World regions (George and Wilding 2002: 123; Stevens 1999: 114). Furthermore, in Latin America political inequality is not as stark as it is in other southern countries. Since the beginning of the nineteenth century, struggles for civic rights commonly registered across Latin American countries. The formation and consolidation of Latin American democracies has been a turbulent process, with ups and downs and sure limitations. However, as a result there appears to be more political equality in most of Latin America than in the many African and Asian states that still lack basic democratic rights and institutions.

Where Latin America shows greater inequality than the rest of the globe is in incomes: the abysmal differences between the rich minority and the rest of the population. Latin America holds the highest Gini coefficient of any world region: an average of 0.522 during the 1990s, compared to the 0.342 in the advanced economies of Western Europe, Japan, Australia, and the United States, members of the Organisation for Economic Co-operation and Development (OECD), and 0.328 in Eastern Europe, 0.412 in Asia, and 0.450 in Africa (World Bank 2003: 1). The distance between the income of the richest 20 percent and the poorest 20 percent is often staggering, at more than 30 to 1 in Brazil, Honduras, and Paraguay (United Nations Development Programme 2003). Precisely speaking, this is Latin America's exceptionalism; it is not the world's poorest region, but the one with the most skewed incomes.

Latin America's peculiarity lies in the fact that the richest 10 percent of the population concentrates more than half of total income (World Bank 2003:1). An illuminating exercise is to analyze the regional Gini coefficient without taking into account the top earners. When the richest sector is excluded from calculations, the disparity in income in Latin America is quite similar to that of the United States: 0.386 compared to 0.353, that is, only a 0.033 Gini point difference. Moreover, Uruguay, Mexico, and Costa Rica would exhibit less inequality than the United States (Szekely and Hilgert 1999). Taking into consideration only the disparity between the middle and lower classes, Latin American inequality is similar to inequality in many other regions in the world, including many developed regions. But when one includes the sectors with the greatest incomes (as is Latin America's social reality), one encounters a vastly different landscape. In all Latin American countries the richest 10 percent earn between 2 and 3.5 times more than the following decile, while in developed but also unequal countries (the United

States, United Kingdom, and Canada) that difference is "only" on the order of 1.6, 1.5, and 1.4, respectively (Szekely and Hilgert 1999: 40).

Therefore, unlocking the key to Latin American inequality requires one to understand how a small stratum is able to appropriate a greater amount of social wealth than its counterparts elsewhere. Even though the question seems simple, the answer is not, since this excessive concentration of wealth depends on multiple factors that implicate the society as a whole as well as the functioning of the state and other institutions. Latin American economic disparity is closely coupled with other forms of inequality and is the product of diverse economic, political, social, and cultural mechanisms. This fundamental question has elicited varying responses from different disciplines and according to how the problem is posed. Historians have emphasized the weighty legacy of three centuries of colonialism as well as the unequalizing tendencies of later liberalism, the primary-goods export economy, and nineteenth- and twentieth-century modernization (Coatsworth 2005; Coatsworth and Taylor 1998; Thorp 1998; Tutino 1988). Neoliberal economists have not much concerned themselves with the problem, because they consider a rise in inequality positive if it indicates that some sectors are out performing others during economic growth (Firebaugh 2003; Martin Wolf 2004). Economists with a structuralist orientation, on the other hand, have emphasized the dualistic nature of the productive structure that separates the high-tech sector from low productivity sectors as well as the division between consumer cultures—luxury goods consumers on the one hand and subsistence goods consumers on the other (Griffin 1969; Furtado 1970; Vuskovic 1996). From institutional perspectives, other economists have stressed the disparities in access to economic opportunities, property rights, and education (Glade 1969; Haber, Razo, and Maurer 2003; Engerman and Sokoloff 2006). Political analysis, for its part, has shown the persistence of clientelism and the overwhelming control that elites exert over the state (Auyero 1997; O'Donnell 1999). Sociologists have advanced arguments about internal colonialism and the gaps between modern and traditional social groups (Centro de Investigación y Acción Social para el Desarrollo Social en América Latina [DESAL] 1969; González Casanova 1964). Anthropologists have underscored how ethnic and racial dimensions of inequality affect indigenous groups and blacks (Castellanos 2004; Poole 1997; Reichmann 1999). Gender studies reveal the inequality faced by women, and cultural studies the roles of status and consumption in the elitist and exclusionary traditions of Latin America. The lack of progressive agrarian and fiscal reforms is often pegged as a debility of state institutions and as due to marked disparities in educational and social capital.

In explaining inequality, the political Right tends to blame the state and populism, in addition to holding the poor responsible for their own plight, while the Left blames the market and neoliberalism, placing responsibility squarely on the rich and their political allies. Some have insisted on dependency and the conditions of Latin America's insertion in the global economy, while others have stressed its internal determinants. Some analysts highlight the limitations of productivity, while others are drawn to problems of distribution and redistribution. To a greater or lesser degree, each of these approaches brings to light one dimension of inequality in the region. But they all suffer from the limits of a unilateral lens, focusing on one angle of the phenomenon without including the rest and rarely adopting broader relational perspectives.

One could add other mechanisms to the long list of inequality's causes, but it is not a question of looking for a single factor capable of explaining the Latin American riddle. There is no "lone gunman" (isolated cause) responsible for the problem, nor is inequality the result of some historical "original sin" (primordial cause). Inequality is a product of the connection and accumulation of all of these processes together. Different contexts are vital, too: some countries have experienced agrarian reforms; in others inequalities are less rooted in ethnic differences, and elite power is heterogeneous. Clientelism is stronger in some countries than in others, as are the capacities of different welfare states; the handicaps of insertion within the world economy vary for every country at different time periods, and so on. It would be futile to search for one common denominator capable of explaining inequalities in every Latin American country.

In contrast, Latin American income disparities are most arguably a product of history. They are the result of the combined accumulation of different factors, such that inequality is greater in those countries and time periods in which there has been a greater concentration and articulation of these factors. This cumulative approach allows one to grasp the nuances of different countries or historical eras. There are nations, such as Uruguay or Costa Rica, that display less inequality because all processes are not in operation at once, or they operate with less force. On the other hand, there are countries, like Paraguay and Brazil, that present some of the world's highest rates of inequality. Argentina was more egalitarian thirty years ago, but inequality accelerated during the final decades of the twentieth century. Mexico has achieved a high index of human development, but at the same time suffers an extreme inequality coefficient. Chile has advanced most in terms of poverty alleviation, but inequality remains persistently high. In Bolivia and Nicaragua, massive inequality and poverty work hand in hand. At some points, inequality has been less pronounced and has even subsided to a degree. Indelible inequalities mark Latin America, but in each historical circumstance the processes that generate them appear quite different.

How can one explain the persistent inequalities of Latin America and, at the same time, underscore the marked distinctions between the varied countries of the region? We need to focus on certain inequality processes that, when working in tandem, leave in their wake vastly unequal societies. My point of departure is an analysis of two processes in Latin America that can be grasped in Tilly's relational perspective: the overlap of social class with ethnic and racial divides, and the strength of social barriers. These two forms of "categorical inequality" combine with two other factors, namely, the resilience of structural forms of economic polarization and the durability of elite privileges. These are not the only intervening factors, but they shed light on the articulation of economic, political, social, and cultural dynamics that reproduce indelible inequalities, as well as join with other processes— land concentration, the weakness of welfare systems, clientelistic and asymmetrical politics—that have long been pinpointed for Latin America.

The Juxtaposition of Ethnic-Racial Divisions with Class Divides

The historical origins of Latin American inequalities conceal a positive core: the resilient capacity for resistance on the part of many indigenous societies in the face of the long-term trauma of conquest. An old ethnocentric cliché laments the region's historic misfortune of having suffered conquest by "feudalistic and un-industrious" Spain and Portugal, while North America was settled by industrious English colonizers, who established its more egalitarian communities. This is the "original sin" from which Latin America has never quite redeemed itself. What this imaginary narrative does not reveal is that the political community of future North Americans included neither natives nor slaves. The majority of the indigenous population was exterminated or fully excluded from the rising new society, while most African Americans suffered bondage until the Civil War or racial segregation into the mid-twentieth century. In Latin America, the Conquest brought dramatic decades of violence, mistreatment, and disease, phenomena that decimated indigenous populations and hastened the disappearance of many ethnic groups. But many of them survived as well, and the region conserves to this day an extraordinary and rich ethnic and cultural diversity. This is more visible in countries with large indigenous populations—Guatemala, Ecuador, Bolivia, Peru, Mexico—while other countries, such as those of the Southern Cone (save Chile) reveal few indigenous traits, whether due to having fewer Indians to begin with or to their historical oblivion. Thus, blacks, mulattos, indigenous peoples, and mestizos have proven to be decisive social actors in the history of Latin America. However, from the beginning, indigenous groups were subsumed into colonial society in deeply unequal ways, resulting in a social matrix with stark differentials of status, power, and material resources.

Comparing diverse paths of colonization in the Americas, Engerman and Sokoloff (2006: 39–41) have highlighted the contrasts between the patterns followed in the territories that now comprise Canada and the United States and those that dominated the rest of the hemisphere. In the more northern regions of the Americas, the abundance of land, scarcity of labor, and initial lack of comparative advantages for large-scale agriculture and mining led to an economy based on small farms that combined agriculture with livestock. These conditions gave rise to societies largely formed by European colonists, with more egalitarian social relationships and a wider distribution of land, economic opportunities, education, and political rights. In contrast, across the greater part of what is now Latin America, an abundance of labor and factors favoring the formation of large-scale units of agriculture or mining led to societies marked by sharp disparities between small European elites, who had privileged access to land and other resources, and the rest of the population, who were of indigenous and African origins. This led, Engerman and Sokoloff insist, to distinctive possibilities for long-term growth.

John Coatsworth has recently questioned Engerman's and Sokoloff's interpretation, specifically their excessive emphasis on institutional characteristics and natural endowments compared to economic and political factors such as forms of production and distinct forms of colonial rule. Moreover, most institutional perspectives (which rarely issue from seasoned Latin American specialists) mistakenly hold that more egalitarian institutions contribute to growth, a thesis unsupported by their own cases in Latin American history. For example, at the close of the colonial era Cuba was Spain's most productive colony, despite its highly skewed institutional basis in slave plantations (Coatsworth 2008). Coatsworth also posits that until the 1860s levels of inequality in North and South America were roughly similar; only in the late nineteenth century did Latin America become notoriously more unequal than the United States and Canada. Apart from any empirical discrepancies between Coatsworth's analysis and that of Engerman and Sokoloff, it is clear that cultural and religious differences of their conquerors did not determine distinct levels of colonial inequality. Much more vital were economic, political, and institutional processes stressed by historians, and in Tilly's terms, the roles and legacies left by categorical distinctions.

In Latin America, colonial class differences were to a large extent constructed on the basis of ethnic, racial, and gender distinctions. Authorities provided special legislation to protect indigenous groups from certain abuses, but this also underpinned the juridical validation of caste distinctions and solidified them in the social imaginary and everyday life. The mass importation of African slaves created yet another social segment exploited and stigmatized based on the color of their skin.

In the nineteenth century, after independence, emerging Creole elites preserved their situation of privilege with respect to the wider population. The unequal matrix created under colonial rule was reproduced under new conditions as the legal distinctions between whites, indigenous groups, mestizos, blacks, and mulattos disappeared. However, beneath liberal legal equality there persisted many economic, social, political, and cultural differences that fostered new barriers between groups. Nonwhite groups were integrated in a disadvantageous and precarious manner within the new republics, which, although far from having explicit racist politics, nonetheless became racialized states (Goldberg 2002; Sieder 2002). This interweaving of ethnic variables with economic and political facts created more inequality, which is typical of what Charles Tilly calls "reinforced inequality," arising when internal categories that divide a group (management-workers, executive-employee, supervisor-subordinate, etc.) become articulated with external categories (black-white, mulatto-white, native-European, native-mestizo, and mestizo-white) (Tilly 1998: 76). After independence such categories may have vanished from law and the state, but they began to be reconstructed in the foundations of everyday life. With time they changed into new blurred categories defined by income, lifestyle, cultural consumption, and length and kind of schooling.

In contrast to other historic situations with clearly marked ethnic or racial boundaries (like apartheid in South Africa or Jim Crow segregation in the

United States), in Latin America's ethnic and racial inequality one does not find strict lines of distinction. In part due to mestizaje (interracial mixing) and in part due to early struggles against slavery and discrimination, these demarcations became vague and ambiguous (Cope 1994). This ambiguity has been used by disadvantaged sectors wanting to avoid stigmatization and to negotiate their position, but it also served for the covering up of ethnic differences under the later national myths of mestizaje and racial democracy. The ambiguity and the relative openness of Latin America's ethnic definitions stood in the way of absolute discrimination, but at the same time allowed the reproduction and persistence of inequalities that were still tied to these definitions in degrees—a veiled form of racism that finds its greatest power in the flexibility of its terms (Castellanos 2004).

In the case of Brazil, one of the countries with the greatest income disparity in the world, recent studies show that, even after one controls for other variables, blacks and mulattos find themselves in a disadvantaged position compared to the white population: blacks have on average 2.3 fewer years of education and their access to higher education is 10 times less than whites' (Hasenbalg and do Valle 1991; Lovell 1991; Reichmann 1999; World Bank 2003). If one were to draw a graph with the percentage of blacks and mulattos in each income decile, one would get an almost perfect descending diagonal line: in the poorest decile, 75 percent are afro-descendants; in the middle fifth and sixth, 45 percent are afro-descendants; and in the richest decile, fewer than 15 percent are afro-descendants (Jaccoud and Beghin 2002: 28).

Likewise, according to a recent World Bank study, indigenous men in Latin America earn between 40 and 65 percent less than non-indigenous men, and in Brazil blacks earn 48 percent less than whites. Combining ethnic and gender variables, indigenous women and afro-descendants have the lowest incomes, while white men enjoy the highest. In Bolivia indigenous women earn on average 28 percent less than white men, and in Brazil indigenous women have incomes that are equivalent to 40 percent of a white man's. This study concludes that "race and ethnicity play a larger role in wage gaps than gender does" (World Bank 2003: 107).

The edifice of ethnoracial asymmetry in Latin America is constructed neither exclusively nor primarily through means of overt discrimination. Ethno-racial discrimination was notorious in the past and still exists, but over centuries has undergone a process of refinement into the unequal distribution of land, property, access to resources, opportunities for education, and qualification. Statistical studies show that ethnic and racial markers account for a portion of inequality, but that the overwhelming share is now explained by factors such as occupation, parental occupation, gender, place of residence, and, above all, the family and individual's education. Ethno-racial determinants function not on their own but in conjunction with others. Today, blacks, mulattos, indigenous groups, and mestizos are at a disadvantage in Latin America not only because they confront discrimination, which is still alive, but mainly as a result of complex historical outcomes, because they presently enjoy less schooling or schooling of poor quality, possess marginal land, or live in remote or depressed urban zones. What was once seen as an ethnoracial hierarchy are now seen as social distinctions based on education, income, lifestyle, consumer preferences, and other characteristics that originate in relational interactions and social styles similar to those of a society organized on the basis of closed status groups.

Some econometric simulations have tried to calculate what would happen if women, indigenous, and afro-descendant wage earners in Latin America had social capital similar to those of white men (in education, job sector, family size) and were to receive equal pay for those same characteristics (World Bank 2003: 112–23). The surprising result of these exercises was that the level of overall equality, measured by Gini or Theil coefficients, would not change significantly. Seen from a different angle, if one were to measure the differences that exist exclusively within the white male sector, one would find levels of inequality as substantial as that of Latin American society as a whole.

There are forces that restrain and counteract ethnoracial domination in Latin America. Indigenous groups, mestizos, blacks, and mulattos have recurred to and invented diverse strategies to limit abuses, gain a variety of rights, and secure social welfare. Since colonial times Latin America has witnessed many black and indigenous movements and rebellions. Their most crucial gains were the abolition of slavery and the elimination of exclusionary or caste juridical systems. Nonetheless, discrimination and ethnic barriers have not yet vanished from everyday life. The conditions of indigenous groups and blacks, as a whole, continue to be adverse. Faced with this challenge, a great number of people have opted for strategies of personal, familial, or community improvement. There are countless cases of "whitening": individuals with indigenous or black ancestry who gain access to middle- or upper-class status through economic, educational, artistic, or athletic

success, which makes them appear "whiter" (Melo da Silva 1991). Whitening
is part of a more complicated edifice of construction, deconstruction, and
reconstruction of ethnic barriers in Latin America. The ruling sectors as
much as the subaltern ones deploy and cross these barriers in their interrela-
tionships. There are strategic uses of ethnicity: on occasion, it is convenient
to accentuate indigenous or black ancestry, but in most situations belonging
to these ethnic groups constitutes stigmatization. This is why Latin Americans resort to different strategies to hide, relativize, and assimilate their
ethnicities. Such tactics can be effective for personal advancement but have
not eliminated discrimination per se. The outcome is a subordinate integration that does not change the rules of the game because the right to cultural
difference is not secured. Alternatively, many blacks and indigenous groups
have taken the historical route of withdrawal and isolation within their own
ethnic boundaries. Doing so allows them to preserve their culture and community ties, but it does not guarantee a decent insertion into the larger
society and, in many cases, has led to greater exclusion. Until recently, the
black and indigenous populations in Latin America have oscillated between
these two unsatisfactory alternatives: subordinated integration, with its consequence of exploitation and discrimination, or ethnic isolation with its high
exclusionary cost. Nevertheless, toward the end of the twentieth century and
beginning of the twenty-first, the majority of Latin American countries have
witnessed an energetic mobilization on the part of the black and indigenous
population that now questions the basic foundations on which inequality
was erected. There are pillars, however, that still sustain inequality, such as
the cultural, educational, and social distance existing between the richest
minority and the bulk of Latin Americans—a distance that is preserved and
policed across an indelible variety of material and symbolic barriers.

Categorical Inequalities, Social Barriers, and Persistent Exclusion

Charles Tilly has argued that persisting inequalities become organized on
the basis of categorical pairs such as man-woman, black-white, or citizen-
immigrant. Such social binaries have pervaded Latin America's history:
peninsular-Indian, white-black, rational people–uncultured peoples, land-
owner-peasant, modern-traditional, integrated-marginal, mestizo-indigenous, included-excluded, among others. Many times such categorizations
transcend a binary scheme to form triads (white-*cholo*-indigenous, white-

mulatto-black, management–union boss–worker) or categories along a continuum of markers and elements, such as colonial ethnoracial differences or the dozens of recognized skin tones in contemporary Brazil. What one should keep in mind, however, is not the existence of categories but the social processes that form and weaken them, the limits that separate them, and the flows of resources channeled by these divides. Levels of inequality are intimately related to the barriers established between social groups. Barriers, which are material and symbolic, geographic and educational, economic and political, configure through categorical devices a larger system of power relations that generates distance, segregation, and isolation. They separate people, mark differences and set limits, make distinctions, and add to the asymmetrical distribution of wealth, prestige, welfare, and power.

In the majority of Latin American countries, a variety of barriers encapsulate the elite and their privileges and keep the rest of the population at bay. It may be the geographical distance that isolates the far-off indigenous region of Chiapas, the Atlantic Nicaraguan coast, or Amazonia—all lacking the minimum of communications and infrastructure—or the educational distance that distinguishes those who complete their graduate education abroad or in the top universities in Buenos Aires, Monterrey, Rio de Janeiro, or Bogotá. These acts of distancing have assumed shifting forms throughout the centuries, from the metaphysical distinction expressed in early colonial debates about whether indigenous peoples had true souls, to contemporary distinctions in symbolic capital between those who speak English, possess higher education, and have Internet access and those who cannot read or write or who have only a few years of primary school.

Take first the issue of physical distance and the material obstacles it creates. When economists use mathematical models to measure the diverse factors that bear on income disparity, they find that in Latin America place of residence is a central component, in particular differences between the city and the country. There is a huge difference between living in a metropolis and living in a remote small village. In Mexico's case, the per capita annual income in the Federal District in 2000 was $22,816, similar to that of many developed European countries. In Chiapas, on the other hand, the annual per capita income is only $3,549, equivalent to that of the poorest areas of Africa and Asia (United Nations Development Programme 2003). According to a study carried out by the Inter-American Development Bank in eleven Latin American countries, toward the end of the 1990s rural salaries were 13 to 44 percent lower than urban salaries. Mexico and Brazil, the two countries with the largest cities in the region, have the sharpest divergences (Eckstein and Wickam-Crowley 2003: 14).

The fact that the richest sectors live in cities can make urban inequality loom larger than the inequality of rural zones, where the vast majority of people live in comparable conditions of penury and marginality. Whatever the case, in Latin America living in the countryside is a big disadvantage. It means being cut off from key educational and career opportunities. This has to do with poor communicational infrastructure (highways, electricity, telephone service, etc.) and the centralization of production, education, government, culture, and healthcare and hospitals. Through the centuries, a disparate resource accumulation sharpened between the capital and the provinces, the coast and the interior, and the country and the city, configuring a centralist and anti-peasant style of development. One must add the stigma attached to the rustic population, especially if they are indigenous. The spatial distance between societal groups is a social construction and not merely a geographic accident. It has a political and cultural history related to those indigenous groups who sought refuge in isolated regions in order to avoid exploitation in reservations, plantations, and *encomiendas* (an early form of colonial fiefdom), and to the history of blacks who fled toward *quilombos* (hinterland settlements founded by runaway slaves) in order to elude slavery. It also reflects decades of political abandonment seen in the maldistribution of public resources: the poor, because they were culturally distinct, could be easily forgotten and receive poor quality services and less social investment. They were not genuinely part of the hegemonic political community, and their voices went unheard. On occasion, such distance was deliberately maintained, but in the majority of cases it was the result of the gradual accumulation of indifference, oblivion, distraction, and the daily assignment of resources that, in the long run, configured the deep contrast between the country and the city across most of Latin America.

Since the 1950s, the rural populations of Latin America have initiated millions of migratory journeys, transitory or definitive, toward the city, to areas with agricultural dynamism, and increasingly toward countries outside their native lands. The encounter with urbanization allows them direct access to job markets and educational opportunities, but it does not guarantee any lessening of distance relative to the ruling sectors, for the urban web produces other relationships of isolation and exclusion. For example, in marginal neighborhoods the poor both lack resources and face arduous commutes to areas with higher job concentration. This is not to mention the starker kinds of urban segmentation described by Teresa Caldeira in her disquieting book *City of Walls* (2000), as demarcated by walls, railings, and the guards of the "condominios fechados" (gated communities) of São Paolo, which keep *favela* (Brazilian slum) inhabitants at arms length and unable to penetrate the fortified enclaves of the rich. Walls and fences are material metaphors for the social construction of Latin American inequalities.

In the past, the cultural and social distance between the elites and the poor, blacks, and indigenous groups was legitimized with the open use of racial typologies and profiling and discriminatory discourse. Even though this still persists, it is less visible today in mass societies, which host periodic elections and adhere to politically correct language. Within this context, educational distance is now one of the best weapons of distinction. Latin America's persistently high illiteracy rates are shocking in societies with their levels of development. Countries with modest resources such as Cuba and Costa Rica have attained far lower illiteracy than wealthier countries such as Mexico and Brazil. Juvenile illiteracy is still substantial in Haiti, Nicaragua, Honduras, Guatemala, El Salvador, and the Dominican Republic. In isolated rural areas as well as in indigenous regions educational lags prevail. Even though Latin America now comes close to universal coverage in terms of primary education, high-school education remains an insurmountable hurdle for the poorest segments of the population. Studies show that almost half of the students registered for high school never finish. This schooling funnel narrows in the tracks toward a university education, which only a minority can attain.

The dilemma of educational inequality in Latin America is due not just to unequal access and availability, but also to qualitative differences. Although enrollment numbers have increased impressively, in the majority of public schools progress is slow, with high failure and drop-out rates. Specialists realize that a large portion of students who enter high school do so with notable deficiencies in reading and writing skills and have a hard time with basic mathematics (Gallart 1999: 123). Segmentation of the educational system pervades Latin America. On the one hand, a privileged path exists for the middle and upper classes, who enjoy access to private—and sometimes public—education of high quality from preschool to high school, and who then enter the best universities with relative ease. On the other hand, the majority of the population has little preschooling and then faces primary and secondary schools of inferior quality. When the time comes to take entrance exams for the university system, most of the poor are defeated in a clean but profoundly unjust competition, because the results of these exams are but a logical outcome of accumulated years of deficient education.

One of the great paradoxes of Latin American education is that just as some poor students obtain a higher education for free, a large number of middle- and upper-class students gain the same benefit. Graduates who are well educated and enjoy the appropriate connections are able to obtain good jobs, but many never do, particularly those who come from the poorest backgrounds (Núñez and Gutiérrez 2004). Disparities in social capital are decisive when breaking into the job market. Regardless of talent, those without friends or relatives in important positions find it hard to get decent employment with possibilities of upward mobility. Deep inside the job market itself the same social distances get repeated: the barriers between repetitive and creative work, between manual and intellectual labor, and between those who follow and those who direct are clearly marked. These barriers then translate into a polarization of job status and salary.

In Latin America the staggering distance between the base and the top of the social pyramid, in addition to the abrupt salary differentials that mark the gaps between them, makes climbing to the next step extremely difficult. Disparities and entrance barriers become more challenging the higher one progresses up the pyramid. Crossing the line that separates predominantly manual labor from intellectual labor is momentous. Those who do cross it can ascend to supervisory posts of medium complexity, but reaching executive or highly demanding management levels is very rare. Finally, in the professional and executive world a novel barrier is segregating the most elite positions, even in what are thought to be egalitarian fields, such as political parties, academia, and NGOs. Whether one can succeed in crossing these borders depends on one's educational credentials and individual capacities, but there are gender, social origin, ethnic, and social-capital filters as well. For example, Latin American women, despite having conquered vital fields in a gamut of economic and political occupations, have hit a glass ceiling that prevents them from scaling the most prominent heights. The same occurs with indigenous and afro-descendant groups, save for rare exceptions.

Across various historical conjunctures and breaks, there have been variations in these barriers, some mobility, a questioning of and erection of new barriers, and attempts to create bridges and relations capable of reducing social distances. Some of these have been notable, such as the process of independence that erased the majority of legal distinctions set by colonial regimes, the diverse revolutions inspired by social-justice projects (Mexico, Bolivia, Cuba, Nicaragua), the educational campaigns in the twentieth century, or the most recent ideals of multicultural citizenship in Colombia, Bolivia, Ecuador, Brazil, and other Latin American countries. One should include in these attempts not only egalitarian protests and rebellions, but also the day-to-day resistance and individual and community-based investments for self-improvement. Among these one finds migration and local development initiatives that chip away at the burdens of living in small, isolated communities. Also noteworthy are familial strategies for raising childrens' educational level, as well as the critique of elite culture via the transgression of symbolic barriers: the use of irony and other cultural strategies that belittle and delegitimize upper-class privilege. In urban areas, popular sectors have attempted to occupy new spaces, construct decent housing, and reduce urban segregation. Thus, simultaneous with processes of exclusion and marginalization are processes of inclusion and desegregation (Peralva 2000). But even these tenacious efforts to trespass and break down the walls between social groups have not been enough to redress the social relations that produce social distancing and stratification. Distances and barriers survive in most contexts not because they have remained immutable, but because they have undergone renovations.

A mutually reinforcing process governs these different forms and levels of exclusion and differentiation. Cultural chasms, income polarization, physical and geographic segregation, educational segmentation, and disparity in social capital become intertwined. This reinforcement naturalizes inequalities. It may seem natural to think that the best positions are reserved for those who acquire educational qualifications, but one must not lose sight of the mechanisms that routinely produce this outcome. Distances between the elites and the rest of society exist in all complex societies. What is problematic in Latin America is the magnitude of such distances and the unjust ways they underlie various kinds of inequalities. The privileges of the elites are thus protected from every angle, while the poor accumulate disadvantages: in terms of ethnic origin, birthplace and residence, gender, income, educational credentials, and cultural capital, and in terms of weak social ties and networks with powerholders. The accumulation of advantages and disadvantages contributes to the persistence of inequality. In his famous book on spheres of justice, Michael Walzer argues that in order to sustain "complex equality" those who are privileged in one sphere should be restrained from domination in other spheres (1983: 19–20). Latin America embodies the opposite of this ideal. To be sure, not all elites are privileged in all capacities, nor do the poor always suffer each and every disadvantage, but there is a clear tendency to an accumulation of advantages and disadvantages at the two extremes of society.

Structural Tendencies to Economic Polarization

"Dualism" is a concept frequently invoked to describe Latin American societies (O'Donnell 1999). This conceptual imagery exists across the board, from DESAL texts of the late 1960s, which depicted cultural superposition and marginalization (DESAL 1969), to Guillermo Bonfil's famous manifesto about the opposition between a "deep Mexico" (México profundo) and the Occidentalized Mexico (Bonfil 1989). One finds this concept in studies about the contrasts between favelas and the world of asphalt in Brazil, in theories of internal colonialism, and in anthropological or sociological dichotomies between tradition and modernity. It also pervades cultural and artistic expression: in classic Mexican films such as Nosotros los pobres and Ustedes los ricos, in García Márquez novels, and in innumerable mass-market soap operas and popular music. At the same time, the overlap and superimposition between these two worlds—worlds that have never been autonomous or never completely merged—are everywhere visible. This is how, since the 1960s, the "myth of marginality" has been easily debunked (Brunner 1978; Perlman 1976). Such analyses reveal the intimate intersections between the formal and informal economy, and talk of "hybrid cultures" became a new academic slogan by the 1990s (García Canclini [1989] 1991). "Hybrid culture" is not so much a "dualism" as it is a polarization in which otherwise disconnected sectors reveal spaces of mediation that reproduce their asymmetries and distances.

At the heart of Latin American inequality beats a polarized economic structure that persistently reproduces privileged or precarious insertions in the circuits that generate and distribute wealth. This is constitutive of what several scholars have identified as "a kind of economy with inequality as its central feature" (Vuskovic 1996: 67) or "a historically guided development which is structurally unbalanced and socially excluding" (Altimir cited in O'Donnell 1999: 77). A sharp contrast runs across the two segments of the economy. One of them is dynamic and productive, composed of a narrow strata of large- and medium-size enterprises oriented in the main toward export or the satisfaction of middle- and upper-class consumer wants. It operates on a large scale, hires highly qualified personnel, uses medium to high technology, and runs under efficient economic conditions. The other segment is made up of a vast number and variety of small economic units, corner stores, stalls, and microbusinesses with limited financial resources, low productivity, and precarious technology. Between these two poles, however, innumerable connections exist. One is not dealing with two economies, one modern, the other traditional, one formal, and the other informal. There is just one, highly polarized economy with multiple linkages between its different component parts. In colonial times plantations and mines could not function without indigenous and black labor. Later, the infrastructure for export economies depended on an enormous reserve of poor workers. Today, *maquiladoras* (foreign-owned assembly factories) and modern businesses still need a large contingent of young workers, largely women, who come from impoverished pools of the urban and rural population. The so-called informal sector has many arteries that flow into the formal sector: it provides labor power, it guarantees the cheap reproduction of laboring families, it contributes to the maintenance of low salaries, it consumes a portion of what modern enterprises produce, it endows those enterprises with greater subcontracting flexibility—in short, it is a central component of the larger process of accumulation (Perlman 2004; Portes 1985; Portes and Hoffman 2003).

Yet the existence of these pathways between different sectors in the economy also points to the possibility of reducing polarization. At some moments, in particular during the mid-twentieth-century era of import substitution, the distance between the two sectors has narrowed, average productivity has grown, and in many countries salaried labor has advanced. During this period, the most productive businesses had the capacity to absorb millions of migrating or underemployed Latin Americans. Some scholars argue that during this process there was a social trend toward convergence and a resultant reduction of the dualism (Altimir 1999; Hernández Laos and Velásquez 2003). Polarization is thus not an immutable characteristic that radically separates the two economies, but one that can be gradually influenced. It is an historical legacy in which the distances constructed between the most advanced economic sectors and the least can widen or shrink. The gap separating salaries and levels of consumption can shorten as well.

It has also long been debated whether economic polarization in Latin America results basically from the region's relationship to the global economy.[1] Some arguments, as in the structuralist or "dependency" schools, point toward the influence of international factors on highly unequal societies. These forces, however, never act in isolation but always in conjunction with internal dynamics. Engerman and Sokoloff (2006) have shown that it was not colonization in itself that created enormous economic disparities, but certain patterns of colonization, which led into institutional configurations that reproduced highly unequal access to economic, political, and social opportunities. Global conditions work together with local processes to produce, or reduce, inequalities. The structuralist and dependency schools argued that unequal exchange has always been a factor in Latin America's relationship with core nations (Furtado 1970). It has taken on different forms, first as the extraction of precious metals built from the violent exercise of colonial power and forced indigenous and black labor in mines and plantations. Other natural resources later flowed toward Europe and wealthier countries: agricultural and livestock products, wood, rubber, oil, and minerals of every kind. Mines, plantations, oil fields, as well as other economic units that functioned as foreign enclaves, have been emblematic of the role that Latin America played in the international division of labor. During the twentieth century, other forms of uneven exchange materialized. Even though manufacturing industries developed in the majority of countries, rarely were they at the forefront of technological development. Latin America continues to be a net importer of technology and capital goods whose prices tend to be higher than the products exported by the region. To this one must add the inequality implicit in financial dependence since, during the last half-century, Latin American countries have paid out considerable capital in servicing their heavy debt. And for a long time Latin America has welcomed direct foreign investment that translates into more currency and jobs, but these earnings are usually surpassed by the wealth remitted to other countries in the form of profits and commodities. This has fed into a long debate over a secular deterioration in the "terms of trade" with developed nations.

For these structuralist *pensadores* and the dependency theorists, Latin America's subordinate insertion in the global economy contributes to internal social inequality for three basic reasons. First, because it provokes an ongoing financial leakage for local economies and public resources, which constrains the possibilities of social programs to guarantee quality health, education, and social services for the population as a whole. Second, it contributes to the division between internal and external markets. From colonial times, the region's exporting capacity meant tapping the wealth of natural resources and the exploitation of local or African labor. The consolidation of the internal market, however, has rarely been as strong. Oftentimes, a dynamic exporting sector remained disarticulated from depressed internal or regional markets (Vuskovic 1996: 42). This historical tendency is still in play and frames a perverse dynamic in which social inequality spawns the conditions for exportation grounded in cheap labor while exports are pursued in ways that reproduce income disparities. This creates a structure of opportunities in which the earnings of the powerful do not contribute to the collective gains of equalizing development. Third, Latin America's asymmetrical insertion in global markets favors the formation and reproduction of intermediary elites, who reap a substantial portion of the benefits of this relationship, as observed today in the management sector of transnational corporations as well as in other related social categories: owners of supply and service businesses, the owners of facilities for rent to foreign-owned maquiladoras, and their technical and professional personnel.

In sum, for many researchers of a Marxist or structuralist orientation, Latin American inequality has a decidedly external edge whose origin lies in the long colonial period, but which later became transformed into newer forms of economic subordination to and disparate exchange relationships with developed countries. Yet this can hardly explain the full extent of the phenomenon. From other perspectives, particularly of a neo-institutional grounding, scholars have questioned whether the persistence of inequalities in the region should be solely or originally attributed to relations with the global economy (Haber 2002; Haber and Summerhill 1997; Huber and Stephens 2005; Sokoloff and Engerman 2000). The external dimension operates in conjunction with endogenous factors: institutional characteristics, categorical barriers, and inequalities between the elites and the rest of the population; the superimposition of ethnic distinctions and class differences; the structural polarization of the economy; and the aptitude of political elites, so-called crony capitalists, for appropriating a disproportionate share of the rents produced in the region.

There are also international factors that operate in a contrary direction, that is, that have helped to soften inequality. The intensity of Latin America's ties with the world has generated genuine resources, compared, say, to most of Africa, a part of which has worked a growth impact in Latin America. Some historians have argued that the colonial economy had multiplier effects across vast regions like the Andes (Assadourian 1982), while others have found that during periods in which exports dominate Latin America's economy has largely grown (Coatsworth and Taylor 1988). Today one can point to the revenues that Mexico and Venezuela obtain through oil exports, or that Chile obtains in other export activities, a large part of which has been ploughed into social and educational programs. Latin America's geographical proximity to the United States has been the cause of many headaches, but has also presented the region with opportunities: the flow of investments, markets, a destination for migrants, development assistance, and so on. The political and cultural ties to the United States, Canada, and Western Europe have also contributed to Latin America's embrace of citizenship and republican ideals and to the illegitimacy of many older forms of ethnic and gender discrimination. It would be absurd to think that all external ties are negative and work only to increase social inequality. Isolation hardly guarantees equality and can, in some cases, generate greater exclusion, as has happened in Haiti for centuries and in Cuba during just the past decade. The focal point is not in Latin America's external ties per se, but in the external and internal mechanisms that regulate an equal or unequal distribution of resources.

Many Latin American countries display striking income differentials. Mexico is a prime example of the enormous disparity in salaries, in particular between those at the top of the pyramid and the rest of the population. This disparity is evident within the private sector as well as in the public and social sectors. In the management sector, the CEOs of the leading companies (those with more than $500 million in earnings) earned average annual salaries of $866,666 in 2001, a figure that ranks among the highest in the world.[2] What comes as a surprise is that they earn more than executives in richer countries such as Germany, Japan, or Canada. This pattern marks the public sector as well: in 2002 Mexico's secretaries of state (a grade equivalent to cabinet minister) received an average salary of $179,000, a higher figure than earned by the prime ministers of Great Britain and Spain ($167,000 and $77,000, respectively). Something analogous occurs at the parliamentary level, where not only do senators and federal representatives enjoy high salaries, but even the most local representatives better their counterparts in developed countries.[3] Such immoderation appears worse if contrasted to the average yearly salary in the formal sector in Mexico, which is still only $6,000.[4] That these salary differentials pervade various sectors of the economy, during different governments and under the rule of different parties, suggests a true structural pattern, one that is politically fixed to a society that has tolerated great disparities in income. The distribution of wealth within a firm, a governmental agency, a university, or a nongovernmental organization depends not only on strict economic variables (supply and demand or the marginal productivity of participants), but also on structures of power, institutional configurations, and cultural determinants. In all countries, executives, managers, and politicians take incomes higher than the average, but in every case the disparity's threshold of legitimacy differs (Kelley and Evans 1993: 76). A salient feature of Latin America is the persisting magnitude of these asymmetries, based not necessarily on majority consent but on the historical correlation of political forces. Rather than a dualism, there prevails a salary structure in which the top of the wage pyramid appropriates a huge portion of the income of economic units. The flip side is that the remaining workers and employees of that unit receive paltry salaries. The high incomes of a specific economic sector cannot be understood apart from the low wages received by the rest.

Elite Capacity for Privilege under
Different Political-Economic Regimes

In May 2003 thirty of Latin America's richest men met in Mexico.[5] Two things about this event were immediately striking: the magnitude of the cumulative fortune of those gathered there, and the attendees' capacity to adapt to new times. Ten of those attending, led by their host Carlos Slim, had appeared on the *Forbes* list of multimillionaires that year. The combined fortune of those ten was $25 billion, a quantity higher than the gross national product of some of the smaller Latin American countries. And these multimillionaires were only the tip of the iceberg of the Latin American elite. According to the 2003 World Wealth Report, conducted by Merrill Lynch and Capgemini, there were 300,000 people with financial assets surpassing one million dollars at the end of 2002.[6]

When one imagines inequality, need and deficiency usually come to mind: millions of people barely getting by under conditions of poverty. But inequality has another side that evokes not limitations, but the unconstrained capacity for accumulating wealth. Latin America is a continent of the poor, but a small section of the population is immensely prosperous, with the region's rich having incomes comparable to their peers in the first world. This asymmetry can be understood from two complimentary perspectives. On the one hand, there is a history of failures and frustrations with reform, a consistent region-wide governmental incapacity to raise the living conditions of the poor. On the other hand, there is a successful history of power and of private appropriation of wealth, the history of a segment of the population that has retained the capacity to keep their privileges and to concentrate half of total income across long periods.

Persistent inequality requires the persistence of elites. In the Latin American case, the resilience of the dominating classes is astonishing: they have been able to reproduce their advantages throughout different historical time periods, under different political regimes, and while following different economic models. From primary-goods export economies at the end of the nineteenth century to the revival of liberal export economies, and passing through the age of import substitution in the mid-twentieth century, the enormous concentration of income at the pyramid's peak has been a constant. It has been maintained under authoritarian governments as well as under populist ones and even under more democratic states.

The reproduction of the Latin American elite is not the outcome of continuity and immobility. On the contrary, it is also a story of conversions, ruptures, and transformations. From a political standpoint, the substitution of governing groups has been the norm: after the wars of independence, the Portuguese, Spanish, French, and British colonial administrators were replaced by new Creole elites, who in some cases were mestizos or descendants of blacks. Later, during the nineteenth century, there were struggles and alternation between the liberal and conservative factions, in addition to the caudillo military's ongoing coup attempts, stirring many abrupt changes in the highest ranks of government elites. In the twentieth century, displacements continued as a result of convulsions such as the revolutions in Mexico, Bolivia, and Nicaragua, as well as military regimes in many countries. Beneath this dizzying history of social and political turmoil, the composition of the elites changed, but a social structure characterized by the existence of select groups with access to economic and political privileges has persisted. At an individual level, a person's situation may rise or fall, but what remains the same is a social regime in which the highest positions stay far out of reach of the majority.

For much of Latin American history, the reason for this permanence was the high concentration of land, a condition that persists in the majority of cases, with the exception of countries where small properties were reinforced (Costa Rica) or that underwent more or less successful agrarian reforms (Mexico). A second factor contributing to the resilience of Latin American elites has been the use of force: many attempts to redistribute land

and wealth were abruptly terminated as a result of military coups and repression, as in Guatemala after 1952–54 or in Chile after 1973 (Hoffman and Centeno 2003). But other elements must be added to the oligarchy equals land-plus-guns formula: the differences in social and educational capital, the superposition of ethnic and class distinctions, and elite sway over state institutions (Birdsall, Graham, and Sabot 1998). Of crucial importance is the inability of most public policies to substantially alter the structure of wealth concentration. In general, high-income groups win the support of the Latin American middle classes in blocking any serious attempts at progressive fiscal reform (Karl 2002; World Bank 2003). Governments have carried out a variety of programs that benefit the middle and lower sectors, but they are rarely successful at or focused on reducing the excessive privileges of the upper class. Not even leaders with populist or left-wing orientations have been able to eliminate these privileges, since it is difficult to govern without the support, or at least the tolerance, of sectors that are able to exert counterpressures, from capital flight, to ferocious media attacks, and even to political destabilization and military intervention.

The political might of the economic elite does not always translate into direct control over state apparatuses. Conflicts frequently register between state technocrats and businessmen. Latin American governing officials absorb pressures from all social strata, in addition to harboring their own bureaucratic interests; this is why they often develop programs and policies that do not correspond to the interests and expectations of the elites. This region has witnessed many social movements and demands for inclusion and for policies to benefit disadvantaged groups, but they have not been able to permanently reorient public policies toward greater social equality. It is more common for mobilized groups to make particular gains or to get clientelistic favors, but these do not translate into universal rights, much less an erosion of the advantages of the most powerful groups. Social demands usually benefit the position of those who carry out the protest.

Latin American powerholders have been able to adapt to the new circumstances while maintaining their place under varying political systems. They have also restructured their businesses throughout distinct periods of economic growth—first as landowners and *hacendados*, later as industrialists, businessmen and bankers, in their capacity as partners or intermediaries of foreign capital, or by fielding true business and financial empires. Those attending the 2003 meeting of mega-businessmen in Mexico are a good example of the preceding: they represent the heads of big corporations, in traditional industries such as cement, construction, beer, and bottling as well as newer fields such as media, pharmaceuticals, and banking. Many of them do not descend from older oligarchies, as new immigrants or of non-European descent, and have recently acquired their fortunes. Faces and family names dramatically change, but the social structure in which a small strata of the population hoards the most privilege is still getting reproduced.

In Sum: Historical Accumulating Advantages and Disadvantages

If Latin American inequality were the result of some theoretical "lone gunman" (land concentration, ethnic prejudice, the plundering of natural resources, educational gaps, neoliberal economic policies, or any other widely accepted suspect), then it could be eradicated by a single focused course of audacious action—be that agrarian reform, full recognition of indigenous autonomy, the nationalization of a strategic resource, massive educational investments, or full-employment economic policies. The popular and sometimes academically held idea persists that one key policy, or one key party or leader hoisted into power, will reverse inequalities that have rooted themselves over centuries. It is not so simple. The region's inequalities are the result of many factors that have articulated themselves over long spans, generating an insidious historical accumulation of advantages and disadvantages. An answer to the riddle of persistent inequality in Latin America is likely found in the overlapping of multiple inequality processes.

One might begin with two key dimensions of the region's Tillyesque categorical inequalities: the juxtaposition of class, ethnic, and gender hierarchies; a system of power relations that reconstructs barriers and social, educational, and cultural distances between privileged sectors and the mass of the population. These dimensions articulate with two other central historical features of Latin America: structural tendencies toward economic polarization, and the capacity of elites to reproduce their privileges. Factoring in as well are the weaknesses and contradictions of fiscal systems, social policies, and other mechanisms that might be able to foster greater equality (Reygadas 2008: 164–72). Along similar lines, social inequality in Latin America is strongly related to the limits on redistributive policies (Huber and Stephens 2005); to the fragility of rules covering property rights, which tends toward the exclusion of majorities (Haber, Razo, and Maurer 2003); and, in a general sense, to the weakness of institutions that are fundamental for equal access to political, economic, educational, and social opportunities

(Abel and Lewis 2002; Haber and Summerhill 1997). Other pieces of the Latin American inequality puzzle explored in this book include the segmentation of health services, everyday practices and relations in shantytowns, the asymmetry in political information and participation, the reconstruction of categorical inequality during migratory processes, and the aesthetics of inequality.[7] It is the conjunction of all these aspects, as well as others that cannot be examined here, that explains the complexity and persistence of inequality in Latin America.

These are interactive processes of long duration, which little by little have built up the historical accumulation of advantages and disadvantages of different kinds. This plays out on the individual level as well as in the social structures of the region. At the individual level, a minority of the population, around 10 percent of the total, concentrates about half the income, has better educational opportunities, and has access to political power and strategic social networks, while the majority of Latin Americans have precarious economic resources, attain only a low level and quality of education, exert little influence on political decisions, and find few chances for decent, well-paying jobs. At a macrolevel, a deeply polarized economic structure has evolved, one that leaves noticeable differences between regions, between formal and informal sectors, and between directing and working strata. A feedback loop then connects the individual level (inequality in the distribution of personal capacities) and the structural level (inequality between privileged and underprivileged social positions). Although the constructive and cultural dimensions of inequalities must be addressed, one should be careful not to ignore such structures.

Between the micro- and macrolevels of Latin American inequality operates a relational logic that can be understood under the "categorial inequality" model proposed by Tilly (1998). Latin America is a sterling case of the superimposition of ethnic, class, and gender categories across long historical periods. This has led to extremely hierarchical classificatory systems that penetrate everyday unequal relations between different social groups. Tilly's focus on categorical inequalities makes an excellent starting point for grasping the persistence of inequalities in Latin America. His proposal is enriched when one takes into consideration the historical and cultural processes that have constructed, reproduced, and modified the barriers that draw and limit social categories in Latin America. Moreover, it becomes an even more powerful tool when linked to ongoing debates about the region's economic history and analyses of institutional development.

Although inequality has prevailed, there is also change and tension in the mechanisms that generate inequalities. In the colonial period, violent expropriation (through the use of force, theft, looting, and caste discrimination) was fundamental to the vast concentration of land and natural wealth. But not everything can be explained by this "original sin" of conquest. What followed colonialism was equally crucial. The everyday workings of exploitation, unequal exchange, the hoarding of opportunities, and exclusion were all at work to produce disparities surrounding novel resources: education, cultural capital, housing, health services, and job opportunities. In this way, old inequalities, befitting agrarian societies, become joined to the new inequalities characteristic of modern urban information societies. Inequalities in Latin America have survived their transformations: from colonial expropriation to unequal exchange mediated by productive and technological competition; from ethnic discrimination to historically ignored needs within black and indigenous communities; from the invisibility of women to their subtle social exclusion; from a forced exploitation of the labor force to the disparities created by polarized job markets under soaring rates of underemployment.

Latin American inequalities cannot be explained by the functioning of the economic system alone (unequal exchange, dependency, polarization of the salary structure, concentration of the means of production, uneven human capital, or relations of subordination and exploitation between the formal and informal sectors). A diversity of political processes intervene as well: excluding or stratified citizenship, the weakness of welfare states, limited democracies, the unrestrained elite influence, the weight of clientelism, among others, as well as cultural dynamics that remake the barriers and limits that preserve differences and hierarchies among social groups.

The indelible inequalities of Latin America are historically constructed, not the sum of inexorable fate. It is frequently acknowledged that the best predictor of future inequality within a society is that society's past inequality. A bedrock of historical advantages and disadvantages, the argument goes, fosters and facilitates the reproduction of unequal practices and structures. But one is not dealing with a closed and fatal circle that reproduces inequalities ad infinitum. One is dealing with historical processes mediated by quite contradictory forces. In Latin America there have existed and still exist diverse actors and forces that counteract inequality. If they have not had the power to substantially reduce income concentration, they have had a moderating influence in other vital realms and have proved crucial for the incorporation of millions of people into the region's modern trajectory of development, even though this integration has been slow, precarious, and full of setbacks and constraints. There are countries, time periods, and experiences that reveal more potential equalities. Uruguay and Costa Rica have both, over long periods, proved more egalitarian than the rest of the continent with their inclusionary and democratic foundations, as well as erecting fewer hierarchical walls between citizens. For a long time, Chile avoided extreme land concentration (Karl 2002). Poverty levels dipped in several countries during the first eight decades of the twentieth century, and in the period between 1950 and 1980 income disparities lessened in some key countries, such as Colombia and Mexico (Hernández Laos and Velásquez 2003; Portes 1985). Thousands of micro and grassroots initiatives generated in the last few decades endeavor to improve the conditions of the poor and reduce the disadvantages that affect women, indigenous groups, and black communities. Latin America may be plagued by distances and barriers between social groups, but it is also host to vibrant movements that strive to break these barriers, scale distances, and build new social bridges. There are good reasons to be pessimistic—inequality is a structural feature that will not drastically decrease in a few short years. But insofar as it is also the result of historical processes, and not an inescapable doom, it can also be reversed and deconstructed. It will not be an easy nor a speedy path, but surely it must be traveled.

Translated by Celina Bragagnolo

Notes

Paul Gootenberg edited the translation.

1. See Gootenberg's essay in this volume.
2. "Salarios ejecutivos: Remuneran bien a los mexicanos," *La Reforma*, 3 December 2001.
3. "Salen diputados de NL más caros que en EU," *La Reforma*, 13 June 2003.
4. "Ganan secretarios más que líderes mundiales," *La Reforma*, 18 December 2002.
5. "Conciliábulo de empresarios de AL en la ciudad de México," *La Jornada*, 24 May 2003; "Celebran cumbre empresarios," *La Reforma*, 24 May 2003.
6. "Tiene el país 80,000 muy ricos," *La Reforma*, 13 June 2003.
7. See respectively the essays in this volume by Ewig, Anderson, Renno, Gray, and Casamayor.

PART II

History, Subjectivity,

and Politics

3

Health Policy and the Historical Reproduction of Class, Race, and Gender Inequality in Peru

CHRISTINA EWIG

Social policies, such as pensions, healthcare, and antipoverty programs, are often conceived of as tools to ameliorate inequalities. Yet, as first observed by the well-known scholar of welfare states, Gøsta Esping-Anderson (1990), social policies provide benefits *and* serve to stratify societies along multiple cleavages. In other words, social policies may in fact (intentionally or unintentionally) reinforce or even create certain inequalities. Because social policies often segment different groups into different kinds of social-benefit systems, the concept of "stratification" has been used to explain the negative effects of social policies on societies. However, as Charles Tilly notes, the idea of vertical and horizontal stratification fosters "an illusion of a continuous, homogeneous two-dimensional grid within which individuals and aggregates of individuals occupy specific cells and move along geometric paths" (1998: 28). Instead, he argues, a relational analysis that incorporates structure and agency is needed in order to move beyond static and unrealistic analyses of social life. Tilly's categorical and relational theory of inequality provides a more dynamic tool than the geological stratification metaphor would allow, for example, how organized groups in civil society, states, and state social policies interact with the "bounded categories" of class, race, and gender to ameliorate or accentuate inequalities over time. The long-term *construction* of inequalities can be uncovered through historical analysis of the formation of health policies in Peru from the late nineteenth century forward. Following Paul Gootenberg's suggestion, I seek to provide a more historically grounded vision of how inequalities are constructed and maintained, but also how these change and indelibly camouflage themselves over the long haul.[1]

In addition to providing more historical grounding to Tilly's theory of durable inequalities, I contribute to broader intellectual debates on the relationship between gender and race and social policies by examining these relationships in the Latin American region. While scholars have offered rich analyses of how social policies perpetuate gender and racial inequalities in advanced industrialized nations, historical feminist welfare state analysis in Latin America is, as of yet, a nascent field of inquiry.[2] While works by Malloy (1979) and Mesa-Lago (1978, 1989) are considered classic comparative-history accounts of social-policy formation in Latin America, they focus primarily on the role of class power and state responses to class-based actions and ignore gender and race.[3] Class may be fundamental to understanding social policy formation in Latin America, but these historical formation processes were also based on gendered and racialized relations of power.

Pre-existing class, race, and gender inequalities in Peru served to shape the formation of Peru's health system in ways that reflected those inequalities. Once established, the resulting health system served to reinforce and perpetuate inequalities by privileging some groups over others, in a feedback effect. Yet such inequalities were neither rigid nor permanent. While the "bounded categories" of gender, race, and class continue to be immensely important in structuring Peruvian inequality, they have morphed and changed along with the transformation of health policies, helping to reshape Peruvian inequalities over time. These changes, in fact, provide clues as to the specific tools one might use to move closer to the goal of greater equality in the future.

Categorical Inequalities and Health-Policy Formation in Peru

Tilly argues in *Durable Inequalities* that bounded pairs such as male-female, aristocrat-plebian, citizen-foreigner and more complex categories such as race (often reduced to white-black despite this category's far greater complexity) "do crucial organizational work." By this he means that social organizations such as communities, workplaces, corporations, and state institutions adopt these categories as a shorthand for deciding who shall be allotted certain privileges or benefits. These allotments *are* often contested, but longstanding belief systems such as religion and "common knowledge" more often justify and perpetuate these categorical inequalities, usually by making these categorical inequalities appear to be the result of individual decisions or traits. These asymmetries are not between separate entities, but rather are intimately bound together.[4] That is, the benefits of the one side depend crucially on the wants of the other and are predicated on the social construction of these binaries.

These categorical inequalities, Tilly explains, are created by two primary causal mechanisms: exploitation, "which operates when powerful, connected people command resources from which they draw significantly increased returns by coordinating the effort of outsiders whom they exclude from the full value added by that effort"; and opportunity hoarding, "which operates when members of a categorically bounded network acquire access to a resource that is valuable, renewable, subject to monopoly, supportive of network activities, and enhanced by the network's modus operandi" (1998: 10). The critical difference between these two mechanisms is that the second mode is accessible to relatively weak groups, while the first is exclusive to real powerholders.

In Peru, the bounded triad of class, race, and gender existed in Peruvian society prior to the advent of the health system and were the result of previous social processes of exploitation and opportunity hoarding. These existing bounded pairs, in turn, played important roles in shaping the terms of the formation of Peru's health system. Once formed, the health system proceeded to use these binaries as part of its justification of its own structure of benefits, thus reinforcing the inequalities inherent in these binaries. Yet Peru's history of health-policy formation demonstrates that these categories were not static and their related inequalities were also not entirely "durable." The categories shifted over time—as did the structure of the health system itself as a result of contestation of particular groups and of government (re)actions. While health policy both reflects and reinforces broader inequalities, Peru's history of health policy also reveals a certain dynamism by showing how these inequalities are renegotiated over time and how social policies play a part in these shifts.

Peru's health system was constructed in a two-stage process. It began, much as in the rest of Latin America, in the late nineteenth century with the development of a public-health system, which was formed in an internal "colonizing" process. I use the term *colonizing* to mean a process similar to Tilly's exploitation, in that "powerful, connected people" commanded the process and sought specific returns, particularly economic benefits. However, this process was quite a bit more complicated than simple exploitation, in that while elites had an instrumental economic interest in improved national public health, they also harbored more nationalist desires for national

development and social progress. They often intensified their campaigns
with foreign cooperation, making this process in some ways akin to foreign
colonization, though it was primarily a nationally motivated internal colonization process. I also use the term *colonization* because it was used by key
protagonists in the founding of state public-health services, figures who
characterized public health as an important tool for the state to gain control
over, or internally "colonize," geographically isolated portions of Peru's
national territory, such as Amazonia or the high Andes. In sum, the formation of the public-health system was a process of internal colonization,
born partially of national development imperatives that included economic
growth and resource exploitation as well as greater political and social control over the national territory. At the same time, however, the state and the
many doctors, nurses, and health professionals in its service saw their project of building a public-health system as part of the betterment of the population and their life conditions, even though the means used to achieve this
were rarely democratic or egalitarian.

This historical process of internal colonization depended on the assumption of the bounded pairs female-male, indigenous-Creole, and elite–
popular class (a division that has a variety of historical nomenclatures in
Peru). In brief, male, Creole oligarchs devised the public-health system in
part out of a desire for the uplift of the targeted populations of women,
indigenous peoples, and the poor, but also in part out of their desire to
exploit these groups so that they might contribute the human resources
necessary for the economic and social development of the Peruvian nation as
a whole. Because its designers employed unequal categorical distinctions to
justify its mission, the public-health system that emerged had important
stigmatizing aspects that served to further reinforce these categorical inequalities over time. These stigmatizing effects were brought into greater
relief during the second major phase of health-policy development in Peru.

In this phase, one can identify an important shift in two of the bounded
pairs and in the process by which the health system was constructed. Industrialization, migration, and urbanization led to the emergence of two new
classes of workers in mid-twentieth-century Peru: urban factory workers and
middle-class professionals. As a result, the elite-popular category in Peru
began to lose some of its significance, and rather than a new binary, a triad
of the poor-worker-elite emerged, with the new urban workers and middle-
class professionals representing a very small and thus new group of elites.
With this shift, one also sees the emergence of a related new racial triad of

indigenous-mestizo-white, which begins to displace the indigenous-white binary, in that a notable portion of urban Peruvian society, including the new class of workers and professionals, begin to identify as mestizo, or mixed race, rather than as white or indigenous.[5]

These shifts in categories contributed to a new process of health-policy formation, one akin to Tilly's notion of opportunity hoarding, but which also involved a government reaction of cooptation. In a context of scarce resources, workers used their newfound political power to demand better health services, but they did so in an exclusive manner that left the existing, poorly supported public-health system intact, while layering on top of it a better, higher-quality system serving only these workers. The state, in a manner reminiscent of Bismarck's Germany, recognized the political advantage to separate but unequal health systems, as this form of organization limited state expenditures and served as a political tool for coopting the emerging political actors.

The layering of a better health system on top of the old, however, reinforced the bounded categories of poor-worker and indigenous-mestizo, as the new health system provided more and better resources to mestizo workers than to the indigenous poor. Moreover, the layering further accentuated the bounded category of male-female. The separate health social-security systems erected for the middle and working classes served primarily male workers, with extremely limited coverage for spouses and children. This change in the health system left the public-healthcare sector feminized in two senses: first, it was the only system free of direct cost to the majority of women and the poor and, second, one of its priorities was to exert control over women's biological reproduction. A further distinction between the two systems was that the newer social-security health system came to be viewed as an exclusive right earned by its beneficiaries, while the services of the public-health system, which had never been explicitly fought for, continued to be viewed as a "welfare" benefit in the stigmatizing sense and as a policy apparatus through which national economic objectives were privileged over individual well-being.

Colonization: Health Care for the Poor

Peru's public-health system was formed largely through a process of internal colonization, a process that included the exploitation and control of human resources in order to serve broader, instrumental national economic objectives. But this form of colonization also incorporated the nationalist objective of national betterment through better health, though the means by which this was achieved were often authoritarian and explicitly drew on racial and gendered bounded pairs.

The establishment of Peru's state public-health system can be traced to the late nineteenth century and the early twentieth, spurred by economic development and the related expansion of the state.[6] From 1890 to 1930, Peru experienced dramatic economic growth. According to one estimate, from 1900 to 1929 the economy grew seven-and-a-half times in terms of gross domestic product (Boloña 1994, cited in Contreras 2004: 177). Economic growth led to an expanding state. Between 1920 and 1928 the number of public servants in Lima almost tripled, from 5,329 to 14,778 (Contreras 2004: 184). At the start of the twentieth century, two issues in particular became major state foci, which in turn shaped the evolution of public-health policy. First was a desire to increase national population in order to meet the labor demands of the expanding agricultural and mining sectors (Contreras 2004; Mannarelli 1999). This goal was sought in the public-health arena through control of epidemics and via policies to reduce infant mortality. A second central focus was a desire to extend state control over interior zones of the national territory with the objective of fostering their economic potential. Public health was seen as an essential tool for such control.

Scarcity of labor, and the related concern about low population levels, became a point of debate in the late nineteenth century as a result of the abolition of slavery, in 1855, and the dramatic era of export growth that followed (Contreras 2004:188). Peruvian elites, like those in other Latin American countries, began to debate the best means to increase the population. Urban elites advocated white European immigration, invoking the premises of eugenics popular at the time, that Europeans would " 'civilize' and populate the country, creating the basis for a robust internal market" (Contreras 2004: 190).[7] Landowners, by contrast, sought cheap manual labor for their plantations and were not willing to pay the high wages necessary to compete with neighboring Chile, Brazil, or Argentina for attracting European workers. Landowners were content with Asian immigrants, who hailed first from China and later from Japan. For a variety of reasons, immigration rates to Peru proved minor compared to other Latin American countries. In 1876 foreigners constituted 4 percent of the population and in 1940 just 1 percent. In 1940, 46 percent of these foreigners were Asian and 21 percent were European (Contreras 2004: 194).

Unable to lure significant numbers of immigrants, the Peruvian state turned to mortality reduction as a demographic and labor policy (Contreras 2004). It did so in two major ways: by actively fighting epidemics and by initiating the first maternal-child health programs with the aim of decreasing infant mortality. In response to the bubonic plague that threatened Peru's coastal cities and towns between 1903 and 1930, the Peruvian government established the first national public-health institutions (Cueto 1997: 27). Key among these was the Dirección de Salubridad Pública (Public Health Board) established in 1903, the precursor to today's Ministry of Health (Cueto 1997: 35).[8] The Dirección de Salubridad Pública was a section of the Ministry of Development (Fomento), a fitting institutional home in that it reflected the views of civilian elite political leaders, who saw state oversight of public-health matters as intrinsic to economic progress and development.

In this colonizing process, in which public health was promoted with an eye toward economic development, crusades against certain diseases became conceptually tied to poverty and race.[9] Justification of these public-health programs and the manner by which they were implemented (often in top-down authoritarian style) were rooted in the reinforcement of unequal categorical pairs of popular class–elites, indigenous-white, and foreigner-citizen. These binaries often bled together in reality: the rates of mortality related to the plague, for example, were higher among persons of indigenous descent and Asian immigrants because these groups were generally poorer and had limited access to healthcare, and thus were more susceptible to disease (Cueto 1997: 50). But race and class convergence was played on by those who acted on behalf of the state, with real consequences for the social policies that resulted. The historian Marcos Cueto writes about the plague in the following terms: "The disease was associated with misery, poor living conditions, and what was even worse: to be considered *chino* [Asian] or *serrano* [indigenous and of the highlands], for some the scum of the earth" (Cueto 1997: 51). As a result, to be targeted by public-health officials was to be racially stigmatized, so much so that upper stratum Peruvians often hid their illnesses. The early public-health system came to be understood as a tool to eradicate disease among populations deemed to be more susceptible to ill health due to their individual "racial" characteristics, rather than due to the structural underpinnings of racial and economic inequality that actually enhanced their susceptibility. Framing health policy in this way not only ignored these real inequalities, but also reinforced them.

While the fight against the plague gave rise to the colonization process that eventually resulted in the state public-health system, that system remained rudimentary until the 1920s. This began to change when the regime of Augusto Leguía (1919–1930) began to strengthen state public-health activities with the aid of foreign counterparts. Having closed the congress immediately after his election as president in 1919, Leguía's "oncenio" regime was notably authoritarian. It was also characterized by its dependence on foreign support—financial and technical—for achieving its development objectives (McClintock 1999: 316; Cueto 1992: 9; Klarén 2000). Leguía enhanced the state in part through spending: social spending between 1920 and 1929 increased annually at a rate of 11.6 percent (Portocarrero, cited in Arroyo Laguna 2000: 190). The fight against another epidemic, yellow fever, served to expand the state's public-health infrastructure with the help of the New York–based Rockefeller Foundation.[10] The outbreak of yellow fever in Peru in 1919 coincided with renewed interest on the part of the United States and European powers in economic expansion into Latin America, Africa, and Asia. The Rockefeller Foundation was alarmed by Peru's yellow fever epidemic, which it saw as a threat to regional trade, potentially infecting ships and spreading the disease to the United States (Cueto 1992). The foundation provided Peru with substantial financial resources and key technical support through the appointment of American physicians to lead Peru's anti-yellow fever campaign.

Reflecting Leguía's governing style and racist attitudes toward Latin America in the United States, the yellow fever campaign was carried out in an authoritarian fashion.[11] The American physician who led the campaign, Henry Hanson, ignored the Peruvian cultural norms and attitudes surrounding healthcare, including the customs of self-medication and reliance on native healers. Cueto writes of the episode, "The attitudes and responses of patients were treated as primitivism to be brushed aside" (1992: 21). Hanson's entourage of forty cavalry and a cruiser of sailors and marines controlled migration from affected areas, prevented public gatherings, and imposed a quarantine on the sick (Cueto 1992: 15). Similar to previous periods, Hanson depended on these strong-arm and technical solutions to attack the epidemic and the individuals affected by it, rather than addressing the social and structural factors related to the spread of the disease.

Next to the focus on quelling epidemics, maternal-child health services formed a second strategy for increasing population levels. The early maternal-child health services in Peru demonstrate once again the resonance of the instrumental objective of economic development behind the formation of Peru's public health system: maternal-child health services were viewed as key to reducing infant mortality and thereby enhancing the labor force and in turn economic development. These services were motivated in part by statistics from 1903–1908 that showed that one-quarter of all children in Lima did not live to one year of age (Contreras 2004: 203–5). While many of the professionals involved in the design and delivery of these early maternal-child health services had a sincere desire to protect and promote human life, a parallel objective of this program, from the viewpoint of the state, was to raise population levels. Population, writes Contreras, was still "viewed as a form of capital" (Contreras 2004: 205n18).

Reflecting the general medical consensus in Peru at the time, the maternal-child health program was premised on the belief that infant mortality could be prevented by mothers (Mannarelli 1999: 73). The new maternal-child health services were to be managed primarily by professionally trained nurse midwives. The initial goal was to appoint one nurse-midwife to serve in each province, a goal that was reached in just half of all provinces by 1916. The government directed these midwives to offer free obstetric services day and night, to provide two hours of daily consultations to pregnant mothers, and to write regular reports to the central government on the number of registered births and child vaccinations. The historian Carlos Contreras notes the authoritarian side of the program, in which infant diets were closely monitored, mothers were compelled to follow the hygienic procedures indicated by nurses, and vaccinations were obligatory (2004).

While racial binaries were central to the fight against epidemics, the maternal-child health program exemplified the ways in which the female-male categorical binary was also at work in the formation of the public-health system. While some may quibble as to whether Peru's early maternal-child health program was indeed authoritarian or simply the practice of the time, the format of the program did demand much of mothers as individuals and identified mothers as the cause of infant mortality. Peru's policy at the time reflected a global early-twentieth-century infatuation with holding women individually responsible for the successful re-generation of the national population. Individualization of the problem of infant mortality, with responsibility falling disproportionately on one side of the female-male categorical divide, diverted attention from the root cause of child mortality: poverty. In the process, individualization drew on and reinforced the unequal categorical binary of female-male. Women became intimately responsible for social reproduction (and in fact blamed for child deaths), while males conversely had little such responsibility, or guilt.

While population was viewed as a form of national capital on the road to development in the early twentieth century, so were the rich untapped resources of the interior of Peru's national territory. The state, led by Creoles of European descent, justified its closer control of distant territories within Peru partially based on the belief that it was necessary for the state to "civilize" the native populations. State public-health services, based on Western biomedical practices, were viewed as an important part of this "civilizing" process and were premised on the indigenous-white binary.

In the late 1930s and early 1940s, amid an economic spurt and urbanization, major efforts were made for an effective state presence in the Amazon jungle region in eastern Peru. Similar but more limited efforts registered in the sierra (Cueto n.d.: 26). State expansion into the Amazon was intrinsically tied to foreign interests, particularly American ones, in rubber and tropical agricultural products. In 1942, the wartime government launched the Peruvian Amazon Corporation (Corporación Peruana de Amazonas), and in 1943 the Board of Eastern Affairs, Colonization, and Eastern Lands (Dirección de Asuntos Orientales, Colonización y Terrenos de Oriente). The former was charged with overseeing rubber production while the latter authorized land use for cattle and tropical agriculture (Cueto n.d.: 14).

Public-health services played a vital role in state colonization of the interior. As a part of this economic oversight, in 1940 the Ministry of Health, Work, and Social Provision established an office to oversee the public-health concerns of the Amazon region. This ministry had been established, in 1935, under the dictatorship of General Benavides and replaced the old Dirección de Salubridad Pública (Cueto n.d.: 17–18). The government of Manuel Prado (1939–45) significantly expanded the financial resources and personnel of this ministry and in 1942 directed it to focus exclusively on health issues, renaming it the Ministerio de Salud Pública y Asistencia Social (Ministry of Public Health and Social Assistance) (Cueto n.d.: 19). This fortified ministry contracted well-known Peruvian doctors, such as Maxime Kuczynski-Godard and Carlos Enrique Paz Soldán, to lead its efforts to colonize the Amazon. Paz Soldán himself explained, "The modern colonizer is a hygienist. Without health, there is no lasting possession of the earth" (quoted in Cueto n.d.: 23).

Paz Soldán and Kuczynski-Godard were both pioneers in the field of social medicine, helping to establish social medicine in Peru beginning in the 1920s (Cueto 2002). Social medicine, which gained significant influence across Latin America in the 1930s, is often dated to the intellectual work of Rudolf Virchow, of Germany, who argued in the late nineteenth century that multiple social conditions, not unitary "scientific" factors, were significantly related to illness (Waitzkin 1998). Social medicine's recognition of the broader social factors behind ill health might have led to an important shift in Peru's public-health system, perhaps toward a less instrumental and ultimately more egalitarian health system. Yet, despite the many noble objectives behind the social-medicine approach of Paz Soldán and Kuczynski-Godard, these men were also products of their times, in which the unequal binary of indigenous-white was widely accepted. As a result, the racial undertones of their hygienic colonization, in both the Amazon and the sierra, were clear.

Paz Soldán, a prominent physician in Peru and the Latin American region, promoted eugenics as a means of "bettering" the population (Stepan 1991). Initially trained by a French medical officer who had worked in Africa as a colonial physician, Paz Soldán believed that public-health interventions in remote areas could improve the "racial" and moral life of the country (Cueto 2002). Similarly, Kuczynski-Godard vaunted the positive role of the mestizo in the colonization effort, arguing that mestizos were more likely than indigenous peoples to develop healthy hygiene habits and to rationally exploit unutilized land. Moreover, Kuczynski-Godard saw the indigenous shamans' and curanderos' opposition to Western medicine as a major obstacle to the colonization efforts in the Amazon (Cueto 2002: 190–91). Similar racial assessments marked the expansion of state public-health services to the Andean region of Peru. Medical officials posted in Puno, the southernmost and highest altitude city in the Peruvian Andes, viewed the spread of Western medicine to the indigenous-descent peasants as akin to the earlier religious crusade of introducing Christianity (Contreras 2004: 203). Despite the expansion of state health services in this period, these services still reached only a fraction of the population. Throughout the 1940s, the poor, in both rural and urban settings, continued to rely on popular medicine and the Catholic charity hospitals in urban areas.

By the end of the 1940s, the formative period of the public-health system was over. Colonization campaigns in the interior had subsided and a new focus took root: the rise of mobilized urban working and middle classes in the coastal cities of Peru. From the 1930s to the 1950s, the state created multiple, separate health systems for these formal-sector and mostly male workers. The process of creating social-security healthcare had some minor impacts on the public-health system. The state social-security system built a few clinics and hospitals in outlying areas to serve those workers who were insured under the newly formed social-security health system yet far from the main social-security hospitals in urban centers. In some cases, these clinics could also be used by public-health-system patients (Mesa-Lago 1978). Other than this indirect form of expansion, the usual trends dominated the public-health system, such as the influence of foreign interests. For example, in 1957 the Pan American Health Organization and UNICEF led new efforts to eradicate malaria (Cueto 1997: 161–68). As a result of foreign cooperation, the public-health system gained growing numbers of personnel, better training, and financial resources.

Statistics can demonstrate, from the 1950s on, the scope of the public-health system, and from these one can begin to assess its distributive character. The construction of most of the hospitals had been financed during the 1940s and 1950s by the Inter-American Cooperative Public Health Service, funded by the United States, while six hospitals were transferred to the ministry from Catholic charities (Roemer 1964: 45, 48). In 1957, the Ministry of Health began "a basic plan of public health" that sought to provide basic health services to the population through a network of clinics, each connected to a hospital, organized in twenty geographic zones. By 1960, the Ministry of Health could report operating 32 hospitals, 71 health centers, 142 medical posts, and 177 sanitary posts.[12] Many of these, however, were empty and provided very limited services. For example, mandated full-time posts in practice offered services only three hours a week (Roemer 1964: 39–45). Each rural post served a population of about 17,000 people, a ratio that was in reality far worse due to inconsistent staffing. In addition to these primary health facilities, the government, in 1960, had 131 "botequines populares," or pharmacies, that made low-cost medicines available to the population.

Contrary to what one might expect, the radical, nationalist, self-proclaimed Revolutionary Government of the Armed Forces, which took power by coup in 1968 and held power until 1980, paid little attention to the public-health system, despite the keen interest in economic development of the first military president, Juan Velasco Alvarado. This government opted for other avenues toward economic development such as agrarian reform, price subsidies, the organization of the poor in government-organized community groups, and worker participation in the management of firms. Although novel experiments followed in participatory development in rural areas and poor urban neighborhoods, formal-sector workers were its key perceived constituency. The military government began only a handful of public-health initiatives, including a basic medicine-distribution program, free medical care for birthing and recent newborns, and a basic healthcare plan that emphasized community participation (Bravo Castillo 1980). Under the military regime in 1975, the Ministry of Health managed a total of 103 hospitals, 344 health centers, and 994 sanitary posts. Given that the total population had grown from about 10 million in 1960 to some 15 million by 1973, the expansion of hospitals and health posts did not keep up with the population. The fraction of the population that primary health establishments served had improved little since 1960; in 1975, one health center served 29,771 persons, and another health post served a population of 14,323 (Orihuela Paredes 1980: 8–10).

While the military regime had scant interest in strengthening the public-health system, population remained a core government concern, as it had been since the beginning of the twentieth century. The first Velasco government made longstanding state pronatalist practices more explicit. Velasco's pronatalist stance stemmed partially from a Catholic tradition, but was also a nationalist reaction to perceived imperialist interference by the United States, which was now actively promoting population control throughout Latin America.[13] When Velasco resigned, ceding to more conservative generals, the centrist and free-market-oriented regime of General Francisco Morales Bermúdez (1975–80) reversed the pronatalist stance and in 1976 outlined Peru's first official population policy. Morales may have been acquiescing to the influence of the United States, but clearly he was reacting to the rapid rise in population in Peru over the prior two decades. This first population policy reflected international currents of the time by making the "Malthusean" connection that population control now was a prerequisite to sustained economic development (Varillas and Mostajo 1990: 380).[14] The new policy included access to artificial contraception, but considered procreation to be the decision of the couple, using the Catholic concept of "responsible parenthood," in which couples are encouraged to use natural means to decide family size (Guzmán 2002: 190). Although it reflected new international trends, this was still a dramatic reversal from traditional policies based on the idea that increased population was a pure economic gain. It shared with previous policies, however, a responsibility placed on women as mothers for the material well-being of the nation.

By the end of the military period, the government faced a severe economic crisis, which contributed to a deterioration of the public-health system. In 1978, the military imposed the first in a series of economic austerity measures that severely restricted the reach of its few public-health initiatives. In 1980, the Ministry of Health budget composed just 3.5 percent of the general budget, down from 17 percent in 1968, prior to the military takeover (Orihuela Paredes 1980: 7). By 1980, with few funds left for social needs, the already weak infrastructure of the public-health system built during the mid-twentieth century was in disarray. The minister of health under President Fernando Belaúnde Terry (1980–85), the first democratic government following the military, described the state of the health system: "The public hospitals—not those of the social-security system—were in a state of calamity. The patients who went to be hospitalized had to bring their own mattress and sheets."[15] In 1980, the Ministry of Health was responsible for providing healthcare to 70 percent of the national population, yet only reached half of that segment.

Public healthcare became even more scattershot under the new democratic government, as part of an overall policy trend toward "crisis" social-policy interventions while allowing the traditional social-policy structure to wither. The centrist Belaúnde administration raised popular expectations as the first government to be elected when the entire population had suffrage, yet it languished under a continuing economic recession.[16] Debt servicing and military spending to combat growing rebel movements in the sierra absorbed most of the national budget, with few resources dedicated to improving the health sector (Davidson and Stein 1988). As the state retracted social-policy commitments on health funding, it turned to "emergency" social policies such as those that funneled international food donations to women's groups in poor communities. As a hedge against the worsening economy, the government encouraged the proliferation of communal soup kitchens run by women volunteers in poor communities, kitchens originally founded by the Catholic Church. The spread of informal kitchens continued after Belaúnde and became politicized as political parties set up their "own" kitchens during subsequent governments (Barrig 1992). With the incorporation of illiterates, a new and substantially poor electorate thus became the object of clientelist politics. This trend hit the health system by siphoning off social spending to a series of emergency programs that served the dual purposes of aid and clientelism.

The late 1980s stand out as a failed attempt to rectify the downward course of the public-health system. Disillusionment with the Belaúnde government resulted in a dramatic turn of the electorate toward the political Left. In the 1980s, the Izquierda Unida united several Left parties, and for the first time the older populist Alianza Popular Revolucionaria Americana (APRA) party was allowed to run a candidate, in the presidential elections of 1985. Following the presidential victory of APRA candidate Alán García (1985–90), his minister of health, Davíd Tejada de Rivero, worked to reverse the decrepit state of Peru's public-health system and to shift its mission toward primary healthcare. Prior to his service as minister, Tejada had worked for eleven years as assistant director of the World Health Organization (WHO), where he had helped to organize the Alma Alta conference, which had defined the original principles of "primary healthcare," in 1974. Primary healthcare shifts the emphasis away from Western hospital-based health services to basic and preventative healthcare services thought to more effectively address the most common health needs of the poor in developing nations (Cueto 2001: 56; Cueto 2004).

In his first year in office García also passed a national population law, which reiterated the church position of responsible parenthood, but also established the right to a choice of contraceptive methods and individual freedom from manipulation or coercion in matters of family planning (Varillas and Mostajo 1990: 322–23). The government then developed the National Population Program (1987–1990), which outlined goals for reducing fertility rates and providing contraception coverage. However, it secured only modest funding. The program's plan spawned the first family-planning programs in Peru's social-security health system and in Peru's state-run public-health system (Guzmán 2002). Notably, the National Population Program was a component of the National Plan for Development, evidence of the continued association of population issues with economic development. Tejada's campaign for primary care and the launching of state family-planning services were overshadowed, however, by the economic and political crises that confronted the García administration.

This history had important results in terms of reinforcing categorical inequalities. Historically, when the state did bring health services to rural and provincial areas, officials viewed the spread of Western medicine as part of a colonization and civilization process, an approach that left little room for utilizing allopathic medicine along with local, popular medicinal practices. These developments also reinforced racial differences between the urban-educated and European or mestizo doctors who strove to bring a measure of modernity to the indigenous "backward" populations. A similar process occurred with the female-male binary. Women's fertility was subjected to economic development, and the binary of female-male was further essentialized, with such control being made to appear acceptably "natural." Moreover, the public system, although it served the majority of the population, received much less state financial support than the social-security health system, which was created through the "cooptation path." Therefore, the poorest and the indigenous populations were left with scant or no access to healthcare. Women, stuck in the public-health system because the social-security system largely excluded them, also faced lower-quality health services than working- and middle-class males. With the advent of a better financed and higher quality social-security health system, some class, racial, and gendered binaries became further embedded. But the story of cooptation also highlights some important changes in these inequalities as well.

Opportunity Hoarding and Cooptation: The Social-Security Health System

Between 1930 and 1950, during a period of rapid economic change and urbanization, Peru began a second important phase in the formation of its health system. This second phase was characterized by Bismarckian-style cooptation of the middle and working classes into the state-run health-insurance programs that became known as social security, and by opportunity hoarding by the coopted groups who sought to maintain exclusive rights to these new benefits.[17] Authoritarian rulers representing oligarchic interests promoted the creation of social security in response to political pressures from particular interest groups, primarily the middle- and working-class employees newly mobilized in both unions and political parties. These groups represented new political interest groups that also forced a shift in the traditional categorical binaries of class and race. Popular groups—elites no longer could suffice here—and new bounded pairs of poor-worker and worker-capitalist emerged. Racial binaries also changed, with the growing consciousness of the mestizo, with which many workers identified. Thus the new triad of indigenous-mestizo-white began to take precedence over that of the older divides of indigenous-white or foreigner-citizen.

While growing in political clout, the organized middle and working classes still constituted a minority of the Peruvian population—the vast majority still being poor peasants and now those in the urban informal sector.

Workers in the middle and working classes essentially constituted their own elite. Rather than banding together and demanding better health benefits for all, this new elite acquiesced to the divide-and-conquer tactics of the state and resorted to classic opportunity hoarding. With their newfound political and economic power, these primarily male union members were able to demand, and then dominate, better-quality healthcare services, services that continued to be denied to the poor, indigenous peoples, and women. This hoarding served to reinforce and even accentuate categorical binaries of class, race, and gender.

General Benavides, appointed president by the congress in 1933, took the first steps in the cooptation process that eventually evolved into social-security healthcare. He came to power soon after the political ascendancy of APRA, an opposition party representing the middle classes and the upper stratum of Peru's working classes. In 1931, APRA held its first national congress, which produced a number of social-policy proposals, including the creation of a social-security system (Cotler 1978: 236). In an attempt to pacify the working-class followers of APRA, the Benavides dictatorship instituted the Ministry of Health, Labor, and Social Welfare in 1935 and decreed social-security health insurance for blue-collar workers in 1936 (the Seguro Social del Obrero, or SSO). With one hand, Benavides launched these programs to appease these class-based demands, while with the other, he severely repressed their political voice in APRA. Besides coopting the demands of urban workers, Benavides expanded already existing social-security health benefits for civil servants (Mesa-Lago 1978: 116). Workers in both of these sectors accepted these separate benefits, thus reinforcing divisions among themselves, and between themselves and the country's poor majority.

After the Benavides regime, restrictions loosened on working-class organizing, and the number of legally recognized unions rose. Thus, the civilian presidency of Manuel Prado y Ugarteche (1939–45) faced increasing pressures from organized class interests. Toward the end of his term, Prado legalized the APRA party, providing a significant opening for class-based political opposition (Cotler 1978). Escalating pressures from the working and middle classes through both union and APRA demands led Prado, in a manner begun by Benavides, to coopt these sectors through expansive social policies, including health policies. Prado expanded the workers' social-security health system established by Benavides, opening six SSO hospitals between 1941 and 1944 in Lima and other cities (Mesa-Lago 1978: 117). The first of these was the Hospital Obrero de Lima (Worker's Hospital of Lima), inaugurated in 1941, the very first social-security hospital in Latin America (Roemer 1964: 26).

Prior to the 1940s, the working and middle classes of Peru had organized separately, each with their own distinct unions or associations.[18] The middle class in fact had a history of its own class-based strikes dating back to 1919 and achieved their first social-policy victory in 1924, under the Leguía regime.[19] By the 1940s, however, APRA had succeeded in blurring the lines between the working and middle classes and had managed to attract the associations of both strata under its political umbrella. The middle class emerged more militant alongside the working-class unions. The intensified militancy of the middle classes came in part from the election of APRA affiliates to leadership positions in key white-collar worker associations in the mid-1940s, including Peru's major middle-class association, the Asociación de Empleados del Perú (Employee Association of Peru, or AEP) (Parker 1998: 218).

While Prado upheld conservative interests, his democratically elected successor, President José L. Bustamante y Rivero, depended on the political support of APRA.[20] The election of Bustamante, in 1945, signaled a brief interlude of influence for the allied middle and working classes. Bustamante recognized a record number of unions in 1946, and white-collar unions in particular reached record levels (Mesa-Lago 1978: 117; Parker 1998: 218). The Bustamante government acted for its constituents by raising the social-security coverage initiated by the prior two administrations. Upper-echelon white-collar workers in specific industries received pensions, and Bustamante established on paper the Seguro Social del Empleado (SSE), a social-security institute to serve the health and pension needs of white-collar workers. Blue-collar workers also claimed new benefits under the Bustamante government, including the inauguration of two new workers hospitals and insurance for occupational diseases. Few of these social-policy measures, however, were carried through prior to the military takeover of General Manuel Odría, in 1948.

Tensions in the working- and middle-class alliance within APRA came to a head with the election, in 1947, of leaders of the middle-class Employees Association. The APRA-backed Employees Association leaders lost the election to opposition candidates, who campaigned on issues that bolstered a distinct middle-class identity—and that explicitly promoted opportunity hoarding rather than solidarity—such as constructing a new social-security hospital exclusively for white-collar workers (Parker 1998: 221–22). General Odría, taking control of the government via coup in 1948, seized on this demand as a way to coopt middle-class interests and further divide the mobilized middle and working classes. The new hospital and Odría's expansion of the SSE succeeded as a pacifying measure, as the middle-class Employees Association lost strength and voice.

In addition to this co-optation, Odría reinforced patterns of special benefits for specific groups that had begun in the nineteenth century. Under Odría, teachers and railroad and streetcar workers won inclusion in the SSE, separate hospitals were created for the police and the military, and benefits expanded for civil servants. Blue-collar workers were not treated so generously, but they did win some larger subsidies for illness, maternity, and funeral aid (Mesa-Lago 1978: 117–18). Social-policy provision based on occupational group continued after Odría, most notably in health policy when President Belaúnde's government laid out a separate health and pension system for fishermen, in 1965.

The 1930s through the 1950s was the critical period for the buildup of the state social-security healthcare systems, though the 1960s also saw some expansion. In addition to the fund for fishermen, in the 1960s the state initiated new social-security benefits for white- and blue-collar workers, some of which had been legislated but not implemented earlier (Mesa-Lago 1978: 118–20). The Ministry of Public Health expanded in the early 1960s, putting up twelve new hospitals in order to serve those insured persons who lived in areas without SSE or SSO hospitals, as well as the uninsured poor.

The process of cooptation led to separate state health-insurance systems for the middle and working classes, each with their own health-insurance programs and hospitals. The white-collar, middle-class, social-security health system was not only separate from the blue-collar one, but clearly superior. The white-collar Hospital del Empleado, constructed by Odría, rivaled the quality of private clinics (Parker 1998: 222). As an indicator of the lavish resources concentrated in this one hospital, its ratio of employed personnel was 3.1 per hospital bed in 1962. In addition, 270 soles (about USD $11) per day was spent per patient at the employee hospital, as compared to 150 soles per day at the worker's hospital. Moreover, if white-collar employees opted to use private instead of state health services, they were subsidized for their expenses. They opted for private services about 50 percent of the time in the 1960s (Roemer 1964: 32, 35).

These systems were financed as "pay as you go" social-security systems, that is, by salary contributions from the employee and the employer into a state fund. These public funds also benefited from other sources of income including fines and donations, as well as yields from investments. When first initiated, employers paid the equivalent of 2 percent of an employee or worker's salary to the SSE or SSO (Mesa-Lago 1989: 187). In 1962 the SSO required from blue-collar workers a contribution of 3 percent of salary, plus 6 percent from the employer and 2 percent from the government. White-collar workers in 1962 gave 3 percent of their salary, and private employers 3.5 percent, whereas public institutions contributed 3 percent and the government just 0.5 percent (Roemer 1964: 25, 30, 31).[21] Unfortunately, the pay-as-you-go health system suffered from evasion of payments by employers (Mesa-Lago 1978: 139). Moreover, workers' contributions, given low salaries and a cap on payments at 500 soles (per a 1950 law), did not come near to covering the real costs of the health services provided. Deficits were often subsidized by the state.

The military government of 1968 was especially supportive of unions and therefore put more resources toward social security, thus insuring a growing share of the population. The share of population covered by social-security healthcare was 8.8 percent in 1969, rising to 10.1 percent by 1973 (Orihuela Paredes 1980: 10), and to 17.4 percent by 1980 (Mesa-Lago 1978; Mesa-Lago 1989: 183). The resources workers received were not just material, but also came in the form of authority and access to power. In 1969 administrative councils composed of representatives of the government, the insured, and employers were formed for both the SSO and the SSE, so that workers would have a role in managing their own pension and health programs.

In 1979 the working- and middle-class systems were unified to some extent when the military government, in one of its final measures, overcame some of the past tendencies toward opportunity hoarding and cooptation, and combined the SSE, SSO, and civil servants' state health-insurance systems. In 1980 the pension system merged with the social-security system as the Instituto Peruano de Seguridad Social (Peruvian Institute of Social Security, or IPSS). This consolidation only partially fulfilled the military's hopes for reform of the health sector. According to Roger Guerra García, who sat on its health-reform commission, the military's plan was a "socialist vision" of a single national health system that would have combined all the components, including "the social security and the armed forces health systems" with the separate public-health system. It faltered, in part, "because there was not the support from the people," an indicator of the degree to which opportunity hoarding had become ingrained.[22]

A number of factors led into a crisis of social security in the 1980s and 1990s. The stratified health systems originating from the cooptation path were poorly managed, especially from the 1970s on. The military used the SSO and SSE funds for other purposes without investing them wisely (García 1998 and Mesa-Lago 1989). According to one source, only 30 percent of payments collected by the state for social-security healthcare actually went to fund health services under the military government (Orihuela Paredes 1980: 8). The inflationary economy of the 1980s also led to a severe deterioration of the real value of social-security deposits. The deepening economic collapse of the 1980s also meant a reduction of formal-sector jobs, curtailing the already small pool of contributors.[23]

The historical formation of Peru's social-security health system resulted in a highly unequal system in terms of the substantive distribution of health resources, which in turn reinforced the categorical inequalities of class, race, and gender. In terms of class, the social-security health system offered urban formal sector workers a "sanitized" health system of higher quality and resources than the public-health system that served the poor. The separate middle-class and military social-security systems were of even higher quality, thus further distinguishing these better-off groups from typical workers. Even after expansion of social-security coverage under the military government between 1968 and 1980, in 1980 only 17.4 percent of the total population was insured (Mesa-Lago 1989: 183). Fifteen years later, in 1995, the state social-security system insured just 26 percent of the population, the public-health system served 52 percent, and a full 20 percent of Peruvians had no access to sufficient healthcare.[24] Despite serving only a fraction of the population, the social-security health system absorbed nearly the same amount of government-directed resources as the public-health system, making Peru's distribution of healthcare resources highly inequitable along class lines. According to the Ministry of Health estimates, based on their own and IPSS data, spending per patient in the social-security health sector in 1995 was more than three times that spent per patient in the public-health sector. Not only did workers gain better-quality health services than the poor majority, but they also gained "voice" through access to decision-making under the tripartite social-security governance system left by the military.

But the impact of the cooptation path on inequality was more widespread than these statistics suggest: the strategy of separate systems for separate groups also further reinforced existing racial inequalities. The population insured by the social-security health systems, by nature of its birth through cooptation of working-class unions and middle-class associations, was overwhelmingly mestizo. Formal-sector workers, even if originally of indigenous descent, through a combination of migration to cities, cultural adaptation to the dominant coastal culture, and economic mobility in formal-sector employment, had become mestizo. The middle-class further differentiated itself from workers in part based on lighter skin color (Parker 1998). The social-security health system rewarded these urban white and mestizo populations. Those departments with the greatest percentage of insured populations were also those with the highest index of urbanization (Mesa-Lago 1989: 182–85). Ninety-eight percent of the self-employed, who composed a significant part of the economically active population, went uncovered in 1981. These included indigenous peoples in agriculture and the large share of female informal-sector workers in "personal services." The separate, stratified social-security system thus reified not only class positions, but also racial privilege.

The dichotomy between the public-health system for the poor and the social-security health system for workers was in and of itself highly gendered. The workers covered by the SSO and SSE were primarily male breadwinners, with few women included, due to their historically low levels of paid employment. Moreover, urban women in paid employment were (and remain) largely in the informal sector or domestic workers, which were not initially covered at all by SSE or SSO. The gendered division of coverage nominally improved in the 1970s, when the military government incorporated domestic workers into the social-security system (Mesa-Lago 1989: 178).[25] However, this reform was mitigated by domestic employers' evasion of payments, which was greater than the already high rate of evasion by employers in general. With the economic crunch of the 1980s, more women entered the workforce, but they did so largely in the informal sector, which remained effectively outside of social security.[26]

Wives or common-law partners of male workers were not much better off. The dependent coverage of SSE and SSO was extremely limited.[27] Originally, wives of insured male workers received only maternity healthcare—all other healthcare for wives was either through the public-health system or paid out of pocket in the private sector. In 1975, children under one year of age were added as dependents (Mesa-Lago 1989: 181; Roemer 1964). It was not until March 1979 that the outgoing military government, as part of its consolidation of the SSE and SSO systems, expanded dependent coverage to include a worker's spouse and children under the age of eighteen. Current legislation covers spouses, minor children, and disabled adult children who are unable to work. Dependents were, and continue to be, covered by the same contribution cap as an individual worker. The legislation of 1979 also allowed independent workers to voluntarily join the social-security health system. However, women workers were not able to carry a spouse or dependent on their social insurance policy until 1992, further demarcating women as lesser citizens. The highly limited dependent coverage for most of the history of the system, and the exclusion of women workers from the right to carry dependents, effectively made social-security care a male domain and feminized the public system. While raising the status of male workers, the social-security health system treats women as actors based solely on their role in the reproduction of the labor force.

Conclusion

The categorical inequalities of class, race, and gender influence the formation of Latin American social policies, and social policies in turn serve to perpetuate or reinforce these inequalities, and even spawn new ones. The historical formation of health policies in Peru was influenced by the discriminatory suppositions of doctors, policymakers, and international agencies about the relationships between gender, class, race, and disease. Commonly held cultural beliefs about categorical inequalities—such as notions that the poor and especially indigenous peoples and nonwhite immigrants were the carriers of disease, or that mothers were responsible for high rates of infant mortality—played into the ways in which Peru's public-health system was structured. The public system that served these groups was top-down and authoritarian, reflecting the disparaging, "colonizing" attitudes of elites toward the poor, nonwhites, and women..The founding of the public system was not premised on citizens' rights to health, but rather on the belief that health and population control was fundamental to economic progress. In the formative period of this colonizing path, the public-health system's target population was not even considered citizens, if one considers suffrage to be central to citizenship. These founding biases help explain the fact that Peru's public-health system has remained of inferior quality and limited reach in comparison to the social-security system that followed it.

But racist, classist, and gendered discourses only partially contributed to the bifurcated nature of Peru's health system. The dual system also reflected broader changing historical power inequalities in Peruvian society, during the transition from an oligarchic to a more modern and urban society of unequals. Those groups that won political voice in the mid-twentieth century, the working and middle classes, effectively claimed for themselves a better state health system—the social-security system—via a process of opportunity hoarding, combined with cooptation by largely authoritarian governments. The male, mestizo leaders of the organized working and middle classes claimed a new and better health system, but it was strictly bounded. They sought to express their newfound influence by perpetuating inequality and upholding their status differences with others through unequal social benefits. Weak Peruvian governments also knew that politically dividing threatening new political groups into competing camps was crucial to their own political survival, resulting in the cooptation pattern.

Disparities in power rooted in class, gender, and race became solidified and reinforced in the two-tier health system that resulted from the combined colonization and cooptation processes. The resulting bifurcated health system also added new inequalities, most clearly in access to and quality of health services, between the working classes, the middle classes, and the rich; between men and women; and between whites, mestizos, and immigrant and indigenous peoples. This inequitable distribution of health services between the social-security and public-health systems continues: in 2000 only 30 percent of Peruvians enjoyed health insurance. The rest paid out of pocket for healthcare or depended on the vagaries of the public system.[28] In the late 1990s clients of the public-health system still faced enormous gaps in recognition between the largely mestizo, middle-class health personnel and their own understandings of health and disease, a rift that has both racial and gender dimensions (Ewig 2006a). Moreover, during the long presidency of Alberto Fujimori (1990–2000), women continued to be the target of authoritarian population-control measures. Fujimori's Ministry of Health led mass sterilization campaigns against indigenous women, premised on the belief that reducing population growth would improve Peru's economic indicators (Ewig 2006b).

The residuals of the historically classist, racist, and sexist foundations of Peru's health system remain in many ways today, yet this history also kindles some hope for identifying paths toward the erosion of inequality in the future. The fact that mid-twentieth-century workers could claim a "right" to healthcare from the central government provides hope for an alternative health system in the future. One lesson to be taken from this history is that the coupling of economic and political empowerment of citizens can lead to the expansion of social rights, including the social right to health. However, one also can glean that key to a more equitable health policy are political alliances that cross class, race, and gender divides, rather than divisions that foster opportunity hoarding.

The history of Peru's health system also suggests that categorical inequalities can and do morph and change with broader economic and social developments. In Peru, one saw a shift from strict binaries to triads that introduced greater racial and class fluidity. While, as Paul Gootenberg argues, racial fluidity in Latin America has sometimes been used simply as a foil to mask inequalities in the region, the fact that new categories can be and are introduced demonstrates the possibilities for change and reinforces the contention that inequalities are constructed, and not necessarily durable.[29]

In addition to a history of political mobilization and changing categories, there are also important egalitarian discourses in the history of Peru's health-policy formation that one can draw on. While these more positive discourses have not yet triumphed, they may constitute the seeds of future, more egalitarian models. Among these discourses is the social-medicine movement in Latin America and its proponents in Peru, which despite its historical shortcomings has laid a discursive foundation that recognizes the centrality of the social determinants of healthfulness, as well as the relationship between broader social policies and well-being (Waitzkin et al. 2001). Social medicine likely influenced former Peruvian health minister and WHO official David Tejada's original formulation of primary healthcare, a notion that remains important in public-health circles today, even though it has moved away from its original, revolutionary meaning (Cueto 2004). Peru's military government of 1968 successfully inculcated Peruvians with the notion of the state as the primary guarantor of social rights (Barrig 1989), a seed that may prove fertile in future efforts toward truly universal healthcare. Finally, in the 1990s Peruvian feminists took up the international call for "reproductive rights," a discourse that has been at least somewhat successful at tempering the long historical practice of population control in Peru, including putting a stop to shameful sterilization campaigns (Ewig 2006b). For those who seek to break the cycle of inequalities begetting more inequalities, these kernels of change must be recognized and strengthened.

Notes

For helpful comments on this essay, I thank Paul Gootenberg and Luis Reygadas, as well as three anonymous reviewers. I also would like to thank the participants in the seminar "Inexorable Inequalities: New Perspectives on Latin American Inequalities," hosted at Stony Brook University on 12 May 2006. I also thank Marcos Cueto and William Jones for comments on an earlier version of this essay.

1. See Gootenberg's comments in the introduction to this volume.
2. Historical comparative work on gender and social policy in advanced industrial countries includes Bock and Thane 1991; Gordon 1990; Koven and Michel 1993; Mettler 1998; O'Connor 1996; O'Connor, Orloff and Shaver 1999; and Skocpol 1992. On race, see in particular Quadagno 1996. Initial works on Latin America include Rosemblatt 2000; Dore and Molyneux 2000; Ehrick 2005; and Pribble 2006.
3. More recent comparative-history treatments of Latin American welfare states have expanded their lens to include the roles of democracy (Haggard and Kaufman 2008) and political parties (Huber and Stephens 2005), but still do not incorporate gender or race.
4. See Reygadas's essay in this volume.
5. Mary Weismantel (2001) would disagree, and argues that the indigenous-white binary persists. Following de la Cadena, however, I would argue that the "mestizo" in the Peruvian context is an important identity category. Yet, as Tilly notes, in practice race is often reduced to simple binaries, dependent on the issue in question. Thus white-mestizo might be the operative in contestation between middle-class professionals and workers in Peru, while mestizo-indigenous would be the binary that takes precedence in moments of contestation over resources between the rural poor and the urban workers and professionals.
6. Historians argue that epidemics lead to the establishment of state public-health policy in Peru. This thesis is not inconsistent with the thesis that economic growth and state expansion led to state health policy. I also focus on epidemics, but see state responses to epidemics occurring within a broader context of state expansion. I rely heavily on the work of Marcos Cueto (2002, 1997, 1992, n.d.), who analyzes the social impact of epidemics in Peru and the state responses these provoked. Epidemics affect primarily the poor, and thus their history provides a clear window onto the creation of public-health systems aimed at the poor.

7. All translations of sources in Spanish are my own. For a broader discussion of race and eugenics in the Latin American region, see Stepan 1991.

8. Prior to this time, public health was the responsibility of the poorly funded municipalities (Cueto 1997: 34).

9. Poverty itself is also a racialized experience in Peru. As one moves up the economic ladder from poor to working or middle class, one's racial and ethnic identity also has the capacity to change from indigenous to mestizo. See de la Cadena 2000 for a discussion.

10. For a history of the Rockefeller Foundation and its ties to public health in the Latin American region, see Cueto 1994.

11. For an engaging overview of the role of racism in U.S.-Latin American relations, see Schoultz 1998.

12. A "*sanitario*," or sanitary technician who had completed primary school and an additional six months of weekly health-related training, staffed the sanitary posts. One or two doctors staffed the medical posts, which were under the loose supervision of a health center (Roemer 1964: 40–41).

13. After the Second World War, the United States led the charge in international population-control efforts. U.S. officials viewed population control as intimately linked to economic development in the Third World and thus vital to its security interests (Hartmann 1995: chap. 6).

14. The classical economist Thomas Malthus argued that population growth, stimulated by the working classes, if left unchecked would outstrip agricultural capacity, leading to a general decline in living standards.

15. Uriel García, former minister of health, interview by author, Lima, 16 April 1998. This phenomenon is not unique to Peru. Throughout Latin America, economic crises led to the collapse of public-health systems, and it became common for patients to provide their own sheets and basic medical supplies.

16. It was not until 1980, which saw the first presidential election after the twelve-year military government, that illiterates were allowed to vote, thereby making Peru an electoral democracy. By disfranchising illiterates until 1980, Peru effectively suppressed the political voice of a large portion of indigenous peoples, the poor, and women (in particular poor indigenous women). As late as 1981, 18.1 percent of the population over the age of fifteen was illiterate. When broken down by sex, 26.1 percent of women were still illiterate and 9.9 percent of men. In rural areas, where indigenous populations dominate, 55.8 percent of women were illiterate and 23.2 percent of men (Peruvian 1981 census data in Blondet and Montero 1994: 61). Literate women were given the vote in Peru in 1955, among the last countries in the hemisphere to grant women's suffrage.

17. The development of the Peruvian social-security health system has much in common with the Bismarckian welfare-state development model in Germany. Both the German and Peruvian health systems were created as largely authoritarian responses to class conflict, and both resulted in systems highly segmented by

occupational group. Milton Roemer's comparative work on world health systems finds that the historically segmented character of Peru's social-security system is not unlike those of the systems of Germany and Belgium, which were also initially subdivided into hundreds of autonomous sickness funds (Roemer 1969: 211).

18. My discussion of the history of the middle class in Peru draws largely on Parker 1998. In Peru, the distinction between *obreros* (workers) and *empleados* (middle-class, white-collar workers) is still important. Parker shows how this distinction came to be, its underlying social (including racial) meanings, and how these evolved in the first half of the century.

19. The policies gained included three months notice prior to firing, compensation for years of service, employer-paid life insurance for employees with four or more years service, and employer-paid disability insurance (Parker 1998: 105).

20. APRA, now legalized, was banned from running its own presidential candidate and thus threw its support behind Bustamante.

21. Mesa-Lago 1978 provides different figures for contributions (138). Roemer's statistics are cited here, as they are more reliable. These percentages increased over time; the most recent rate, since 1996, requires the employee-worker to make the entire contribution, 9 percent of her or his salary, which is deposited by the employer with the Social Security Health System (known as ESSALUD, formerly IPSS).

22. Interview by author with Roger Guerra García, interview by author, Lima, 11 September 1998. See also Bravo 1980.

23. I do not have specific data on informal sector employment for 1981. However, in 1970, 31.6 percent of Lima's workforce was employed in the informal sector and another 9.8 percent as domestic laborers. In 1990, between 40.7 and 46.8 percent of Lima's workforce was employed in the informal sector and 5.1 percent was employed as domestic laborers (Sheahan 1999: 98).

24. Numbers provided by the Ministry of Health.

25. Between 1984 and 1993, females comprised between 88 and 99 percent of domestic workers (Gárate and Ferrer 1994: 75–76).

26. For specific data on women in Peru's informal and formal workforce from 1980 to 1993, see Gárate and Ferrer 1994, esp. 73–76. I say "effectively" excluded because informal-sector workers could voluntarily join the social-security system, but the majority opted not to due to the cost. In 1987 only 12.1 percent of the nonsalaried workforce was covered by social security (Verdera 1997: 30).

27. Mesa-Lago 1989 points out that Peru was particularly restrictive in its social-security dependent coverage among Latin American countries.

28. Figure from the website for the Ministry of Health, "Ministry of Health Website, Seguro Integral de Salud Program Page," accessed 15 February 2006.

29. See Gootenberg's essay in this volume.

Incommensurable Worlds
of Practice and Value

A View from the Shantytowns of Lima

JEANINE ANDERSON

The measurement of poverty and the framing of inequality constitute one more site for the exercise of oppression against subaltern groups in countries such as Peru, in particular the oppression of nonrecognition, or "misrecognition," in the language used by Fraser and Honneth (2003) in their much-cited debates on redistribution and recognition. Urban shantydwellers in Peru cannot avoid being assessed and evaluated by the nonpoor; sometimes (as in tuberculosis-control programs) they are literally weighed and measured. Meanwhile, their own ideas of what constitute legitimate and illegitimate measurements, and what should be considered the defining elements of poverty, are rarely consulted. Their perceptions of inequality are hidden from dominant groups because of the pain or risk of revelation and the confrontation it might entail.

My concern in this essay, however, goes beyond ensuring opportunities for opinion, consultation, and frank conversation between the poor and the nonpoor. This is because of the way value is created in modern complex societies and the imbrication of value in questions of poverty and inequality, distribution, and recognition. If value emerges from praxis, and is not simply present in some preexisting set of hierarchies, then poor people have at best very limited channels for claiming value for their persons, aspirations, and ways of life. Shantydwellers have projects of transcendence that express their understandings of a valuable life; what they do not have is access to arenas that would permit their understandings to enter into competition with—to be "measured" against—the understandings of the rest. In addition to enduring inequality's more familiar economic, social, and political consequences, shantydwellers experience inequality as a limited capacity to be cultural agents endowed with the potential to define the future course of Peruvian culture and society in central dimensions that turn on value, recognition, prestige, and respect.

Poverty usually presupposes a standard of measurement, and inequality often does. Many of the debates that swirl around these concepts are in fact debates about how one establishes metrics for poverty and quantifies patterns of inequality. (What, for example, is the distance between one social segment and the next? Which societies have the greatest disparities between those at the top and those at the bottom, and are, in that sense at least, the most unequal?) A huge literature has accumulated on these questions, much of it quite technical. Milanovic (2005) proposes a radical new methodology for calculating inequality among the world's citizens, independent of the national units in which they are located. Pogge (2005) questions the use of averages and other kinds of statistical legerdemain that lull one into setting modest and misleading goals for poverty reduction.

Mitchell (2002) makes a general claim about the functioning of modern societies and the knowledge practices that serve to maintain the hegemony of powerful groups.

> The new forms of economic and statistical knowledge did not stand in relation to the economy in the simple relation of a representation to reality, the way a map is thought to represent the real world. And yet this is how it would appear. The removal and concentration of knowledge into new sites opened up a distance, a gap that came to seem an absolute divide. The movement from the field to the survey office was not to be experienced as a chain of social practices, but as the distance between reality and its representation, between the material and the abstract, between the real world and the map. (Mitchell 2002: 116)

Of interest are Mitchell's "chain of social practices" and the divide between those who are licensed to establish definitions and measurements (ex oficio, by virtue of their academic titles, given a position of power) and those whose situation makes them the subject of measurement, with their quite different understandings of the world. In seeking to match one's assessments of poverty and theories of inequality to actions for addressing them, and in seeking to match both of these to the understandings and actions of the poor themselves, one may be, in profound and irremediable ways, moving in incommensurable worlds.

Measurements of poverty have important practical consequences. Though not the only consideration, they guide the programs that governments apply for alleviating or eliminating poverty. For example, in recent years in Latin America, social policymaking has been tightly bound to ideas of "targeting," and the demand for careful targeting of public subsidies, investments, and expenditures increased the centrality of measurement. However, there is no greater consensus today about the metrics to be applied, nor is it evident that social programs designed around targeting strategies have been more effective than the "universalistic" or self-selection mechanisms of participation that characterized the programs they replaced.

The policy implications of inequality metrics are less clear. The comparison by Verba et al. (1987) of Sweden, Japan, and the United States suggests that some governments and political movements incorporate Gini coefficients and other inequality indicators in their definition of political programs that seek to shape a particular kind of society (egalitarian), ensure democratic access, or promote social peace and integration. Esping-Anderson (1990) highlights the different levels of priority assigned to reducing inequality in his comparison of social-welfare regimes. Communist governments, in their heyday, created leveling programs based on their own particular metrics: number of hectares privately owned, years of formal education, time of residence in cities as against the countryside. These translated into policies that ran the moral gamut from genocide (eliminate class enemies) to the provision of social services guaranteeing a living wage and basic necessities to all.

Do such metrics have any significance to the experience of inhabiting particular places in social hierarchies ("inequality") and the material conditions of people's lives ("poverty")? The question emerges from the observation that the people normally relegated to the categories of "poor" and "subordinate" do not, as a rule, focus their lives or build their identities around the issues the categories pretend to index. They, like anybody else, are involved with projects that reflect their own definitions of what a good human life is all about (Nussbaum 1993).

Still, poor families develop strategies for moving from point to point, they make comparisons between themselves and others, and they enumerate their goods and achievements in ways that track their progress. The word *strategies* of the poor has echoes of the debates around survival strategies that occurred in the 1970s. Although the militaristic, strategic-planning connotations of that concept have come to be regarded as suspect, the narratives of shantydwellers and other segments of the urban poor commonly refer to objectives and dreams, calculations of their likely fulfillment, references to the resources needed to act, and self-evaluations of progress made along not just one life path, but a jumble of simultaneous, evolving, contingent pathways, one of which may actually lead to some kind of happiness and sense of transcendence. Better than mere "survival strategies" is the concept of "life strategies" that include aspirations focused on the meaning of a worthy life, a personal legacy, and a life well lived.

The notion of strategies (or strategic action) needs further underpinnings, and these can be found by linking that notion with practice theory, one of the dominant theoretical currents in sociology and anthropology in recent decades. Ortner (1996) has critiqued some of the more prominent innovators in this field (Bourdieu, Sahlins, Giddens) for the way they put individual agency in play but shy away from the problem of the actor's intention. Their approaches tend to exaggerate the influence of habitus, history, and structures over agency and personal visions of the good. Ortner proposes a new version of practice theory that promises to yield better accounts of the lives of women and subaltern, postcolonial, and minority groups of all kinds: "One can do practice analysis as a loop, in which 'structures' construct subjects and practices, but subjects and practices reproduce 'structures.' Or one can do—what shall we call it? subaltern practice theory?—and choose to avoid the loop, to look for the slippages in reproduction, the erosions of long-standing patterns, the moments of disorder and of outright 'resistance' " (1996: 17). Ortner deploys definitions of practice as "games" as well as projects, dramas, and stories. Lives, and pieces of lives, however, are "serious games," and the actors play with "skill, intention, wit, knowledge, intelligence." Signaling the fact that the game is "serious" is meant to foreground the way power and inequality pervade the games of life. While there may be playfulness and pleasure involved, the stakes in these games are often very high (Ortner 1996: 12). As a gender specialist, Ortner incorporates the concept of transcendence, with reference to Simone de Beauvoir's vision of women's condition as the search for transcendence over nature, human biological reproduction, and the limits of the female body. Her notion of games draws on Jean-Paul Sartre's description of life projects as a "moving unity of subjectivity and objectivity" (Ortner 1996: 20).

As such references to French philosophers suggest, transcendence appears more commonly in philosophical and theological discourses than in social-science research. There, it alludes to overcoming human finitude, achieving goals, or reaching a place that expresses what each person understands to be the profound, unique significance of his or her individual life. People labeled poor and subaltern in rank are as much concerned with projects of transcendence as they are with their conditions of poverty and relations of subordination, although the transcendence projects of some may include a large component that deals with overcoming poverty and confronting inequality.

One of the bitterest of injustices inflicted against the poor is denying them the possibility of their own diverse visions of transcendence. Poverty as a denial of rights—above all, political and economic—and a negation of the agency and capacity of the poor to seek and exercise rights is a problem that is increasingly recognized, even in the rarified boardrooms of the World Bank. Recognizing the place of transcendence in the logic of the dispossessed and disregarded takes one well beyond the current debates around participatory policies, "voices" and "choices" of the poor, and rights-based antipoverty programs. It also raises questions of incommensurability with renewed force.

I bring to these debates the detailed register accumulated from and about a small group of families at a particular juncture in the recent historical process of Peru. The families live in what began, in 1970, as a squatter town on the southern edge of Lima, Pamplona Alta. With support from many sources, I was able to carry out three formal waves of interviews (1978, 1992, 2001) with members of what started out as seventy-four households and ended, after death, migration, and sample attrition, at around fifty. Along the way I amassed a large amount of information through ethnography (attending baptisms and community anniversaries, walking the streets, visiting men and women leaders) and applied anthropology (participating in projects to strengthen women's organizations, create a daycare system, and promote adult education). In a series of articles and conference papers, I worked through various possible interpretations of the processes in which these households were caught up over more than three decades. By the standards of anthropology and sociology, this represents the *longue durée*.[1]

The founders of the households were almost all part of the twentieth-century rural to urban migratory wave that, in the eyes of the actors themselves, was explicitly concerned with reducing inequality and finding a better life. Politicians, social scientists, and journalists who document and analyze the processes of occupation of open land around Peru's cities agree: what was under way was one kind of project for reducing the vast differences in wealth and opportunities between Peru's rural poor and the rest.

Incommensurability and Poverty Reduction Praxis

In the conditions of urban Peru over the three past decades, in sectors of the so-called Conos (areas that originated with informal occupation of the land and that still suffer from deficient services and communication with the rest of the city), the dynamics of movements in and out of poverty appear to be coupled to six major factors: (1) becoming trapped in a small number of occupational niches highly exposed to economic cycles, shocks, and politics; (2) meltdowns in the households' care economy; (3) the absence of synergies among the social supports and programs that families access; (4) predation by the wealthier and better positioned; (5) limited understanding of the complex systems that affect poor households; and (6) recognition failures, loss of prestige, and the difficulties of maintaining self-respect. This short list reflects the patterns found in the detailed household histories compiled in Pamplona Alta, but it is supported by other studies of poverty in Peru.[2]

Families in Pamplona Alta fell into occupation traps because of their very limited access to job training and experience outside the possibilities offered by their networks of family and neighbors. This meant that entire family groups depended for their daily or weekly income on a single sector or subsector of the urban economy: transport, construction, market- or street-vending, domestic service, repairs of specific products, and low-level government jobs such as municipal garbage collection, where posts might even be transmitted as inheritance from father to son. Under these conditions, extended families could not insure themselves against downturns in one sector or another.

Families can plunge into deep poverty by meltdowns in the household-care economy: that is, the goods and materials, time, energy, and emotional resources needed to meet daily maintenance requirements of household members (feeding, clothing, hygiene), and the integration and long-term reproduction of the family group. Demands that go beyond housework and childcare tend to be invisible, yet they place a huge burden on households that are also deploying all their able-bodied members in the labor market.[3] Some of the implosions that I observed in Pamplona Alta originated in catastrophic illnesses, spikes in the need for care of aging family members, accidents, and disabilities. Others involved a breakdown in cooperation among family members, including violence and exploitation.

The problem of establishing synergies among social programs and benefits shows up in my data from the opposite standpoint: the advantages enjoyed by the few households that do manage to create a kind of "career ladder" that they can climb over time. Social programs in Peru tend to be simple, directed to primary needs generally understood to affect the majority of the poor. The problems poor people face, by contrast, tend to be extraordinarily complicated. Creating synergies involves using the benefits provided by one program or service to access another stream of opportunities, accumulating information and "cultural capital" on one rung that can be applied for a successful lunge to the next.

All too often the families of Pamplona Alta are the victims of what can only be called predation, carried out in particular by a category of actors that Harriss-White (2003) typifies as the "nearby rich." They may be neighbors: shopkeepers and moneylenders, informal employers in sweatshops, *socios* in unlikely entrepreneurial ventures. They may be government employees engaging in any of the myriad forms of petty corruption that target the poor and uneducated as their prey: teachers, health workers, legal-service providers, police, judges, gatekeepers at the offices of local government. These nearby actors engage in daily relations with the poor and are intimately aware of their needs and vulnerabilities.

The need of the poor for information is generally recognized, but in Pamplona Alta I found a deficit that goes beyond the problem of gathering facts. It has to do with fitting the facts into interpretative frameworks of great complexity and understanding these as systems of interrelated phenomena. Thus, "complexity literacy" seems to capture best the advantage enjoyed by a few families and the predicament of many others. Gaining this kind of literacy seems to come from lived experience within complex, hierarchical organizations rife with conflict and political countercurrents. Few people in Pamplona Alta had such experience, except for older men who had worked for large unionized industrial firms in the 1960s and 1970s. Such people were able to apply their understanding of complex systems to the challenge of scaling up, diversifying, and improving the efficiency of their businesses. They had advantages vis-à-vis anticipating future scenarios and protecting themselves against political uncertainties.

Losing one's good repute, being a member of a family that falls into disgrace in the eyes of its neighbors, struggling for recognition of one's abilities and trustworthiness, and losing one's self-respect are also grave risks for the poor. All are varieties of what Fraser and Honneth (2003) discuss as misrecognition and nonrecognition, here applied to the local

Mechanisms of Persisting Poverty in Pamplona Alta

Deliberately impoverishing	Unintended effects
Predation	Unsustainable pressure on care economies
Non- and misrecognition in all forms	Occupation traps
Complexity illiteracy	Synergies (lack of) in social programs

scene. In Pamplona Alta, losing standing and confidence in this way led to being excluded from the networks that circulated vital news, from groups that were formed to take advantage of subsidized food and other goods, and from job opportunities shared among neighbors. Some families spun into downward spirals of stigma, self-destructive behaviors, and unbearable pressures on the family group, leading to new rounds of negatively sanctioned behaviors and relationships.

The six patterns summarized here unquestionably contribute to the perpetuation of poverty or (where households come down on the positive side) mark routes of escape from it. But do they also perpetuate inequality, or even help to widen the gap between the privileged and the excluded in contemporary Peru?

That question returns one to the problem of understanding structures and their force, as well as interpreting the actions ("practice") of the nonpoor. Which of these actions have the direct intention of keeping the poor poor, of holding them at a distance, of preventing their access to valued resources? One might imagine a continuum running from one extreme, where structures and practices are clearly designed to maintain conditions of vulnerability and deprive the poor of assets and resources, to the other extreme, where the disadvantages suffered by the poor seem to be more an unintended consequence of decisions with apparently unrelated objectives.

Thus, care economies are strained because governments fail to invest in basic services and because they seek to transfer to families what ought to be the functions of systems of public health, education, and safety. With no one accounting for the costs to households of these actions, they appear innocent of ill intent. Occupation traps form where free labor markets run rampant, and neither governments nor the private sector (including educational institutions) intervene to ensure that young and recycled workers can diversify and learn new skills. Again, the fact that most of the problems reflect acts of omission creates an appearance of "no harm intended." Finally, that social programs operate as islands with little flow of information to make them transparent to the users seems to be a side effect of the organizational structure of the agencies responsible for the programs, the training of public servants, and the institutional cultures they inhabit. It flows from the logic of secrecy and self-preservation of bureaucracies and, at a more profound level, from the absence of political consensus with respect to social policy and its role in promoting welfare and equity in Peruvian society.

By contrast, predation, the denial of recognition or studied ignorance, and the denial of information and understanding that would permit poor people to defend themselves more effectively are part of the active "games" or "projects" of privileged minorities in Peru. All of these involve practices of exclusion and border policing between "them" and "us." All support a hierarchy of access to material resources (akin to Tilly's "opportunity hoarding"), as well as a hierarchy of prestige and value that threatens the poor's self-respect. All erode the capacity of the poor to act strategically and to find coherence in their lives and surroundings.

In this picture, where do antipoverty programs fit in? They are, ostensibly, actions and practices emanating from non-poor people who seek to collaborate with the poor in their efforts to improve their position. Over the span of my research, a wide variety of programs have been attempted by the Peruvian government, and many NGOs and civil-society organizations have also carried out projects they believed to represent a positive contribution. Nonpoor people develop, plan, and execute these policies, programs, and projects. But are they commensurate with the poor's own strategies and practice vis-à-vis poverty?

If this were so, the conscious efforts of the poor to improve their position, the actions they took that, while not strategically directly to this end, did actually have the effect of protecting them and enhancing their possibilities —all this should have coincided or linked with the government's antipoverty activities and those of important private actors (Cáritas, large NGOs). Such a convergence would provide evidence of an underlying "commensurability" in the practice of one sector and the other.

A quick review of the research done on the impact of Peruvian social programs over the last decades suggests this is not the case.[4] Poverty, by the official metrics, affects half the population, and this figure has barely changed over two decades. The strategies and content of social and antipoverty programs reveal a weak capacity to affect the fundamental determinants of poverty. The six sets of factors that have driven the dynamics of poverty in Pamplona Alta over the past three decades have almost no correspondence with the strategies and objectives of antipoverty programs in Peru or other Latin American countries. Under those strategies, any kind of employment creation, even if destructive of other capacities and goods, is understood to be a benefit. The household-care economy is viewed as a private matter, not as a responsibility of the leaner neoliberal state. The need for coordination and synergies among social programs is recognized but translates into the elimination of nuanced mechanisms capable of responding to the changing needs of poor families, while resources are concentrated in a few highly visible, easily policed, wide-spectrum "one size fits all" solutions. Periodic campaigns to control fraud, theft, and corruption are disconnected from discussions of poverty reduction. Basic education is failing dramatically and complexity training unimagined. And, finally, any bridges linking dignity, respect, and recognition to alleviating poverty are viewed as secondary issues, a luxury unavailable for poor countries.

Subaltern Practice and Its Projects

If one is attentive to issues of agency and vantage point, one must take seriously the fact that poor people do not limit their understanding of their lives to matters of poverty or inequality. Poor and oppressed people are not singlemindedly dedicated to not being poor and oppressed, nor to not seeming poor and oppressed, nor to not feeling poor and oppressed. They have other concerns and agendas. Based on hundreds of interviews accumulated from members of dozens of families in Pamplona Alta, I have been surprised at the scarcity of comparisons with those who have more (except the "nearby rich"). Instead, there are many references to people's struggles against the "misery and incoherence of life in the urban centers" (Devisch 1995: 595). The interviewees' descriptions of their personal trajectories and ideas of the good impose coherence by foregrounding particular events, memories, and aspirations and organizing them in what the narrators consider to be meaningful patterns.

Some narratives reveal multiple "games" or projects in play, but most seem focused on a particular, personal vision of meaning and transcendence. Five major categories of transcendence projects emerged in Pamplona Alta: business and wealth accumulation; house and "house"; religious reform; political projects; and projects of self-improvement.[5]

Projects of Transcendence 1: Business and Accumulation

Most of the households in the Pamplona Alta sample derive at least part of their income from some kind of business activity. They may be self-employed, have a store or workshop employing family members and occasional outside help, or have a small business that uses family and outside labor on a regular basis. Such enterprises fall solidly within the tradition of rural-to-urban migrant families (Gölte and Adams 1990; Ypeij 2000; Aliaga Linares 2002; Cancino 1995). Self-employment and microbusinesses are a fallback for people who lose salaried work, but for those who invest their life projects in these activities, they carry deeper significance. They are a channel to the Andean ideal of economic independence and self-sufficiency. They are a showcase for skills involving production, planning, budgeting, and abstemiousness. Businesses that accumulate wealth permit their owners to become generous patrons. They select from members of the kin network and invest in the careers of brothers and sisters, children, nieces, nephews, and grandchildren they deem most loyal and worthy. This is how informal enterprises and businesses that emerge from "popular capitalism" are often portrayed in the literature.

The passion and hopes with which people pursue these projects are independent of the scale and even respectability of the operation. One woman single-mindedly involved with her business project was a reseller of second-hand shoes and leather goods. She rents a tiny stall in an informal market on one of the main avenues of the district. Her family has endured much hardship, with, for example, four out of six of them getting tuberculosis during the crisis years of the late 1980s and early 1990s. Her oldest son, who acquired a drug problem when he worked as a private guard in the coca-producing area of Tocache, now does repairs on the shoes and occasionally on leather jackets or gloves that the mother buys. One of her daughters works the stall with her, and three others work independently, all buying and reselling used clothing. Their daily sales are minuscule and barely keep the household in food. Yet the woman has left a space in their semi-finished house for a future convenience store, which already has a name: "Minibaratilla."

In Pamplona Alta, small business pursuits run by men included carpentry, electronics repair, metal-working, tire repair, auto repair, paint and body shops, fiberglass molding, and silk-screening, among many others. Women ran small businesses involving put-out work for handicraft markets, knitting, manufacturing baby clothes, catering, wholesale and retail market stalls, street vending, Internet and videogame shops, hair dressing salons, and home-based stores. Not all of these were life projects in a strong sense, but many were.

Several families had larger businesses that were more likely to assume the characteristics of projects of transcendence. They took years to build up, and their survival and flourishing attest to the investment of many talents and many hours stolen from more relaxed forms of family life. A number of households had home-based workshops for manufacturing baby strollers and playpens; these had hived off from a single innovator, who had contacts with Lima and provincial markets. Family groups bought vehicles for use in urban transportation. Some ran construction businesses. One had a local bakery, and another had a dental technician's shop in a middle-class neighborhood. Although married couples were usually at the heart of these enterprises, in some cases it was a group of siblings, especially two or three brothers who might form an association. Some of these businesses had expanded into areas outside Lima, although many had been forced to retrench by the recessions of the 1990s.

Some of the interviewees were committed to collective enterprises on an even larger scale. A group of families from Cuzco had organized a credit union, which was a life project for those most involved in its management. One man had invested heart and soul in a transportation cooperative involving both owners of buses and the drivers they hired on a daily basis. His dream was to arrange a deal whereby all would be able to get loans for buying vehicles under government programs that encouraged this kind of private investment. At the same time, as part of a tiny minority of Afro-Peruvians in the area, he wanted to unite the "gente de pelo" in a mutual assistance project. Finally, several dozen women of the community, with the critical stimulus and support of an NGO, tried to establish a handicrafts and bakery cooperative. The business component was interlaced with a range of projects on women's education, women's rights to family planning and freedom from domestic violence, working women's right to onsite childcare, and recognition of women's initiatives by the community authorities.

Projects of Transcendence 2: House and "House"
For some people and even some entire families, transcendence meant devoting efforts to building a house and building a "house," in the sense in which anthropologists (and historians of royalty) speak of "house-based societies": "The house as a grouping endures through time, continuity being

assured not simply through succession and replacement of its human resources but also through holding on to fixed or movable property and
through the transmission of the names, titles and prerogatives which are
integral to its existence and identity" (Carsten and Hugh-Jones 1995: 7). The
original inhabitants of Pamplona Alta, most of them born in towns and
villages of the rural Andes, were familiar with the polysemy of houses as
physical places and as signs of social groups cooperating on many different
levels (Allen 1988; Mayer 2004).

According to Gudeman and Rivera, throughout much of rural Latin
America, "material practices are organized through the house, and the lexi-
con for them comes from the vocabulary for the physical dwelling: the house
as shelter is a metaphor for the house as economy" (1990: 2). Furthermore,
though they say little about social and ceremonial ties beyond the household,
Andean data show that where houses are concerned, economy, wider social
interaction, and ritual are not always easily disentangled (Carsten and Hugh-
Jones 1995: 5).

Rural kinship is created out of ties to house, land, and locality. In the city,
people try to bind their children and grandchildren to the house or, at least,
to houses in neighboring settlements, including new squatter invasions
farther up the hill.[6] In Pamplona, in the most recent round of interviewing,
large numbers of older children with incipient families of their own were
found to be living in their parents' house or nearby. Ideally, new stories or
new rooms are added for each offspring who brings a spouse to live in the
house. Such additions are more desirable than parents helping to set children up independently, as they provide tangible proof of the flourishing of
the generations, numerous descendants, and the promise of companionship
in old age.

The importance of the house as a building is indisputable. Having a
house of one's own is the most frequent reason given for participating in
new squatter invasions and suffering through years of privation. For most,
the ideal is a freestanding house with outside areas that can be used to grow
vegetables, keep chickens and ducks, and possibly install a workshop. In
fact, a majority of houses in Pamplona Alta do combine living and work
areas. Riofrío and Driant (1987) have written about the architecture and
aesthetics of Lima's shantytown houses. Brick walls are left unplastered;
space is not wasted on such things as living rooms; staircases and closets are
distributed without much prior planning; and the decoration is sparse. Such
houses tend to be built over years or decades with the help of neighbors and

relatives. Each added-on space is proof of gradual improvement in the family's economic capacity and capacity to pull together. As in other societies, "the house as name, concept or building provide[s] an image or demonstration of the unity achieved" (Carsten and Hugh-Jones 1995: 8).

The home of one of the families I interviewed exemplified a successful house project. The couple (case 62), having finished their house in Pamplona Alta and launched their children into productive adulthood, was able to accumulate enough to accept the role of sponsors of the annual patron saint festival in their home village. This role involves recruiting labor and resources from a wide network, as well as taking on debts. For the couple, however, it was a means of establishing a physical connection between their house in Lima and the houses they had left behind in the Andes decades before.

The house marks status and is material proof of success. Houses are "vehicles for rank" (Carsten and Hugh-Jones 1995: 8), and in fact the residents of Pamplona Alta make constant comparisons among neighbors who have built up to three or four stories and even purchased land in other parts of the city, and a few families who are still living in shacks. In the 2001 interviews, however, following the latest recession, the residents commented about large houses with impressive facades occupied by families who had barely enough to eat.

Projects of transcendence focused on the "house" can fail, like any other. One woman, victim of her husband's violence, considered her project a failure.

> Frankly, I've failed. By way of the failure of my marriage. At first, he would work, making some money. But afterward the money just disappeared in partying, getting drunk. When we got here, this place was just shacks, an invasion. He didn't even want to stake a claim to a house. But I wanted to have my own house. [Francamente he fracasado. Por medio de mi matrimonio he fracasado. Los primeros días él trabajaba, ganaba su plata. Después se le iba en fiesta, tomadera. Cuando venimos acá era sólo una choza solamente, invasión. Él no quería siquiera agarrar casa. Yo sí quería tener mi casa propia.] (Case 211)

Houses too crowded, unfurnished, left for years with corrugated tin roofs are signs of failure. One drunken and abusive man was finally expelled from the house by his wife and children (case 65); the principal charge against him was that he had not made the effort expected of him and had therefore forced his family to live in unacceptable conditions. In general, fathers who use resources for their personal ends, or are simply not good providers, are condemned in similar terms. Wives may be accused of being slovenly and poor housekeepers. In a few dramatic cases, wives, disgruntled with their living conditions (added to other factors), have simply left the house to return to their natal homes or to start or join another household.

House projects also failed through breakdowns in cooperation and mutual respect between the generations. One young man was thrown out of the house by his father after he had brought three successive women home as wives, had procreated several children who were cared for by their aunts and grandmother, and had generally behaved in a violent and unstable manner (case 62). Being part of a house project requires rising to certain standards of moral conduct and loyalty to the collective good.

Projects of Transcendence 3: Religious Reform

A small number of people cherished projects of transcendence that were explicitly religious and revolved around ideas of saving of one's self, saving others, and implanting morality in an immoral world. The projects frequently involved conversion from a formal, perfunctory Catholicism or a nonreligious life to leadership within one of the Protestant evangelical congregations, which have grown explosively in Peru as in the rest of Latin America in recent decades (Marzal, Romero, and Sánchez 2004). Many such projects reflected dramatic ruptures with a former life—mediocre, frivolous, even criminal—and the adoption of a new lifestyle and set of social relations. The role of religious vocations and religious splinter groups in lending meaning to the lives of the downtrodden poor, especially in chaotic cities of the developing world, is often noted (on Kinshasa, for example, see Devisch 1995).

Among those I interviewed, the most dramatic tales of self-reinvention come from a few male evangelical preachers, leaders of tiny congregations of the faithful that often meet in the houses of their pastors. One of these pastors, C. Huamán, had a conversion experience that saved him from a life of crime and violence. A gang member since adolescence, he suddenly found himself at a crossroads after a term in prison. His epiphany occurred while listening to the evangelical network Radio del Pacífico and was later reinforced, during a dream in which he saw himself on a surgical table, his entire body opened up, with all his internal organs putrefied and deformed. He was impelled to seek out a preacher in a nearby settlement and he was eventually incorporated into the church (Assembly of God) and training for the pastorate. His congregation initially consisted of his wife and two pre-school daughters. For a Seventh Day Adventist pastor, conversion entailed the ridicule ("burlas") of his friends, who placed bets on how long he would last. But his resolve was firm: "I'm sticking to it" [Pienso mantenerme].

Similar projects of personal religious commitment and self-perfection were fewer on the Catholic side. One example was a master builder who for many years was the secretary of public works in the Pamplona Alta community. He underwent a change of life in his early forties, many years after separating from his wife. Although he had retained custody of and raised his children, as young adults they faced an uncertain future: one daughter was schizophrenic, and a son who had dutifully helped him in supervising construction sites was increasingly distant. This man's religious project focused on obtaining the forgiveness of his estranged wife and on working as a volunteer in catechism and the vocational training activities of the local parish. A few women participated in prayer groups, and some had formed a group around a Maryknoll nun who lived in the community for several years. They studied the bible and discussed their faith, but they also participated in social programs such as tuberculosis monitoring.

The evangelical Christian church leaders have ambitious projects for combating social evils and instructing others in better ways of living as families and among the neighbors. They do house-to-house visits and run outreach programs for the needy, bringing food and comfort to the sick, elderly, and abandoned. One specializes in ministering to prisons and hospitals. One of the evangelical pastors dreams of establishing in Pamplona Alta schools, centers for technical training, job exchanges, shelters, and soup kitchens, all as means of saving the young people from drugs, unemployment, desperation, and meaninglessness. Another pastor attends to new squatter towns as they form and tries to help the people organize themselves. Yet another, the leader of a locally based congregation—that is, one without the connection to a foreign mother church that many other congregations have—plans to install an Internet service in the church office (a house), to raise the cultural level of the community with a bookstore, and eventually to operate a radio station.

Though some bearers of religious projects belong to the poorest families in Pamplona Alta, others are relatively prosperous. A recent rash of Latin American television evangelicals pitch the association of religious faith and practice with material success. One pastor says of his congregation,

If they aren't merchants they're businessmen or white-collar employees. They're successful because God doesn't say you need to be poor. God doesn't want us to be poor people. All wealth obtained with God's grace is well received. [Si no son comerciantes son empresarios o empleados. Ellos tienen éxito porque Díos no dice que seamos pobres. Díos no quiere que seamos pobres. Toda riqueza obtenida de la mano con Díos es bien recibida.] (E. Quispe, personal interview, Pamplona Alta, 2001)

Another speaks of the scholarships his church offers to young people who otherwise would be unable to attend college, of income-generating women's groups, and of other economic projects.

The church has its own banks. The church doesn't speak of staying poor. Or that Christ is about to come. Nope! The Church of God is not that sort. The Church of God opens eyes: that yes, there's prosperity. That's what it sounds like. [La iglesia tiene sus propios bancos. La iglesia no habla de quedar porque tiene que ser pobre. O que ya viene Cristo. ¡No! La Iglesia de Díos no es de ese tipo. La Iglesia de Díos abre los ojos: que, sí, hay prosperidad. Por eso suena así.] (E. Aguayo, personal interview, Pamplona Alta, 2001)

One Pamplona Alta family is headed by an elder in the "Israelita" movement, a congregation that originated in Peru and has spread to Chile, Ecuador, and Colombia. The couple and their four children are dedicated followers of the faith, but deftly combine that commitment with their economic activities. Father, mother, and son run a trucking and urban-transportation business. Over several years in which they were engaged in long-distance trucking of produce from the interior of Peru, they used the trips to preach the faith and ferry messages among Israelita congregations spread around the country. In Lima, the mother and daughters run stalls in an open market founded by the congregation. (The Israelita organization also has a political party, Frente Popular Agrícola Fia del Perú, FREPAP, with a pro-agrarian, quasi-socialist ideology.) This family thus combines in a single project a religious, an economic, and a political agenda.

Religious projects confer a sense of transcendence because of their connection with the deity, eternal truths, and eternal life. But some also offer mundane connections to larger-than-oneself social actors, as is the case with churches whose headquarters are in the United States and that occasionally send preachers and administrators to Peru, injecting dollars to finance projects and opportunities for foreign travel, education, and further self-improvement.

Projects of Transcendence 4: Political Projects and Careers
Some men and women in Pamplona Alta seek meaning and transcendence in explicitly political projects, but they are few and their ranks have thinned over the years. Their levels of commitment have also waxed and waned. In the early years of the settlement, many of the men were politically involved at the community level. In 1976 a "women's council" was created to take on projects identified with the women's sphere: nutrition, health, preschool, activities for children, literacy, and other educational activities. Meanwhile, the men's committee, with delegates elected from each housing block and a core of leaders as its executive organ, occupied itself with getting electricity and potable water, sidewalks and asphalted streets, a school, and a health post, with brief incursions into income-generating projects like a cooperative hardware and building-supplies store.

The core of men who, in varying combinations, were elected to leadership posts over the years are notable figures in the community, even though many ended their terms accused of corruption or incompetence. The women are less well known, but a few developed long political careers, moving from community organizations to NGO-sponsored projects and programs. During the 1980s, some of these men and women, together with others from neighboring sectors of the district, formed a Left splinter group with its own program. Several graduated from community to municipal politics, including a pair of unsuccessful candidates for office as district councilors. Many have ties to national political parties or movements, wherein they receive training, socialization into the political system, legal advice, and financial support for campaigns. In return, they are expected to bring in the votes and organize marches and other demonstrations of popular will in favor of their parties' positions. This kind of local clientelistic politics has generated a vast literature in Peru, as in other Latin American countries.[7]

During the 1980s and early 1990s, being part of such projects exposed many to threats from Peru's Sendero Luminoso (Shining Path) guerrillas. One woman told of how Sendero detachments would sweep through the area at midday, when the collective kitchens were finishing the preparation of the day's lunch rations, demanding to be fed without paying even the few cents that regular beneficiaries of this government-subsidized program were asked to pay. She would remind them that she had "seen them in diapers" and had been working for a better Peru since before they were born. Indeed, some Pamplona residents did subscribe to the political strategy of Sendero Luminoso. One, who joined and later repented, was assassinated in his shack.

A common accusation brought against those who pursued political projects pointed to their mixture of idealistic and material objectives. One woman, who along with her husband was a militant of the Alianza Popular Revolucionaria Americana (APRA) party, received a teaching appointment at a convenient neighboring school during the APRA government of 1985–90. Two or three of the men who pursued political projects were wooed first by Fujimori's operatives and later by Toledo's, with promises that job training and service centers would be established, thus resolving their underemployment problems. While some went with the political winds, many were either truly convinced that their ideals could be housed under successive parties or recognized their very limited power to change political reality: decisions made by national party organizations, clientelistic networks already established in areas like Pamplona Alta, and overwhelming contradictory demands welling up from below.

One would be wrong, however, to dismiss as clientelism and manipulation the genuine search for transcendence and for a better world that is expressed in these projects. Middle-class politicians and social scientists have a poor record in interpreting the elusive organizational life of the poor. Throughout the decades of the Pamplona Alta study, debate swirled in academic circles about the poor as "new social actors" and their potential for reforming Latin American democracy. Such debates depended on a highly selective reading of association in urban poor areas. An inventory of organizations in Pamplona Alta in 1992, when these debates were at their peak, showed that one-third were soccer clubs, one-third were women's organizations connected to government social programs and NGO projects operating in the area, and the other third was a mix of religious groups, parent-teacher committees, economic organizations (bus committee, association of home-based stores, cooperatives of various sorts), musical and artistic clubs, and local party committees. Those with political projects could use any of these as a base.

Projects of Transcendence 5: Self-Improvement
Many of the inhabitants of the Pamplona Alta community were passionately involved in self-improvement, self-expression, and make-over projects that expressed a vision of transcendence and an effort to overcome limitations.

These personal projects were often associated with projects for improving closely connected others, usually family members, and it seems fair to group such projects together, because family members in intimate relations of mutual commitment ("diffuse enduring solidarity") can be considered extensions of the self. Those who struggled to change their parents, children, or spouses were working to change the relationships between these people and themselves. They were working to move the dyad or family group in new directions.

It is worth noting, in this context, the rich aesthetic and creative life many poor people have. Among the Pamplona Alta families, there were musicians, both traditional Andean, *salseros*, and young rock musicians. One man who defined himself as an "inventor" experimented constantly in his carpentry shop with new gadgets that might have practical uses. Another man spent years as a member of an itinerant political theater group. Honoring a long Andean tradition, women focused their aesthetic impulses largely on weaving, knitting, sewing, and embroidery, intended for themselves, their children, or for sale (Arnold 1997).

Many of the men had projects for "improving" their wives, particularly in the early years of migration, when the men enjoyed the advantage of wider social networks and work relations that took them all over the city. The women, whose urban experiences were often limited to a few months or years as domestic servants, were more easily intimidated by unfamiliar people and situations. Many of the wives had difficulty speaking Spanish, and almost all had lower levels of formal education than did their husbands. The husbands' projects for the women thus had overtones of the "civilizing" projects of the middle classes in relation to the poor. One such husband (case 492) said, for example, "She really doesn't have a clue. She lacks a whole lot" [Es que ella no tiene pues idea. A ella le falta bastante]. Men saw their wives as traditional and countrified. They spoke of the "preparación" that the women lacked, and many launched specific programs combining study and exposure to new experiences that would provide such preparation.

Yet some of the wives had studied the lifestyles of the families for whom they had worked as domestic servants, and their own ideas began to impose themselves as the women gained self-confidence. Thus it was that by the 1990s one was more likely to find wives with projects for refashioning their husbands than to encounter the opposite. By that time, many of the men had sunk into hopelessness, alcoholism, violence, infidelity, withdrawal, and total irresponsibility with regard to home and children. Some wives tried to draw their husbands into new religious groups as a way of straightening them out.

Parents also had projects for improving their children that explicitly aimed to prevent those children from ending up like their parents: "She's got to become another kind of person" [Ella tiene que ser otra gente], said one mother of her daughter. Most of these projects involved promoting children's education, and parents thus had first to educate themselves. The development project that generated Pamplona Alta's strongest consensus was the creation of a preschool in the late 1970s. Parents felt the school offered a way to set their children, from the earliest possible age, on a path to urbanity and middle-class status. Parents also nursed projects for their children to attend college and become professionals even as it became abundantly clear that the quality of public education available in the area made that dream almost impossible.

Children, especially during adolescence, likewise had improvement projects for their parents. By the 1990s some of the children looked on their fathers and mothers as hopelessly traditional and ignorant. In the 1992 interview adolescent boys and girls were asked about the lessons they had learned from their parents. Said one young man about what his father had taught him: "Not to be like him" [No ser como él]. Children complained that their parents were authoritarian and intolerant. Although their parents had pushed on them the necessity of learning to work with skill and discipline, many children saw their parents as drudges who accepted degrading treatment and insufferable working conditions.

Meanwhile, the children were fashioning themselves as various degrees of hybrid between their migrant parents and their Lima-born peers, including friends and models from different social classes. Some spoke of this very explicitly as a self-creation project. They made thoughtful decisions about their clothes and hairstyles, their friends and social networks, their studies, their tastes in music and what that expressed, their way of walking and talking, where and how they circulated around Lima, and their recreations. Some were creating themselves as hard-working responsible future citizens: "It's always the youth that are supposed to be the future, and I feel like the type of person in which hopes can be invested" [Siempre tienen la esperanza en la juventud y yo me siento como una persona que en mí pueden depositar una esperanza] (case 494).

Interviews with the second generation of residents in 2001 revealed that many young people were trying to remake the model of marriage and gender relations that had prevailed in their families of origin. Their project was to establish more democratic relations in which the young wives could seek work without limitations and young men would share in housework and childcare. They were struggling to avoid the conflict and dissatisfaction that many identified in their parents' relationships and consciously sought to be better parents than their own had been for them: more patient, willing to listen, and accepting of their children's points of view.

Finally, there was the collective self-improvement project pursued by the founders of the community. This was the self-improvement project at its most inclusive, focused on maintaining the fervor of the early years of mutual aid and generalized communal solidarity. In Pamplona Alta, as in similar settlements, the shared adventure of coming to live on a barren hill and creating a functional community is spoken of years later in almost utopian terms. The dream of achieving a perfect union dies hard, and the migrants are faced with a reality that includes neighbors robbing neighbors, child rape, corrupt leaders, marital infidelity, domestic violence, disputes over houses and lots, street-corner fighting and other forms of public nuisance, youth gangs, and even a vacant lot on one perimeter that is given over to drug dealing. No matter how successful the personal and family transcendence projects, the deterioration of the surrounding context, in so many aspects, is hard to ignore.

Conclusion

Many transcendence projects converge (or could be helped to converge) with the antipoverty programs sponsored by government or civil society. The self-employed and owners of small businesses could be assisted in locating economic pursuits with more likely prospects. Running the businesses could be facilitated with training, credit, and connections to markets. House projects are firmly on track, both in their search for strong family organization with built-in insurance and assistance mechanisms, and in the demands they bring for improved urban infrastructure and the consumer goods associated with household furnishing and operation. The religious projects may have otherworldly aspects, but they also have strong elements of solidarity with the downtrodden and outreach to the most stigmatized of the poor. The political projects could be nudged toward greater relevance through political education, increased access to information, procedural reforms to make entry to the system easier, attacking corruption in the political and judicial systems, support for people with leadership potential, and the creation of participatory mechanisms that reach farther down into the society (thus creating training arenas and contexts for building political movements). Finally, many of the self-improvement projects contain obvious elements of a Weberian transformation in the spirit of capitalism and liberal democracy.

These different projects of transcendence are not mutually exclusive. Some (house and business; self-improvement and religious) are easily combined. "House" projects probably did, in the conditions of Pamplona Alta, exclude more collective, communitarian, and political projects. That would help to explain the collapse of many community organizations and the turn away from dreams of a utopian urban settlement of neighbors who recognize each other and interact in solidarity.

The projects of transcendence that the people of Pamplona Alta were embarked on are not projects for overturning the relations of inequality in Peru. But neither are they projects for passive accommodation to inequality. All of them could be imagined to flow into—harking back to Ortner—"slippages" in the existing machinery of society and its political economy, "erosions" of prevailing norms and expectations, "moments of disorder" seized to assay a new order. All express, to one degree or another, resistance to the prevailing system, especially as it operates on the ground: producing insecurity and material privation, difficult family relationships, continuous petty injustices, and the quotidian insults embodied in the limited and distorted significance that other Peruvians attribute to the objects, roles, and persons that constitute the world of the urban poor. All occupy a space of "subaltern practice" and agency that Ortner proposes to reposition in social theory, just as they need to be repositioned in political programs for reducing inequality and the categorial differentiations that sustain it.

Thus, despite all their efforts, the people of Pamplona Alta, and those like them, cannot make their life projects and the value they express commensurate with those of the nonpoor. They are restricted to certain spheres of the economy, certain sets of social relations, a particular geographic range (though broader than one may think, especially given the new reality of international migration), and a prestige and value hierarchy that is often incomprehensible, even irrelevant, to others. All this serves to dissuade and deflect any direct competition with the wealthy and the powerful of Peru. Poor people cannot—or can only very rarely and exceptionally—locate their projects on a larger stage. This would require disputing not only the grounds staked out by others, but also the metrics others use to guide their actions and put value on their lives. No matter how well built their businesses, their houses, their churches, and their political projects, the poor take part in "tournaments of value" (Meneley 1996) almost exclusively among their own.

The incommensurability of value and practice between the poor (as represented by the families of Pamplona Alta) and the rest (middle-class and wealthy Peruvians, as well as local technocrats and politicians and members of the global institutions whose habits of thought and decisions have broadranging impact) takes its place as the ultimate expression of inequality in Peru and, arguably, other countries of Latin America. It incarnates the vast social distances discussed by Luis Reygadas.[8] Following Tilly, one can see the incommensurability of life projects as a sign of categorical inequalities: the poor see and judge themselves as a distinct category from the rest of Peruvian society. The absence of a participatory debate about the meaning as well as the measurement of poverty and national development, and the impositions, silencing, and injustices this entails, can be read as a massive failure of communication that interacts to tragic effect with spatial segregation, racial and ethnic discrimination, economic exclusion, and other more familiar components of inequality. When the poor and the non-poor live in worlds apart, their encounters channeled through predatory interactions or well-intentioned but essentially irrelevant attempts at assistance, incommensurability and inequality become mutually reinforcing.

Indeed, in Pamplona Alta, only two projects may be said to have emerged on a national stage. The Israelita religious group with its political party is one. Despite its minuscule size, the party has elected a handful of representatives to congress in the past, and despite its eclectic theology, Peruvians recognize it as a home-grown contribution to religious expression. The other project falls into the category of economic strategy and was deployed by a few families whose interests have diversified to farming activities on the tropical eastern slopes of the Andes. Pamplona Alta was the childhood home of a woman who was elected to congress, in 2006, as representative of the coca growers of Peru. The *cocaleros* may foreseeably play a role in the current political process, reinforced by the presence they have gained in neighboring Bolivia.

Like the poor, the rich are also constrained by structures, norms, and habitus. The key seems to be visualizing arenas of national culture where structures and individual agency, habitus, and projects of transcendence from both sides of the inequality divide would come face to face. These arenas, somehow, would serve as tournament grounds where the worlds of the rich and the worlds of the poor would meet and compete for value, recognition, resources, and power, and indeed, fleeting signs of such tournaments can be found in Peru today.

Notes

USAID Office of Nutrition underwrote my first wave of research in the late 1970s; the International Development Research Centre, Government of Canada, supported the second, in 1992; and an award from the Global Development Network made possible the third. The latest round of analysis was supported by the MacArthur Foundation through a grant shared with the University of Wisconsin, the University of KwaZulu-Natal, and the International Food Policy Research Institute for the comparative study of the persistence of poverty in Peru and South Africa. The Rockefeller Foundation's Durable Inequalities in Latin America program allowed me to spend a year at Stony Brook University (2003–4), reading and writing. I also wish to note the contributions of my students and colleagues at the Catholic University of Peru, who have constantly challenged and enriched my reflections on this research.

1. There are few similar studies in Latin America: long-term follow-up or restudies of urban poor families. Two that have come to my attention are Janice Perlman for Río de Janeiro (2010) and María Eugenia Zavala de Cosío for Mexico City (Coubés, Zavala de Cosío and Zenteno 2005).

2. In a forthcoming book in Spanish, I discuss each of these patterns and present the evidence that supports them. Here I can only suggest briefly the kinds of predicaments the families experienced, which further my argument about the incommensurability of the practices that poor people and the non-poor put in play even when the non-poor bear no ill will or explicitly wish to benefit the poor. I connect the argument with the practice involved in antipoverty programs applied by the government of Peru.

3. Aguirre (2005) documents for Montevideo the necessary crisis-management functions.

4. See Zárate 2005; Vásquez and Mendizábal 2002; Mauro 2002; Saavedra and Chacaltana 2001; Vásquez et al. 2001; Figueroa 2001; Figueroa, Altamirano, and Sulmont 1996.

5. I venture that the five categories of transcendence projects would extend to other urban centers in Peru, but further research will have to show whether and how they might be relevant in other parts of the world.

6. The phrase "rural kinship," famous among specialists in kinship, is David Schneider's.

7. See, for example, for Argentina, Auyero 2001a; for Ecuador, Burgwal 1995; for Bolivia, Goldstein 2004; for Brazil, Gay 1994.

8. See Reygadas's essay in this volume.

Inequalities of Political Information and Participation

The Case of the 2002 Brazilian Elections

LUCIO RENNO

Inequality and exclusion are trademarks of Latin America, past and present. Latin America has been characterized as the "lopsided continent" and singled out among all regions of the world for its radical divides between the rich and poor, blacks and whites, and men and women (Hoffman and Centeno 2003; Korzeniewicz and Smith 2000; Portes and Hoffman 2003). The great majority of the population controls only a tiny slice of economic resources and is destined to lives of hardship. Furthermore, the voice of the excluded is barely audible, resulting in public policy that rarely aims at reducing inequality in the long haul, providing only shortsighted *asistencialista* (palliatives). The long history of economic and social exclusion is, in itself, a powerful testimony of how little demands for equality have effectively filtered into the state.

The lack of political voice of large portions of the population also reflects an accumulation of inequalities that are present in the social, economic, and political spheres. Inequalities appear to cut across different dimensions of life. Indeed, the crosscutting and cumulative nature of inequality is probably the essence of its resiliency and drives an indelible cycle of exclusion that further reinforces inequalities (Tilly 1998).

If cycles of exclusion are formed by the self-reinforcing cumulative nature of inequalities, then a central issue in the study of Latin America is how distinct forms of inequality transfer across distinct resource realms. How are exclusionary cycles perpetuated? This key problem can be evaluated by mapping inequalities along the distribution of political information and electoral participation in Brazil and by testing if such inequalities mirror the other gaps in equality that have traditionally permeated Brazilian society.

Therefore, my primary goal in this essay is to test how gender, race, and income affect access to political information and participation in Brazil. It is well documented that gender and race categories themselves are root causes for differential treatment among individuals in Latin America, especially in the educational system and labor market (Skidmore [1974] 1993; Lovell 2000a, 2000b; Andrews 1996). However, the impact of categories of gender and race does not stop there. They may lead to unequal access to other crucial resources, such as civil and political rights. Furthermore, income and educational gaps may also become causes for inequalities in other realms. Political rights, which include access to political information and voting, are certainly prone to be affected by gender, race, and income.

Inequality refers to the systematic distortion in the distribution of re-sources among social groups. Inequality is generated when a specific group seizes control over a resource, through mechanisms like opportunity hoard-ing and exploitation, and monopolizes their allocation (Tilly 1998). This necessarily creates a situation in which there are insiders, who benefit from access to the scarce resource, and outsiders, excluded from access. In some cases ethnic cleavages set the borders of inequality. In others, it is race that defines insiders from outsiders. In most societies, gender is also a constant source of differentiation between "haves" and "have-nots." Wealth, social status, or caste are also mechanisms of social exclusion.

Wealth and income play a lead role in this equation because they are generally a consequence of prior inequalities, but have become sources of differential treatment in the present. Rich people enjoy better resources with which to defend themselves in the judicial system, to influence public policy, and to assure deferential treatment by the police. Furthermore, social mobil-ity is so sluggish in Latin America that income and wealth merge into cate-gorical differences between individuals: differences that cannot be overcome in time and that are dichotomous with clear borders. Hence, social class or economic status, basically defined by income and wealth, are sources of cur-rent differential treatment and privileges and cannot be ignored as causes of other types of inequalities.

In fact, if differences in income affect other resources, such as political information, this is strong evidence of the cumulative impact of inequalities. If those who lack access to one resource, such as income or wealth, also lack access to other resources—such as the law, technology, information, decent housing and heathcare, political voice—then inequalities are accumulating across social groups. Tilly (1998) refers to the process of accumulation of inequalities as "adaptation" or "emulation," meaning that inequalities spread from one resource to the next. The spread of inequalities through varied resource realms, caused by a singular categorical difference between individuals (race, gender, class), is a key mechanism for the persistence and durability of inequality over time. Hence, understanding how inequalities transfer from one resource to the next is vital to explain the resiliency of inequality in Latin America.

Distinctive forms of inequality can affect political resources and abilities. Among the political resources voters have, political information and voting are central to an active democratic citizenship. It is through informed choices that voters are able to punish and reward incumbents and to select among competing alternatives. Therefore, accountability hinges on information, and if there is unfairness in access to information, there will be distortions in accountability.

This is the point where political information and inequality overlap. Several researchers have mapped systematic biases in the distribution of information based on historical inequalities (Delli Carpini and Keeter 1996; Mondak and Anderson 2004). In other words, inequalities in the distribution of economic resources flow into and are reinforced by inequalities in the distribution of political information and voice. Obviously, such systemic biases are attributable not to personal characteristics of members of underprivileged groups, but to constraints that have been structurally imposed on these groups over time.

The differences in levels of information have strong political implications. A classic discussion in Latin American politics concerns the role of clientelism as a political relation based on unequal, hierarchical relations between politicians and voters.[1] The essence of clientelism is the idea that voters exchange political support for public or private goods distributed to their localities by politicians. Politicians exert power to allocate resources and are interested in the votes of the population for political survival. Voters lack resources and need them to survive, period. Hence, inequality generates clientelism. But it also allows clientelism to persist in time. A key, albeit rarely researched, mechanism for the durability of clientelistic networks is the lack of information: on the voter's side, of his or her rights and of the existence of other means for obtaining public goods, including information about competing candidates and partisan alternatives. Identifying how certain voters, particularly poor people, are prey to shortfalls of political information may shed light on yet another facet of clientelism.

Inequality in the distribution of distinct resources, caused by similar social dynamics and with identical roots, is the essence of the cycle of exclusion. If varied social groups, especially the underprivileged, are also less politically informed and less participative in politics, their ability to influence public policy will be further reduced, thus perpetuating inequality. The cycle of exclusion generated by the accumulation of inequalities in the same groups—the poor, the undereducated, women, afro-descendants, the indigenous population—is what sustains inequality in Latin America over the long haul. Analyzing inequality in political information and participation is therefore an illuminating way to investigate the cumulative mechanisms in the cycle of exclusion.

The Case of Brazil

Brazil is a compelling case study of inequality in political participation and information because it is a highly unequal country that has recently made impressive efforts to democratize access to political information and to open the political "market" to greater popular participation. Thus, it is possible to contrast how entrenched forms of discrimination may have endured, even after clear policy innovations to combat inequality.

Several persistent forms of inequality affect the daily lives of Brazilian citizens. Race, though defined in extraordinarily complex ways in Brazil, has always been a determining force in social and economic relationships. There is compelling evidence that race is a central facet of discrimination in the educational system, in the courts, and in the job market, albeit little is known about the implications of race in the political realm.[2] Gender discrimination is also a growing issue in contemporary Brazil (Lovell 2000a), so much so that partisan gender quotas have now been stipulated for the nomination of candidates for the Chamber of Deputies. Still, the number of women holding office is quite low in comparison to their share of the population. Abundant evidence from a range of countries indicate that substantial gender gaps in political information benefit men (Mondak and Anderson 2004). Such a gap may also operate in Brazil, further dampening the political participation of women. Finally, income is a key differentiating factor among Brazilians (Andrews 1996). Poor Brazilians have limited avenues of social mobility and reduced access to alternative sources of information. In addition, the educational levels of the poor are clearly lower than those of the rich and middle class, who enjoy easier access to better schools. In fact, education and income are so highly correlated in Brazil that by measuring the impact of income one is also taking into account the influence of education. It is reasonable to suspect that poor people may also possess lower levels of information.

On the other hand, since the 1990s, Brazil has developed innovative electoral legislation that guarantees media access to all competing candidates in elections, called "free electoral airtime." Such programs, aired during television and radio prime time, allocate time to candidates to publicize their candidacy and platforms. In addition, news broadcast coverage of elections, especially in 2002, is much fairer and balanced than in any time in Brazil's history. The electoral law stipulates that equal time segments need to be allocated to each presidential candidate in news programs, a clear effort to reduce coverage bias, rampant in previous elections, and in nominally democratic societies at large (Lima 1993; Miguel 1999).

Therefore, there is no reason to believe that the message content about the candidates and issues during campaigns has been significantly biased. Furthermore, Brazil enjoys widespread availability of television and radios; exclusion is not due to a lack of access to the minimally required equipment. In short, the availability of political information, coming from fairly balanced broadcasts and from diverse news sources, is seen as a free "public good." Moreover, no studies of Brazil indicate that information is packaged to specific social groups and therefore absorbed differently by social groups due to content alone. The message per se is not leading to skewed access to political information. If biases exist, they are caused by other social mechanisms. The fact that the Brazilian government has made significant investments to reduce informational biases among distinct social groups adds another fascinating piece to the puzzle of how inequalities persist over time. Has purposeful governmental action to reduce biases in coverage and raise access to distinct voices in the media made inroads against political inequalities?

The dramatic election of the left-wing candidate, Lula da Silva, of the Workers' Party (PT), to the presidency, in 2002, was surely an example of how the hurdles created by inequality can also be overcome in Brazil. It may also indicate that stark inequality hindered expected clientelistic ties. Indeed, this might well be the case for the presidential election, which was not, however, the only race that occurred in 2002. Brazil's general elections are concurrent: voters must choose candidates at various levels and for different offices. Only by considering the races for all such offices can one get a clear picture of the role of information and informational biases on political participation.

By mapping the existence of informational biases while controlling for other possible explanations for persisting informational distortions or disparities, one can determine if there are deep informational biases caused by gender, race, and income. If such biases do exist, then it is certain that the traditional sources of inequality reinforce one other, creating a cycle of long-term exclusion that perpetuates gaps in resources between social groups.

The Data: The Two Cities Panel Study

To map systematic biases in the distribution of information in Brazil, I rely in this study on a unique public-opinion dataset that contains information at the individual, neighborhood, and city levels. The data comes from a panel study conducted in two midsize Brazilian cities during the elections in 2002. The first wave of interviews took place in March and April 2002, before the campaigns started, to capture benchmark measures of information before exposure to the electoral campaign. The second wave was implemented in September, before the first presidential debates and the beginning of the free electoral airtime. The final wave occurred in October 2002, after the first round of the elections and before the second round of the presidential and gubernatorial contests. Hence, the third wave of interviews allows for the measurement of voters' final levels of information, after being exposed to the entirety of the electoral campaign.

The interviews were conducted in two cities, which were chosen because they provide variation in the characteristics of the political environment while being relatively similar in socioeconomic and demographic terms. Juiz de Fora, in the state of Minas Gerais, is a city in which political parties are poorly organized and display weak or diffuse ideological divides. Furthermore, the elections for federal deputy are quite complex there, with a very high number of candidates competing for the local vote. Caxias do Sul, in the state of Rio Grande do Sul, has a very long history of deep ideological cleavage between left- and right-wing parties. This schism dates back at least to Brazil's first modern democratic period, from 1945 to 1964, where there was a clear clash between supporters of the Brazilian Labor Party (PTB) on one side and supporters of all other parties on the other. During the military dictatorship (1964–1986), the city was divided between the opposition party, Movimento Democrático Brasileiro (MDB), and Aliança Renovadora Nacional (ARENA), the party that supported the military government. Finally, with re-democratization, after 1986, the city maintained its tradition of bipolarity, this time defined by the rift for or against the Workers' Party (PT). The political system of Caxias has well-structured left- and right-wing parties and a clear ideological divide that replicates economic class boundaries. Poor voters support the PT, and wealthier ones the right-wing parties.[3]

The difference in political environments between the two cities allows for assessment of how distinct political orders may attenuate or intensify biases in information distribution. As political learning appears to be affected by environmental factors, it is plausible to hypothesize that electoral environments may affect biases in the distribution of information, which calls for a clear comparative analysis of how distinct contexts impact informational gaps.

In addition to the intercity variation, the dataset includes neighborhoods within the two cities as another level of analysis (Huckfeldt and Sprague 1995). Around 100 interviews were conducted in 22 neighborhoods, which were selected using a stratified probabilistic sample, allowing for the construction of aggregate indicators of the characteristics of each neighborhood. The entire sample comprised around 2,500 interviews per wave in each city, thus totaling almost 15,000 interviews in the three waves.

Information, Inequality, and Voting

Discussions of political sophistication, understood as the amount and type of information voters possess, is a cornerstone in the academic study of voting behavior and political psychology (Niemi and Weisberg 2001), going as far back as the pioneering research of Campbell et al. (1960), at the University of Michigan, and Lazarsfeld et al. (1944), at Columbia. Although informational demands expected of voters by early analysts were very high, and consistently proven to be unrealistic, nowadays a consensus exists that voters do not need an "encyclopedic" knowledge about politics in order to make reasoned choices (Lupia and McCubbins 2000).[4] Summary information, in the form of shortcuts, cues, and heuristics about candidates, abound and suffice to instruct voters about candidates' issue positions and policy preferences. However, it remains unclear what type of summary information most affects voter choice and how informational distribution is shaped by institutional and contextual variables (Lupia and McCubbins 2000). Informational shortcuts are nonetheless real information, and their distribution and impact in voter choice can be problematized and evaluated empirically (Luskin 2002).

For informational shortcuts to be effective, voters must have certain information about politics. Almost all accounts of the functioning of political cues concur that voters should be able to identify the candidates, either through their names or party affiliation, know whether a candidate is an incumbent or a challenger, know who endorses that candidate, and understand what the different parties stand for (Delli Carpini and Keeter 1996). But voters need not have factual information about a specific issue position or know how an incumbent voted on different legislative proposals. It suffices to know, for instance, the party of the candidate and the policy reputation of the party. This summary information is enough to instruct voters about the candidates' potential choices in the future. The literature is clear that there are minimal informational requirements for voting.[5]

However, and more important to the interests of this study, even these minimal levels of information are not equally distributed through different social groups and may be affected by institutional environments. Hence, informational shortcuts, because they are information and require some investment to obtain, are not equally distributed throughout society (Luskin 2002; Delli Carpini and Keeter 1996).

The acquisition of information is dependent on environmental, institutional, and historical characteristics, as well as on individual traits. For instance, Lupia and McCubbins (1998) argue that for political parties to serve as a source of information for voters, parties must be linked with specific policy preferences or ideological positions and must have consolidated "brand names" (reputations) that the electorate can easily discern. In other words, the impact of partisanship is contingent on the historical factors that affect party strength. Lupia and McCubbins (2000) then explicitly claim that the role of informational shortcuts is conditioned by institutions.

For instance, where political competition is fragmented between several candidates, it may be harder to acquire even the minimal informational requirements about all candidates (Rahn 1993; Bartels 1988; Lau and Redlawsk 2001). In political systems where the choice set is unclear or more complex "either because of the chaos of institutions or the enfeeblement of ideology," voters will find it more difficult to learn about politics (Sniderman 2000). Hence, particular configurations of the political environment further hinder voters' ability to learn by making information more convoluted or costly to gather.

How information and inequality affect vote choice is a matter for empirical verification, especially in Latin America, where there are so few studies on the impact of information on elections.[6] Given that the effects of information on voting varies by institutional environment, one cannot assume that shortcuts that aptly assist North American voters will also do so south of the Rio Grande (Lupia and McCubbins 1998; Shugart, Valdini, and Suominen 2005). Therefore, it is necessary, before focusing on the gaps in information, to verify what type of information matters to concrete political choices in Brazil. In addition, analyzing this information alongside classical sources of inequality allows one to evaluate how information may affect participatory biases set by gender, race, and income.

Table 1 presents the results of a multivariate analysis of the impact of information on turnout and casting a straight-ticket vote.[7] While voting is mandatory in Brazil, it is not excessively difficult to abstain. Therefore, it is worthwhile to explore if there are biases in the first step to making political demands: turnout in elections.[8] The turnout variable is coded from 0 to 5, indicating the number of offices for which the voter cast a vote for a candidate.[9] Ten percent of the voters in both cities did not vote for any office in 2002. Around 40 percent voted for all offices. The remaining population is scattered among the other four options. The hypothesis is that better-informed voters are more likely to turn out and vote.

Straight-ticket voting is operationalized as a dummy variable indicating if the respondent voted for candidates of the same party in the elections for president and federal deputy.[10] Casting a straight-ticket vote is a signal of a partisan vote (Mainwaring 1995). It can be seen as a more sophisticated form of voting, one that takes into consideration national and partisan issues more strongly than just local ones. In order to cast a partisan vote, the voter must be well informed not just about candidates, but also the national parties. This is especially true in Brazil, where most of the population does not vote a partisan ticket. Thirty percent of the voters in Caxias do Sul and 24 percent in Juiz de Fora cast a straight-ticket vote in the elections in 2002. This is much lower than the 70 percent of voters that do so in the United States (Lewis-Beck and Nadeau 2004), which is an indication that political parties in Brazil still do not mold vote choice as effectively as do their counterparts elsewhere (Mainwaring 1995).[11] The hypothesis is also that better-informed voters will cast a straight-ticket vote.

Furthermore, the model controls for a series of political factors and for differences in participation attributed to gender, race, and income. However,

Table 1. Full Maximum Likelihood Coefficients for Impact of Information and Opinionation on Turnout and for Straight-Ticket Voting, Brazil, 2002 Elections

Variables	Turnout: Caxias	Turnout: Juiz de Fora	Straight-ticket voting: Caxias	Straight-ticket voting: Juiz de Fora
Information				
Knows candidate names	0.14[b]	0.09[c]	0.16[c]	0.04[c]
Information on federal deputy	0.64[c]	0.66[c]	1.02[c]	0.78[c]
Generalized information	0.08	-0.05	0.19	0.05
Opinionation				
Opinionated: privatization	0.02	0.03	0.02	0.03
Opinionated: land reform	-0.02	0.04	-0.05	-0.07
Places presidential candidates on feeling thermometers	0.19[c]	0.19[b]	0.04	-0.04
Places political parties on feeling thermometers	0.02	-0.02	0.02	-0.01
Inequality				
Male	-0.17[b]	-0.23[c]	-0.23[a]	-0.03
Black	0.21	0.05	0.09	-0.00
Top 10% income	0.06	-0.15[a]	0.26[c]	0.03
Neighborhood income	0.01[a]	0.01[b]	0.01[b]	0.01[b]
Proportional reduction in error (PRE)	0.41[c]	0.45[c]	0.28[c]	0.21[c]
Number of strata	22	22	22	22
Number of observations	2,490	2,524	2,490	2,524

Key: a = significant at .05; b = significant at .01; c = significant at .001.

"race" is not as straightforward to measure in Brazil as, for example, gender, and thus deserves special attention. As much scholarship has confirmed, defining race in Brazil is a complicated affair. Racial attribution is usually based on physical characteristics and in most recent studies measured by self-placement scales, which are then recoded into white-nonwhite dummies. However, those most at risk of facing hardship because of skin color are people who self-identify as blacks. Blacks are the ones who have endured the suffering of exclusion in Brazil. Hence, distinguishing self-identified blacks from mulattoes and whites may capture clearer differences that become invisible when mulattoes and blacks are placed in the same category. Thus, the race variable receives a value of one for those who self-identify as black and zero for all others.

Here, too, the race variable is based on voters' self-identification using the traditional skin-color categories employed by the Brazilian census: black, white, brown (*pardo*) being the overwhelmingly predominant options, and a small percentage selecting yellow (Asian) and red (indigenous). The breakdown of this variable varies by city. Caxias do Sul is mostly white (76 percent), with 15 percent claiming they are pardo and 5 percent black. In Juiz de Fora, the racial distribution resembles more closely the national Brazilian pattern, with 55 percent claiming they are white, 25 percent pardo, and 14 percent self-identifying as black.

Interviewers were also asked to classify respondents according to color.[12] The results between the two race measurement strategies are practically identical with a slight inflation of whites (80 percent in Caxias and 59 percent in Juiz de Fora), but without affecting the pardo and black classification. Yellow (Asian origin) and indigenous classifications were quite small in the self-placement question (about 2 percent each in each site) and practically vanish when interviewers classify respondents. Hence, attribution of racial traits is not dramatically distinct between self-identification and external evaluations. It does not affect the percentages of pardo and black in the population.

Finally, the economic state of a voter was measured in two ways. The first relies on individual-level indicators based on family income. The variable was recoded into a dummy to differentiate the top tenth percentile from the rest of the population, in order to verify if the very richest part of the population is more informed and politically active than the rest. The idea is that the effect of income on the individual level is nonlinear, and that the main differences exist between the richest sector and the rest of the population.[13]

Income was also measured at the neighborhood level, as the mean neighborhood income, to capture the environmental characteristics of voters. This two-pronged strategy allows for a fuller evaluation of the impact of economic status on information acquisition and political participation.

The analysis controls for other variables that are also related to economic status in Brazil. Variables included in the analysis are educational level, age, participation in civil society organizations, identification with the Workers' Party, ideology, media attention, propensity to engage in political conversations, and the number of discussion partners. Of these factors, the most consistent influence on straight-ticket vote and turnout is identification with the Workers' Party, which increases the likelihood of both. The other variables present inconsistent results and are not further studied.

Table 1 partially confirms expectations regarding the effect of information. Factual summary information about politics, indicated by the variables Knows Candidates' Names and Federal Deputies' Index, is decisive in positively affecting turnout and party voting. Hence, specific information about the election is a strong determinant of concrete political behavior. Generalized information and opinionation are not nearly as vital as specific factual information. Generalized information has no impact on electoral choices, which confirms that voters do not need encyclopedic knowledge about politics to make electoral decisions. In addition, the only opinionation variable that matters is being able to place presidential candidates on "feeling thermometers," and that affects only turnout. In Brazilian elections, being informed about specific factors in campaigns increases voters' likelihood of voting and of casting a partisan vote.

Notably, formal educational level does not have a consistent impact in these distinct forms of voting when political information is brought in the equation. That is, political information, when educational level is controlled, matters more for political participation. In other words, educational level per se is not sufficient to increase political participation when it is not enriched by political information. Income and gender also condition political participation. Female voters with the same informational level as male voters are more likely to turn out and to cast a straight-ticket vote. A tiny bit of information makes a big difference for women. When women gain knowledge, they are very likely to engage in politics. However, when the gender variable is entered in a simple bivariate regression of turnout and straight-ticket voting, then the difference either favors men or is not statistically significant. In other words, when informational levels are not a factor, men seem more likely to participate. Therefore, in addition to directly influencing political activism, information is also a central intervening variable that affects women's political participation. Political information boosts women's participation. When women and men are on a level-playing field in terms of political information, differences in participation no longer favor men. This is a strong indicator that greater information leads to a narrower participatory gap between men and women.

Income measured at the neighborhood level also has a positive mark in both of the political participation variables. People who live in wealthier neighborhoods are more likely both to turn out and to vote along partisan lines. Hence, there is a participatory bias that favors the already well off, another case of the accumulation of inequalities through distinct resources. On the other hand, one needs to highlight that the impact of race is not statistically significant in either city; race thus does not seem to affect political participation and vote choice in these two Brazilian cities.

A Model of the Impact of Inequality on Information Acquisition

A gender and income gap thus exists in political participation, conditioned by political information. Unequal political participation is mediated by unequal information. The question then is how information itself is affected by more durable forms of inequality. A core hypothesis of this study is that informational biases are caused by gender, race, and economic divisions. In Brazil's informational gaps, these variables should have a statistically significant impact on the dependent variable analyzed: knowledge of the names of candidates running for different offices. Knowledge of candidate names is vital in Brazil because voters vote on candidates, not parties, and because knowledge of candidates is a straightforward indicator of more awareness about voters' options. Clientelism is intimately related to voters' lack of information about political alternatives. Therefore, knowing about more candidates most likely reduces the viability of clientelistic relationships. This approach tests if fundamental inequality affecting the distribution of varied resources is transferred across to the political realm. Specifically, my first hypothesis is that groups that have been historically marginalized in Brazilian society, women, blacks, and the poor, will also have little access to campaign information.

Hypothesis 1 is tested within a larger model of information acquisition. The model takes into consideration that learning results from the conjunction of opportunity, motivation, and ability (Luskin, Fishkin, and Jowell 2002). Opportunity refers to the environmental factors that facilitate information acquisition. Electoral campaigns are usually viewed as amplifiers of the typical political information environments of voters. A second hypothesis, then, rests on the fact that information acquisition is facilitated by electoral campaigns, which reduce the cost of information and make its distribution more equitable.[14] Hypothesis 2 is that the informational gap linked to race, class, and gender divides should decrease during the course of an electoral campaign.

To test this hypothesis, an indicator of the passage of time is included in the model. This variable signals participation in each of the three waves of interviews in the panel study. A positive coefficient for this variable of the multivariate analysis indicates that voters gained information during the electoral campaign. The time variable was recoded so that the first wave receives value 0 and subsequent waves receive values 1 and 2. The model interacts time with race, gender, and income to check any changes in the impact of such variables over time. By coding the first wave as 0, the "main effect" variable for race, income, and gender indicates the effect of these variables on the first wave of interviews, the benchmark measure for information levels. The coefficient for the interaction between the time variable and race, income, and gender indicates change in the impact of these variables over subsequent waves.[15] The analysis therefore permits an evaluation of race, gender, and income bias in information early in campaigns and how this bias is then attenuated or augmented by the electoral campaign itself. It uses a growth-curve model to evaluate biases in information gain (Singer 1998).

The model is also tested separately for each city, to see whether distinctions between the different city-level environments affect information gain. Theory suggests that simpler environments should facilitate access to information (Lupia and McCubbins 1998; Sniderman 2000; Rahn 1993; Lau and Redlawsk 2001). Electoral complexity is usually related to the number of political actors in the system and the visibility of their messages. Therefore, simpler environments, with fewer actors who have recognized reputations, facilitate information gain. Caxias do Sul may for this reason provide more fertile ground for political learning.

However, it is also possible that the polarized environment of Caxias do Sul leads to starker class divisions in which poor and richer voters cease to bother learning about candidates and parties other than their "own." In addition, the less-polarized environment of Juiz de Fora may increase opportunities for cross-class, cross-race, and cross-gender political deliberations, bringing overall higher levels of information. My third hypothesis is that environments will affect the informational gaps, but the direction of the impact is not explicitly specified by existing theory and needs to be verified.

In addition to environmental and temporal determinants of information acquisition are motivation and ability at the individual level. The model includes several factors that may influence the amount of information voters possess. More motivated voters pay closer attention to the media, engage more often in political conversations, watch Brazil's free electoral airtime, and talk with party and candidate supporters. It is natural to speculate if such motivated voters are better informed.

Finally, the model controls for factors influencing learning abilities, including education, employment status, age, or status as a housewife or student. Political orientation, measured by identification with the Workers' Party and Left ideological leanings, may also affect political learning, so it is included in the model. The model also controls for respondents' propensity to guess.[16] Guessing is said to be a factor that especially pervades the gap between men and women.[17] Controversy surrounds whether men are generally more likely to guess than women, with different authors wielding contradictory evidence for this hypothesis. Still, to control for guessers, a variable focusing on risk-taking was placed in the analysis.

Information Inequalities in Brazil

To analyze the actual impact of gender, race, and class on political information in Brazil, it is vital to devise and fully specify the model of information gain to ensure that possible gaps caused by gender, race, and class are not in fact attributable to other, extraneous factors, such as individual differences in educational levels. This provides a more robust test than evaluating differences in means without controlling for other sources of variation in information acquisition. That said, discussing the impact of all the different factors that influence learning about candidates is beyond the scope of this essay: suffice it to say that more educated, more media attentive individuals are likely to be better informed. On the other hand, housewives and older people are less likely to be better informed. The crucial question, however, is if race, gender, and income affect political information even when accounting for these other potential causes for informational biases.

Table 2. Full Maximum Likelihood Coefficients for Knowledge of Candidates'
Names, Brazil, 2002 Elections

Variables	Knows candidates' names: Caxias	Knows candidates' names: Juiz de Fora
Intercept	4.11[c]	3.72[c]
Inequality		
Male	0.95[c]	0.84[c]
Black	-0.16	-0.49[c]
Top 10% richest	0.33[a]	0.08
Neighborhood income	0.00[b]	0.00[c]
Time	2.62[c]	2.07[c]
Male * time	0.13	-0.04
Black * time	-0.47[a]	-0.15
Top 10% richest * time	0.18	0.02
Mean neighborhood income * time	0.00	0.00[b]
Level 1 N	6973	7165
Level 2 N	3384	3250
Level 3 N	22	22
Proportional reduction in error (PRE)	53%	48%

Key: a = significant at .05; b = significant at .01; c = significant at .001.

Table 2 presents findings about candidates' names, measured over time.[18]
The first part of the table shows results for the three main inequality variables when regressed alongside the full information-acquisition model esti-
mated over time. The time variable indicates how the mean level of information changes over the three waves of interviews. The coefficients for the
gender, race, and class variables indicate the size of the gap in the first wave
of interviews, before the campaign started. The coefficients for the inter-

action terms between time and gender, race and class indicate how the early campaign gap changes over time.

Regarding hypotheses 1 and 3, it is clear that a gender gap favoring males exists in both cities. Levels of information among men are higher than among womens early in the campaign, as the main effects for the male variable indicates. Although women with the same informational level as men tend to participate more in politics, women in general are less informed about politics. This is independent of the environment embedding women and men. In both cities, the gender gap is the most pervasive one. Hence, given how information activates women's political engagement, if women were as informed as men, they would probably display more voice in the political system. This gap exists even when controlling for other possible factors that attenuate gender differences, such as educational level and insertion in the labor market. Women with educational levels and jobs similar to those of men are still likely to lag in political information.

The racial gap is wider in Juiz de Fora than in Caxias do Sul early in the campaign. This shows that complex electoral environments, like that of Juiz de Fora, have higher learning costs for scarcer information, a finding supported by the results of the "main effects" of the race variable.[19]

The individual level variable for income in Caxias also indicates a difference in informational levels early in the campaign. Even though race does not matter early in the campaign in Caxias, income level does. The top tenth percentile is better informed when information is less available. This is expected because the class divide between rich and poor is quite strong and clear-cut in Caxias, in contrast to that in Juiz de Fora. Again, the cost of information early in a campaign may hinder voters' ability to learn in Caxias. The strong ideological divide between rich and poor accentuates this and may further obstruct the spread of information. In Juiz de Fora, where such a divide is weaker, class differences are not decisive in affecting political information. Rich and poor, in a less divisive environment, do not appear that different when it comes to political information levels. However, neighborhood income is a factor influencing informational levels independent of the city, indicating that income differences when taken as a larger environmental factor do affect information.

Hypothesis 3 was that the passage of time during the election campaign will lower the cost of information and therefore decrease the gaps caused by race, class, and gender. First of all, the positive statistically significant coefficient for time indicates that voters do in fact learn during the campaign.

They also learn slightly faster in Caxias do Sul, in its simpler electoral environment. However, the gaps stemming from gender, race, and income do not seem to change dramatically over the course of the campaign. In both Caxias do Sul and Juiz de Fora, no statistically significant changes occur in the coefficient for the difference between men and women. There are also no statistically significant changes for differences between rich and poor as measured at the individual level. The only changes linked to inequality indicators appear with race in Caxias do Sul, where Afro-Brazilians' levels of information actually decrease during the campaign, and with neighborhood income in Juiz de Fora, where voters in rich neighborhoods become even more informed. Therefore, although an electoral campaign raises voters' levels of information overall, these gains do not favor historically underprivileged groups. The rate of learning does not vary by social group, and when it does, it benefits the already privileged groups.

Figures 1 through 3 facilitate analysis of the main informational gaps in Brazil. Figure 1 shows the gender gap in Caxias do Sul, which is identical to that in Juiz de Fora. The rate of learning, indicated by the slope, is constant, but men and women start at different levels and that gap is maintained throughout the three waves of interviews.

Figure 2 shows the gap between Afro-Brazilians and the rest of the population in Caxias do Sul, where the information gap diverges. The gap becomes clearly wider over the course of the campaign, indicating some kind of bias in the distribution of information in Caxias during the campaign. Underscoring the salience of this finding is the fact that ideology, partisanship, and other factors related to learning are accounted for in the model. This finding reveals a pattern of race-biased distribution of information in Caxias, where the Afro-Brazilian population is more of a population minority than in the rest of Brazil. Race certainly does matter in Caxias, where Afro-Brazilians remain disadvantaged in learning about more candidates relative to white Brazilians. They are even more excluded from information access in Caxias than in other Brazilian cities, such as Juiz de Fora. Figure 3 shows the informational gap by income measured at the individual level in Caxias do Sul. It highlights a distinction, albeit a very small one, between rich and poor.

However, the difference measured at the neighborhood level is far more substantive. Figure 4 shows the difference between respondents in rich and poor neighborhoods, confirming it as in fact the largest and most significant distinction in this analysis. Income captured at the individual level does

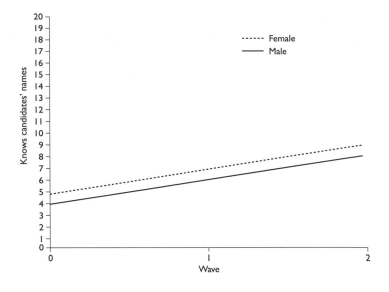

Figure 1. Gender Gap in Knowledge about Candidates' Names.
Source: Juiz de Fora, Minas Gerais, Brazil, 2002.

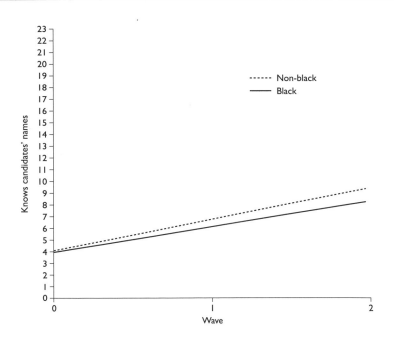

Figure 2. Race Gap in Knowledge about Candidates' Names.
Source: Caxias do Sul, Rio Grande do Sul, Brazil, 2002.

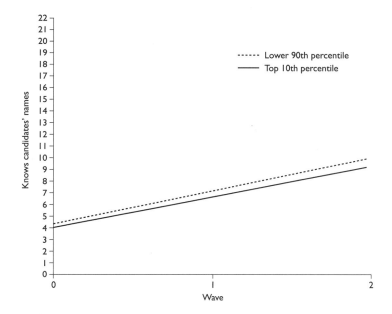

Figure 3. Economic Gap at Individual Level in Knowledge about Candidates' Names. Source: Caxias do Sul, Rio Grande do Sul, Brazil, 2002.

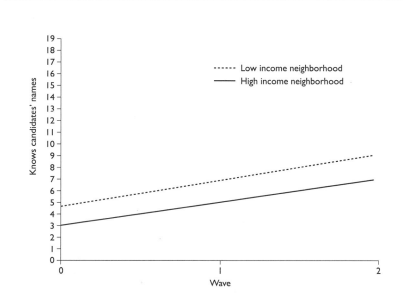

Figure 4. Economic Gap at Neighborhood Level in Knowledge about Candidates' Names. Source: Juiz de Fora, Rio Grande do Sul, Brazil, 2002.

not differentiate voters' levels of information, but the environmental characteristics of the neighborhood play a decisive role in the range of information voters get exposed to.

Conclusions and Implications

In testing whether historical and social inequalities based on race, gender, and income transfer into the current political sphere in Brazil, my study confirms that there are indeed biases in the distribution of information and in political participation, and these are due mostly to gender and income gaps.

Voters living in rich neighborhoods, with the same informational level of voters living in poor neighborhoods, prove more likely to participate in politics. The transfer of income inequality to political participation certainly contributes to further deepening the gap between rich and poor in Brazil. Moreover, a consistent informational gap is caused by income differences. Not only are citizens who live in wealthier neighborhoods more likely to participate when they enjoy the same range of information as citizens from poor neighborhoods, but they also are in general better informed than citizens who live in poor zones. The income gap clearly affects political resources and is at the root of the urban poor's lack of voice and influence in the Brazilian policy-making process. Because the poor are less informed and less likely to participate, they are less visible to public authorities, and their demands are either ignored or take longer to filter into the state.

However, it is neighborhood mean income, characterizing the overall economic condition of the neighborhood, rather than individual income, that best distinguishes between haves and have-nots in terms of political information and participation. The neighborhood environment overrides individual differences and conditions access to information more clearly than individual-level variance.

The persistent gender gap is slightly different. Women with the same informational level as men are actually more likely to throw themselves into politics. However, the difference between men and women, without considering extant information levels, favors the former. Hence, information is a crucial intervening factor influencing the political participation of women. Better-informed women are more politically active than equally well-informed men. Information enhances women's active roles, though two problems remain. First, men are consistently better informed about candidates running for office than are women, and this persists during the course of a campaign. A clear gender gap persists in political information, one that remains even when several other potential explanations for its existence are controlled for, such as education, employment status, media attention, and interest in politics. Second, when informational differences between men and women are controlled for, men are still more likely to participate in politics. In sum, only well-informed women are politically active, while men, independent of their informational level, tend toward more activism in politics. Therefore, poorly informed women face the most challenging hurdles to political participation.

Finally, it seems that environmental characteristics affect the impact of durable inequalities. In more complex political environments, the costs of electoral information are high throughout the campaign. Consequently, it is hard for those groups hit hardest by the costs of information to attain the levels of information of more privileged groups.

What are the implications of these findings for inequality in Brazilian and Latin American politics? First, this research indicates that voters are actually learning during campaigns, but that such learning does not attenuate some of the costs of gaining information for specific groups. Worse, the sectors with narrow access to information are the same ones that are historically excluded from access to several other resources in Brazil. In short, the informational bias favors richer, whiter males, especially those in more complex political environments. Inequalities thus appear to cut across different spheres of life in Brazilian society and to affect the distribution of various resources simultaneously. Those historically excluded from a multiplicity of resources—the poor, blacks, and women—also seem less prone to engage in politics and to actively obtain political information, further perpetuating the cycle of exclusion.

Second, the informational and participatory gap caused by income differences clarifies the mechanism through which clientelistic relations work in Brazil. Voters who are easy prey for clientelism, those marginalized from economic resources, are also those more likely to be less informed about their political options. Inequality of information may thus help to explain how clientelism persists in Latin America.

It is notable that even in the 2002 election, which elected a genuine representative of the Brazilian people—Lula shares their social background and has personally faced the difficulties most Brazilians face in their everyday lives—informational inequalities were still widespread and resilient.

Therefore, focusing only on the presidential election and ignoring other races for legislative and state-level offices provides an inaccurate picture of the role of informational inequalities in elections.

Information intensifies the propensity toward political activism and those who are attentive to the media and the free electoral airtime grasp more about politics. This shows that investing even more in democratizing access to political information is crucial to combat the cycle of exclusion. Brazil's current policies for qualitative equality are important, and no doubt making a difference, but have yet to accomplish their goals. This could be simply due to the fact that legitimate elections, especially presidential ones, are still a novelty in Brazil when compared to the democracies of Western Europe and North America. Hence, the passage of time and the continuation of the current policies, which aim at opening access to balanced and fair political information, could result in shrinkage of the informational gaps found here. Increasing access to political information remains a necessity in countries plagued by resilient inequalities. Though Brazil faces a long road ahead, it is at least moving in the right direction by investing in this democratizing access to political information.

What is troubling is that even in a country like Brazil, which has made notable investments to attenuate informational inequality, the problem lingers. As Paul Gootenberg and Luis Reygadas point out, inequality is a humanly constructed phenomenon that is fluid and malleable through human agency.[20] While Brazil has made an effort to democratize access to information and restrict broadcasting biases, the deep gaps of the past are not easily erased. The historically indelible processes that bequeathed today's chasms between rich and poor, white and black, men and women will require long, continuous, and purposive action to reverse.

Furthermore, given that few Latin American countries have made comparable efforts in increasing access to political information, it is probable that the inequalities found in Brazil are more pervasive where there are no mechanisms in place for democratizing political information. Informational gaps may therefore be even more profound in the rest of Latin America.

Appendix: Measuring Informational Levels and Opinionation

Political information refers to how much factual information voters have about politics (Delli Carpini and Keeter 1996). When using survey data, this is measured by a simple count of correct answers on a politics "quiz." Other survey research strategies for measuring information include external evaluations of respondents' knowledge about politics, usually performed by the interviewers themselves (Bartels 2005), and indicators that refer not to concrete factual data but to factors that depend on respondents' opinions about certain topics, that is, "opinionation." Some types of opinions reflect an informational awareness of the political system. Indeed, Delli Carpini and Keeter find that the formation of opinions depends on information (1996). The different measurement strategies derive from distinct conceptualizations of the types of information voters use in elections. Some voters may be generalists: they know a little about various different political issues. Other voters may be knowledgeable about specific issues; they may know, for example, all there is to know about gender issues or international politics. Basically, this is the distinction between generalists and issue specialists.[21] External evaluations of respondents' levels of information are not issue specific, but assess how informed voters are about all subjects. It is an indicator of generalized knowledge. On the other hand, responses to items on specific topics are a more focused form of information and indicate that the respondent is an issue specialist.

These two types of information were operationalized in this study following guidelines in the literature (see table 3). General information is operationalized by interviewer evaluations of respondents' levels of information ("Generalized Information"). Specific information here refers to specific knowledge about actors in the electoral process and is indicated by an index of voters' ability to name candidates for different offices ("Knows Candidates' Names"; alpha = .77) and by an index of information about Federal Deputies ("Information on Federal Deputy"; alpha = .65). These questions are based on factual information about central actors in the elections and offer no margin for speculation.

Opinionation, on the other hand, refers to the voter's ability to formulate an opinion about a specific issue; it refers exactly to voters' speculations about politics (Krosnick and Milburn 1990; Delli Carpini and Keeter 1996). Even though opinionation differs from information, the former is dependent on the latter. Having an opinion is an indicator of political awareness. In this study, because of the way opinionation variables were deployed, opinionation is also as an indicator of information, but not in any concrete factual sense. In all waves of the panel, respondents were asked to place candidates and political parties on "feeling thermometers" that measure feelings about a candidate or party on a scale from 0 to 10, and they were also

Table 3. Description of Variables

Variables	Description
Information	
Knows candidates' names	Index composed of four variables that ask respondents to name candidates for different offices, including president, governor, senator, and federal deputy. The variable ranges from 0 to 23 and is a count of correct names.
Information on federal deputy	Index composed of three dichotomous variables that indicate if respondent knew if the candidate he/she voted for federal deputy was elected, if respondent knew the party of the candidate he/she voted for, and if respondent knew if the candidate was running for reelection or running for the first time.
Generalized information	Variable based on an item that asked the interviewer to evaluate the respondent's level of knowledge about politics. It was recoded into a dummy to contrast those who have high and very high levels of information from the rest of the population.
Opinionation	
Opinionated: privatization	Index composed by four variables indicating if respondent knows if the four main candidates for president (Lula, Serra, Ciro, Garotinho) are strongly against, mildly against, neutral, mildly in favor, or strongly in favor of privatization. Those who did not know how to answer were coded 0. Those who gave an answer were coded 1. Answers were not checked for accuracy because the positions of all candidates are not absolutely clear and can give margin for more than one correct response.
Opinionated: land reform	Same as above, but for candidates' positions on land reform.

Table 3. *Continued*

Variables	Description
Places candidates on feeling thermometer	Index composed of four variables indicating if respondent can place the top four presidential candidates (Lula, Serra, Ciro, Garotinho) on feeling thermometers. Respondents who expressed an opinion toward a candidate received value 1. Those who did not express an opinion, received value 0.
Places parties on feeling thermometer	Same as above, but with regard to four of the main political parties in the Brazilian political system (PT, PMDB, PSDB, PFL).
Inequality Indicators	
Black	Response to self-description of item on skin color. 1 = black, 0 = all other responses.
Income	Coded 1 if respondent is in the top tenth percentile of income distribution. Based on item that asks respondent to state approximately total family income per month.
Mean neighborhood income	Mean of the individual level income by neighborhood. Average response given to item on how much money the family earns in a month. Measured in Reais.
Male	Gender of respondent. 1 = male, 2 = female.
Individual political predispositions	
PT identification	2 = Identifies strongly with the Workers' Party; 1 = Identifies weakly with the Workers' Party; 0 = Does not identify with the Workers' Party.
Left-wing ideology	1 = Self-places on the Left on a 5-point ideological continuum from Right to Left; 0 = Does not self-place on the Left.
Individual Motivations	
Participation in neighborhood association and participatory budget	1 = has participated in a meeting of these organizations at least once in the past year.

Table 3. *Continued*

Variables	Description
Political conversation	Index composed of responses to items on habits of talking about politics with neighbors, friends, co-workers, and family members. Min: 0. Max: 1 Cronbach's Alpha: .59
Media	Index composed of responses to items on frequency of watching the top two television-news broadcasts most watched by the respondent in a week and the frequency of reading the top two newspapers most read by the respondent in a week. Min: 0. Max: 26.
Free electoral airtime	Dummy variable for having watched the free electoral airtime programs for federal deputy.
Individual characteristics	
Education	Response to item on last school year attended. Ranges from 0, illiterate, to 15, completed graduate school.
Age and age^2	Age of respondent based on response on year of birth; square value of age.
Married	1 = is formally or informally married.
Student	1 = is currently a student.
Housewife	1 = is currently a housewife (*doña de casa*).
Employed	1 if respondent is employed; 0 otherwise.
Design controls	
Replacements wave 2	1 if the respondent was part of a fresh cross-section interviewed in wave 2; 0 otherwise.
Replacements wave 3	1 if the respondent was part of a fresh cross-section interviewed in wave 3; 0 otherwise.

Table 4. Descriptive Statistics of Juiz de Fora, Minas Gerais, and Caxias do Sul, Rio Grande do Sul

Variable	Juiz de Fora	Caxias do Sul
Population	456,796	360,419
Literate population more than 10 years of age	367,844	290,772
Hospitals	17	4
Enrolled in elementary school	79,836	57,410
Enrolled in high school	26,705	15,268
Voters	312,474	229,614
Number of business enterprises	16,132	17,991
Employed personnel	106,787	115,328
Banks	35	41
Municipal tax revenue	R$ 48,059,512	R$ 30,423,079
Budgetary expenditures	R$ 203,254,396	R$ 121,228,965
Federal transfers	R$ 11,077,834	R$ 9,794,410
Federal educational fund	R$ 15,410,839	R$ 18,337,539
Wages paid by local businesses	R$ 527,387,654	R$ 753,334,828
Deaths, external causes	273	231
Deaths, younger than 1 year	217	123
Deaths	4,080	2,014

Source: Instituto Brasileiro de Geografia Estatística, Brazilian Census, 2000.

asked to indicate whether they knew the positions of candidates on privatization and land reform. These variables were recoded to differentiate between those who could provide a valid response to these questions, that is, recognize and place candidates and parties by feeling thermometers while also knowing the position of candidates on issues, and those who said they did not know.[22] Voters able to express a judgment about candidates and parties through feeling thermometers and who admit to knowing something about the candidates' positions are likely more informed about politics than those who cannot. However, because candidates' positions on certain issues can change and sometimes are not clear-cut, knowing candidates' preferences is often a matter of speculation, not concrete factual information. Still, these opinions reveal a minimum awareness of the political system and its main actors.

For this study, four opinionation indices were created, indicating candidate placement on feeling thermometers (alpha = .81), party placement on feeling thermometers (alpha = .90), opinion about presidential candidates' position on land reform (alpha = .88), and opinion about presidential candidates' position on privatization (alpha = .89).

Notes

I would like to thank Paul Gootenberg and Luis Reygadas for comments that greatly improved the final version of this essay. I also thank the participants of the Janey Program conference series in the New School for Social Research, colleagues at the Center for Latin American Studies at the University of Arizona, and members of the Brazil Studies Group of Columbia University for comments on preliminary versions. Finally, I am grateful for the suggestions of Duke University Press's anonymous reviewers.

1. Gay 1994; Fox 1997; Abers 1998; Auyero 2000; Archer 1990; Banck 1999; Brusco, Nazareno, and Stokes 2004.
2. For an exception, see Oliveira 1999.
3. For descriptive socioeconomic and demographic data on both cities, see table 4 in the appendix at the end of this essay.
4. Lupia and McCubbins define a "reasoned choice" as one in which an individual knows the consequences of their action (2000: 47–48).
5. Obviously, those who know more than the minimal levels of information are always better off. Bartels argues that fully informed voters act differently from other voters (Bartels 1993). In addition, better-informed voters tend to vote more moderately than less-informed voters (Luskin, Fishkin, and Jowell 2002) and are less hesitant about candidates' policy positions (Alvarez and Brehm 2002).
6. See the appendix for a technical discussion on the measurement of political information.
7. See the appendix for a description of the variables used in the analysis.
8. Voters can only vote in the cities in which they are registered. If they are away from home, they can't vote and must justify their absence, which is done on election day by filling out a justification claim in any voting zone. The justification forms are provided in polling centers, so the voter simply has to go to one of them and fill in the form. Voters may also do so after the election, by going to the electoral court of their home municipality and paying a nominal fine.

9. Brazil has general elections every four years, with voters choosing candidates for president, governor, senator, federal deputy, and state deputy. The turnout variable does not include the vote for state deputy and does include the two votes for senator that were required in the elections in 2002, which is why it varies from zero to five. If the voter voted blank or cast a null vote, this was considered an invalid vote and coded as zero.

10. The measure includes the citizens who did not cast a valid vote for either election. These individuals necessarily fall in the split-ticket voter category.

11. If one excludes the invalid votes from the count in Brazil, the percentage of straight-ticket voters increases to 50 percent in Brazil, which is still twenty percentage points lower than in the United States.

12. To avoid classification contamination, interviewers were instructed to classify the respondent silently and before asking the respondent to self-identify.

13. Income was imputed for around one hundred cases. The variables used for imputation were race, gender, educational level, being employed, and age. The variable was then logged to normalize the distribution.

14. Popkin (1991) claims that electoral campaigns reduce the cost of information.

15. See Jacard and Turisi 2003 for a discussion of interaction terms in regression analysis.

16. This variable was developed in studies of Mexican elections by Morgenstern and Zechmeister (2001). The assumption is that guessing is more likely among risk-taking than risk-averse respondents. To operationalize risk-aversion, respondents were asked to choose between two well-known popular sayings in Brazil. The first option was "a bird in the hand is better than two in the bush." The second was "nothing ventured, nothing gained"(quem não arrisca, não petisca). Those who chose the second option were considered risk-acceptant and thus more prone to guessing. In fact, confirming previous studies, women are more likely to be risk-averse; of the risk-acceptant, 57 percent are men and 42 percent women. A final control refers to technical aspects of the research design. Because panel conditioning can affect measures of the same individual over time (Bartels 1999), and because information variables are particularly sensitive to panel conditioning (Brehm 1993), fresh cross-sections were interviewed in waves 2 and 3 to control for differentiation between the panel respondents and the rest of the population. Dummies for replacements interviewed in waves 2 and 3 were added to the model.

17. Mondak and Anderson 2004; Frazer and MacDonald 2003; Hayes 2001; Kenski and Jamieson 2000; Verba, Burns, and Schlozman 1997.

18. The data includes measures at different levels of analysis. It has measures within individuals over time, between individuals (which is the same as within neighborhoods), and between neighborhoods. Therefore, the most appropriate estimation technique is a hierarchical model that estimates both fixed and random effects. Given that all variables are counts, but not highly skewed and with

various categories, I model their distribution using an identity-link function. I also tested the same models using a Poisson link function; the results do not vary. Given that the identity-link function facilitates interpretation by leaving the metric of the dependent variable untouched, I opted to present these coefficients instead of Poisson functions.

19. The "main effects" indicate the effect of being black on information about candidates in wave 1.

20. See Gootenberg's and Reygadas's essays in this volume.

21. These distinctions are not mutually exclusive and are taken as extreme points in a continuum.

22. Again, I refer to these variables as indicators of "opinions" because candidate's positions on issues are quite often unclear and difficult to identify, so there is no way to affirm if the respondent is correct or incorrect in his or her assessment.

PART III

Culture across

Borders

6

Between *Orishas* and Revolution

The Expression of Racial Inequalities

in Post-Soviet Cuba

ODETTE CASAMAYOR

"For those who don't like it. For those bugged by it. I am a rapper, black and from East Havana," sings the group Hermanos d'Causa.[1] It's a cry. A chant that, though it comes from the hip-hop scene in Cuba, has turned into the cry of many Cubans. A muzzled, suffocated, and hidden shout. A cry deemed unnecessary for the first fifty years of the socialist revolution. But a cry that beginning in the nineties burst into the open. A movement that at first took many by surprise but has now proved its staying power. The demand for the cultural recognition of black culture has now become a crucial part of discussions about race within Cuban intellectual circles.

The current reality in Cuba was shaped by the fall of the Berlin Wall, in 1989. With this collapse came the inevitable tottering of what were once certainties and illusions sustained by a total faith in the socialist system. In addition to continuous economic calamity, Cuban society has also witnessed a social and ethical disaster. Cuba, adrift as a country, now merits many of the "post-" labels: postrevolutionary, post-Soviet, post–Cold War, postcolonial, and postmodern. In the arena of racial equality, one is dealing with a country that for decades considered the differences between black and white to have been abolished and then suddenly awoke, in the nineties, to find the opposite to be true. The measures adopted immediately after the triumph of the 1959 revolution, which sought to eliminate racial inequality altogether, were not enough in the end. This failure is difficult to confront and conceals a crucial problem: how can one explain the persistence of Cuban racism when "underlying" economic, social, political, and ideological conditions no longer offer adequate answers? In this respect, the isle of Cuba, a castaway site during the closing era of the grand metanarratives about modernity, can be viewed as a laboratory. The nation's racial paradox demands a search for other methods for grasping the permanence of racial inequality. At first glance, this paradox would seem to refute Charles Tilly's thesis that persistent inequality is due to the use of categorical divides such as black-white or man-woman in assigning social resources, for the Cuban Revolution has eliminated these kinds of categorical binaries between black and white, and the biased distribution of opportunity rooted in such categories. Nonetheless, a closer look reveals that while such categorical divides vanished from official language, they persisted in the everyday interactions between people in Cuba. Racism and racial inequality were suppressed in aspects of public policy relating to employment, education, and access to nutritional and health services, but they survived in many cultural, emotional, ethical, and aesthetic dimensions of life. Thus, rather than undermining Tilly's idea of categorical inequality, one needs to enrich it with a finer analysis of the historical and cultural processes that reproduce inequities. Thus, I propose in this essay to examine the indelible inequality between whites and blacks under an ethical-aesthetic lens, one that approaches racism from the intimacy of being, one rejecting determinism yet incorporating the suggestions of economic, political, social, and historical analysis.

Thinking about these dilemmas helps to focus research about Cuban hip-hop as a sociocultural phenomenon that embodies a discourse about the recognition of black culture in contemporary societies. In this realm, Cuba is not estranged from a transnational movement that has shaken afro-diasporic communities throughout the Americas. The Cuban situation, however, has its own particularities, since its national hip-hop is generally considered an underground scene that integrates what is known in the island as the Alternative Cuban Music (Música Cubana Alternativa).[2] Although not all Cuban hip-hop artists express their social and political commitment through their work, the hip-hop arena is in general regarded as a space of protest and social criticism. The rap groups Obsesión, Anónimo Consejo, Hermanos d'Causa, and Fabri-K are representative of this militant hip-hop and stand out among other groups for their sharp critiques of racism in today's Cuban society. For instance, the groups Obsesión and Doble Filo joined forces and created the collective Fabri-K, which is considered one of the most interesting new hip-hop phenomena. One of their primary goals is to raise the political consciousness of marginalized black Cubans.

I examine these rappers in parallel with the painter and multimedia artist

Juan Roberto Diago, because a similar stance of nonconformity, social resistance, and antiracism characterizes his works. Their message, overall,
responds to the necessity of putting an end to a historical condition of
subalternity. Even though they recognize the efforts of the revolution to
improve the well-being of black Cubans, their anger results from years of
feeling the discrimination against Afro-Cuban cultures and religions, the
persistent silence around their problems as blacks, and the official denial of
any need to open a serious discussion on the racial question. In short, they
are asking for visibility within civil society and for real recognition as blacks,
Cubans, and, in certain cases, even as the authentic revolutionaries of postmodern times.

Blacks in Post-Soviet Cuba

On the island, hip-hop emerged during the nineties, in the midst of general
anxieties wrought by the early 1990s crisis of socialism. Many Cubans faced
the stark challenge of finding new survival strategies—economic, political,
social, and ethical. They sought everyday answers to Jean Baudrillard's provocative question: into which garbage can does one toss Marxism, the ideology itself responsible for inventing the phrase "dustbin of history"?[3] At issue
was how to understand a wildly contradictory situation, reinterpret the past,
and find meaning in a chaotic present lacking a secure vision of the future.
Capitalism and socialism were equally challenged on a daily basis. Traditional Cuban morals as well as socialist morals gave way to present imperatives, characterized by individualism and the dire need to acquire the resources for daily sustenance. At this point, prostitution, delinquency, and
drug trafficking—unknown to Cubans after 1959—resurfaced.

In this context of abandonment, drift, lost certainties, and a novel wind of
neoliberalism, racial inequality became an unavoidable problem. Until the
eighties, open questioning of the official narrative of Cuba's absence of
racial differences was rare. The Cuban Revolution, profoundly nationalist
and identifying itself since 1961 with Marxism-Leninism, had among its
main objectives to consolidate a national identity that would guarantee the
unity and continuity of its project and to eliminate any and all inequalities
that undermined national cohesion. In this way, the struggle against racial
discrimination became a vital task for the revolution from its inception.
Chapter 5 of the socialist constitution explicitly and specifically condemned
racial discrimination for the first time in Cuban history, and the state aban-

doned all segregationist barriers. Compared to other Latin American countries, the black population of Cuba was able to integrate within revolutionary society in surprising ways. Measures were taken to ensure the poorest of Cubans, blacks in their majority, not only primary schooling but secondary and higher education as well. This considerably raised educational levels while eliminating obstacles that impeded access to certain jobs. Within a few years Cuban authorities reached the conclusion that having officially abolished the objective causes of discrimination, racial inequalities would disappear from the new society, fading into a mere memory.

As noted by Mark Sawyer, Cuban postrevolutionary racial politics draw from Latin America particular considerations on race (chiefly the myth of color blindness) and from the socialist, anti-imperialist, and Third World ideologies adopted by the Cuban revolution. In this sense, it is interesting how "racial politics within Cuba have followed patterns of opening and retrenchment that have been driven by the need of the state to mobilize blacks to support state projects and to protect the state from hostile forces. Once the state's projects have been completed or the threats against it neutralized it has consolidated around new racial orders. Within this process, racial ideology has played a critical role in setting the boundaries for improvement on racial issues and providing justifications for retrenchment" (Sawyer 2006: xix).

In the nineties, the inequalities between blacks, whites, and mestizos acquired relevance again. This does not mean that racial inequality had been actually eradicated during the revolution's first thirty years, as official discourse proclaimed, or that the crisis revived an extinct phenomenon. Racism has always been present in Cuban society, some times more surreptitiously than others. But after the fall of the Berlin Wall, the state became incapable of assuring basic welfare for the entire population. As the economic depression spread, every Cuban was left to his or her own devices, which strongly affected blacks (De la Fuente 2001: 319–26). In contemporary Cuba, possession of foreign currency is the required form of capital for integration, and those without means for its procurement were rapidly left behind. For the majority of the black Cubans, dollars proved hard to get within legal parameters. On the one hand, they were disadvantaged with respect to their white compatriots in terms of remittances, since, as it is widely known, blacks were never a sizeable portion of Cuban émigrés, especially those who thrived economically abroad.[4] On the other hand, within the new mixed and foreign businesses rooting in Cuba, blacks occupied a minority of positions, usually of lesser rank. As a result, a substantial group of marginalized Cubans had no alternative but to seek means of support in the black market, in delinquency, or in prostitution. There was nothing extraordinary about this process: it was the revival in Cuba of the downward spiral linking poverty to marginality and delinquency. A part of this reality was the exacerbation of racial prejudices and a revived discussion about blacks within the Cuban society and nation.

This is when the resurgence of a radical discourse of cultural recognition emerges in Cuba. Its description of neglect, rootlessness, and marginality is not far from conditions that have favored the birth of hip-hop in places like the South Bronx, Rio de Janeiro's favelas, the poor barrios of San Juan, or Loiza in Puerto Rico. These marginal enclaves of the Americas, along with the East Havana neighborhoods to which the Hermanos d'Causa proudly pay tribute, are the neglected peripheral zones of the post-industrial urban landscape. These spaces reflect a stark institutional or leadership vacuum, where traditional practices of contestation disappeared or become obsolete and social ties loosened to the point of destroying the community. These contexts are laid out in Tricia Rose's book on North American hip-hop, *Black Noise*. As she lucidly explains, "Hip-hop emerges from the deindustrialization meltdown where social alienation, prophetic imagination, and yearning intersect. Hip-hop is a cultural form that attempts to negotiate the experiences of marginalization, brutally truncated opportunity, and oppression within the cultural imperative of African-American and Caribbean history, identity, and community" (Rose 1994: 21). Rose limits her analysis of hip-hop to the North American experience, as do most hip-hop scholars, but her assessment is useful for looking at other sites. It is indisputable that hip-hop as an aesthetic can be traced to an American artistic creation of African origin, and that ideologically it emanated from traditional African American nationalism. Nor can one dispute its roots in marginalized North American urban communities composed, for the most part, of African and Caribbean populations. Beyond these circumstances, however, hip-hop now answers to global predicaments and is transnational in character.

Through hip-hop, the youth of Western societies with concentrations of afro-descendants find a medium through which to find identity and expression in a world that marginalizes, alienates, ignores, and forgets them. In Cuba this phenomenon is striking in that it constitutes a kind of a "tribal" claim, in a context that since 1959 has aspired to full societal cohesion, to the suppression of factions, of the tribal, or of all that is "different." Hip-hop practices came to the fore only as globalization made its impact. After a half century as an enclosed enclave of the communist empire, an island as far geographically from Moscow as it was politically from Washington, Cuba has finally been re-exposed to global events and trends. Demands for cultural recognition of black culture in Cuba today could be read, then, as a protest against two different types of homogenization: one stems from a nationalist power, whose aim was to obviate or denigrate anything "black"; the other derives from a form of globalization that sorts, cleanses, and domesticates the unruly. Thus, as the Hermanos d'Causa fervently affirm an identity pivoting around hip-hop, race, and belonging to impoverished neighborhoods such as Habana del Este, the artist Juan Roberto Diago enthusiastically shows off his black identity. The work of this young black painter can be studied in conjunction with the works of Cuban rappers because the stylistic and ethical spirit of hip-hop heavily infuses both genres.

Black Cries

Another cry: Diago's art damages the senses, interrupts daily routines, questions official history, and demands reflection and memory. It is explicitly performative. His canvases question and demand answers. A painting such as *Cuba Sí* does not pass unnoticed; it expresses the repressed rage that finally erupted with increasing intensity at the beginning of the nineties. As in the more politically committed rap lyrics, the violence in Diago's painting embodies the call for consciousness while transmitting some hope for the transformation of society. It is protest and social criticism of our age. However, all this seems contradictory when observing this immense painting: 2 x 3 meters of reconstituted jute fabric in bleak tones simulating a damaged, filthy wall. An enormous red blot at its center emanates the word SCREWED ("JODIDO"). Precisely speaking, such an exclamation of abandon is not an explicit proposal for social change. Its social agency manifests by how it subjects the viewer and society to the recognition of being "screwed," the condition suffered by marginal blacks. The painter is demanding a space for himself and the right to exist socially. Diago's is thus a gesture for social change, or at least for wider recognition of those who are screwed, marginalized, or alienated. Coincidentally, the thrust of hip-hop is to guarantee continuity for the marginalized individual within his or her secular discontinuity, opening the possibility of being, even on the margins. Confronted with an orderly movement toward progress perceived as something external, the margin-

Figure 1. "Cuba Sí." Photo of the painting by Juan Roberto Diago.

alized agent decides to disrupt, to break the regularized rhythm of ordinary reality—a beat that bypasses and says nothing to her. To break, to tear, to fracture, to hurl a scream, or leave a tag, better still if on the side of a train moving anonymously through the city. The forced immutability of marginals attains a kind of motion, as their invisibility explodes before everyone's eyes. Blackness is exposed with vigor and anger. In the end, the person who is "screwed" has been screwed by someone, and Diago and the rappers do not seem hesitant to point fingers at institutions of power as the instrument of discrimination in Cuba's long history.

Critique and protest become more explicit in the lyrics of the Hermanos d'Causa. Their version of the famous *son* "Lágrimas Negras" (Black Tears) erupts in bitterness, nonconformity, and an urge for social change.

> Confronting things, a realist all the time.
> Don't tell me there's no racism where there is a racist.
> Always and when, wherever I find myself
> Prejudice of some kind is always present.
> Delinquent negro, legendary concept,
> Seen as adversary, any time of day. . . .
> They have it stuck in their heads that because of my color
> I'm a brute. . . .
> I feel a deep hatred of your racism

Your irony no longer confuses me
And I cry without you knowing that my weeping
Carries with it black tears just like my life. . . .
There is no punishment better than the one we carry in ourselves
Which will end when you shout, "Enough!" . . .
Where will all this end? I don't know
I will not be silenced by things happening around me
I will not let bad deeds pass with impunity
I will not let lies become the truth
Hermanos d'Causa, as usual, telling it like it is
Giving afro-struggle continuity.
[Yo de frente, todo el tiempo realista.
No digas que no hay racismo donde hay un racista.
Siempre y cuando, donde quiera que me encuentre,
El prejuicio de una forma u otra siempre está presente.
Negro delincuente, concepto legendario,
Visto como el adversario en cualquier horario. . . .
Tienen metido en su psiquis que por mi color
Yo soy un ordinario. . . .
Siento odio profundo por tu racismo
Ya no me confundo con tu ironía
Y lloro sin que sepas que el llanto mío
Tiene lágrimas negras como mi vida. . . .
No hay peor condena que la que uno mismo arrastra
Que acabará cuando tú grites ¡Basta! . . .
¿A dónde vamos a parar? Yo no lo sé.
Ante cosas que están pasando yo no callaré
No dejaré que lo mal hecho sea impunidad
No dejaré que la mentira sea la verdad
Hermanos D'Causa demostrando como siempre
Lo que es y lo que hay.
Dándole a la afrolucha continuidad.]

Black Cubans of the nineties felt the catharsis of denouncing the persistence of racism after almost fifty years of the revolutionary regime. Diago, for his part, reappropriates in *Cuba Sí* slogans that had a huge visual presence on the Cuban streets of the time, a core of national identity invoked by authorities to recover a crisis-ridden sense of unity and patriotism. Murals or revolutionary marches frequently chanted "Cuba Sí" or "100% Cubano," phrases immediately redolent of the government's nationalist affirmation in the face of a political, economic, and ideological void. Diago admits a Cuban identity, but impetuously demands recognition of his racial condition and for Cuba's negated black history. Despite the mottos of official history, the black person in Diago's painting is still "screwed." For Diago and many rappers, this is not a mysterious predicament. Though they offer no fixed explanations, they present what they have—their own ordeal as blacks in revolutionary Cuba—as testimony of the perseverance of racial inequality. After decades of silence, they finally shout out:

> Don't tell me that there isn't
> Because I have sure seen it
> Don't tell me it doesn't exist
> Because I have lived it
> Don't tell me there isn't hidden racial prejudice
> That condemns us and treats us all as equals
> Don't let yourself be fooled
> Open your eyes wide
> Don't let yourself get tangled up
> All is well, nothing bad.
> There are those who can't accept
> That blacks can think, study, and be professionals
> Without being antisocial, potential delinquents
> If you walk hand-in-hand with a white girl
> Many will start to talk
> Many are intrigued by both as we pass
> We are slandered by the many as we go by
> They are shocked even though the watch has not stopped
> Others say, "I am not a racist"
> Of course not
> While they tell their daughter
> "Sweetie, blacks won't do" . . .
> For the police with or without a whistle
> The darkest ones are their favorite dish
> The others here are saints . . .
> It's easier to blame a darker one
> Supposedly guilty for how he looks.

[No me digas que no hay
Porque yo sí lo he visto
No me digas que no existe
Porque lo he vivido
No me digas que no hay oculto un prejuicio racial
Que nos condena y nos valora a todos por igual . . .
No te dejes engañar
Abre los ojos de par en par
No te dejes envolver
Todo bien, nada mal.
Hay a quien le cuesta aceptar
Que un negro pueda pensar, estudiar
Y ser todo un profesional,
Sin ser un antisocial,
Potencial delictivo.
Al caminar si es del brazo de una blanca
Muchos se ponen a hablar
Con respecto a ambos hay intrigas al pasar
Con respecto a ambos hay calumnias al andar
Con chocar, a pesar de que el reloj no se paró.
Otros dicen no soy racista yo,
Claro que no,
Diciéndole a la hija,
Niña un negro no sirvió. . . .
Para el agente policiaco con silbato o sin silbato
Los más prietos son el plato preferido
Los otros aquí son unos santos . . .
Más fácil es culpar alguno de color oscuro
Supuestamente involucrado por lo que aparenta.]

Here, as in lyrics of other MCs, a wave of anger produces unease within the Cuban public. In fact, this denouncing or militant rap is not at all popular in the island.[5] After years of alleged racial equality, society has little desire to know about blacks trying to reclaim racial difference—blacks who prefer to shout their racial pride, expose their cultural marginality, even knowing, or because they know, that for Cubans "shouting is something blacks do." In doubt here is the utopian idea, omnipresent throughout Cuba's national saga and present, of a Cuba "without races." Put in play by José Martí in the nineteenth century, fostered by canonical national ideologues, and foundational in the revolutionary ideology since 1959, in this ideal a national identity trumps racial identity.

> The revolution [of the 1890s] is what restored the black race to humanity; it is what made the horrible act disappear. She was the mother, she was the saint, she was the one who snatched the master's whip, she was the one who enabled blacks to live in Cuba, the one who lifted blacks from their shame and embraced them, she, the Cuban Revolution. The abolition of slavery . . . is the purest and most transcendental achievement of the Cuban Revolution. The revolution, brought forth by slave owners, declared slaves to be free. Every one who has been enslaved and is now free, together with all their offspring, are children of the Cuban Revolution. (Martí 1963: 27)

Considering Creole slave-owners the principal agents of the revolution, exalting their altruistic gesture of liberating their slaves, making blacks eternally indebted to their "liberators," the quote of revered Martí makes clear that all Cubans should first and foremost be patriots and revolutionaries. Blacks become truly human when they become revolutionaries since they are "born" out of revolution. Before the revolt, in Martí's simplified representation, blacks were merely beasts. In short, racial feeling was buried by the founding ideas of Cuban national identity, and so demand for cultural recognition of this identity is possibly antipatriotic. "A man is more than white, more than mulatto, more than black," preached Martí in 1893.[6] Meanwhile, in twenty-first-century Havana, the rap duo Anónimo Consejo (Anonymous Advice) conveys in lyrics that "easy it is to be a man, hard to be a black." A similar retort flows from Diago's work *España, devuélveme a mis dioses* (Spain, give me back my gods) (2002).

Mestizaje and Black Identities

On another front, the vitality of black culture has been concealed behind the magical solvent of "mestizaje" (racial intermixing), considered by many Cubans as an ideal solution to the national problem. Consider, for example, the sociologist Fernando Ortiz's seminal notion of "transculturation" and the national poet Nicolás Guillén's "color cubano."[7] In many ways, the celebratory recognition of mulatto identity erases blackness. The claim that national culture is a product of the intermixing collision of elements of

Figure 2. "Spain, give me back my gods." Photo of the painting by Juan Roberto Diago.

different origins, mainly African and Spanish, is hard to dispute. But if the mestizo dominates in Cuba's ethnic composition, or if one accepts Guillén's observations on the island's mulatto spirit, recognition of these homogeneous mestizo claims brings with it the dissolution of blackness. When the mulatto is considered most authentically Cuban, a new form of ethnic and cultural hierarchy is produced. Over-valorization of mestizaje results in a distancing from blackness or whiteness. When mestizo culture is incarnated as the sole truth, as Cuban reality, as the national ego, then blackness and whiteness become reduced to mere roots of mulatto identity. They become prehistoric and now superseded subjectivities.

Mestizaje ends up constituting the final, finished, and harmonic product of Cuban identity—capable of obliterating by its synthesis all variety of contradictions at the center of the national soul. This utopian exaltation of mestizaje has been astutely analyzed by the French sociologists François Laplantine and Alexis Nouss. To them mestizaje constitute neither an essence nor a substance, neither a content nor a true category. If it does not represent a true identity, neither does it point to alterity. For them, mestizo is alterity, identity, reason, and unreason all jumbled into one vessel. Mestizaje is a noncoincidental irresolution. It cannot be depicted as synthesis or symbiosis, that is, as a realization, because for Laplantine and Nouss mestizaje relates to a process of becoming and transformation. It must be viewed as a process and a never-finished product. It is an imperfect, unsatisfactory phenomenon, always within an unending back and forth journey. The notion of mestizaje, therefore, "cannot be mobilized as a response because it is the question itself that perturbs the individual, the culture, the language, and society in their tendency toward stabilization."[8]

Definitive ideas about mestizaje are still vaunted by intellectuals in Cuba and national identity continues to be commonly considered as the raceless mix of all ethnicities, but the reality corresponds more to Laplantine's and Nouss's ambiguous account. The dream of ethnic-cultural unity embraced during the twentieth century by the likes of Ortiz and Guillén is not yet visible in present-day Cuba. While genetically Cuba's population is becoming more mestizo, deep cultural divides reign between what is considered "black" and "white" in Cuban society.[9] On one side, the state, the elites, and both national and international media persevere to promote the ideal of the Cuba "mestiza"; on the other, darker side, racial considerations weigh more in recent years, when the state has lost the absolute power it enjoyed from the sixties through the eighties. The openness—even unwanted—of Cuban society to neoliberalism and globalization increased inequalities and the awakening of racial prejudices, which were mitigated before by the effectiveness of egalitarian state policies. More than ever since 1959, how black or white the individual is, or the way in which a black or mulatto Cuban exhibits his or her blackness, is influential in social inclusion and marginality. However, a real discussion on racial problems has not been promoted in civil society.

Therefore, beginning in the nineties, the rappers under discussion began to demand attention to race. They seemed tired of such silent indifference on the racial question. The violence and determination with which this demand flows through hip-hop aesthetics was unheard-of in revolutionary Cuba. The rappers of Anónimo Consejo boldly declare their nonconformity and denounce racial oblivion:

Today we are the bad guys
Today we are the thieves
Power has shown those others as gentlemen.
[Hoy somos los malos
Hoy somos los ladrones
El poder ha demostrado que son los otros los señores.]

Meanwhile, the Fabri-K collective sings,

> I am what I will be
> I will still go to the tenement to catch Negra Mercé
> I will not stop drinking Mamá Inés's coffee.
> I will not renounce the verse that became the "peanut vendor cry"
> No one will ever do away with me. . . .
> Sharing my joy with the *orishas*[10]
> I am more Cuban today.
> [Soy como seré.
> Yo seguiré yendo al solar a pillar a la negra Mercé.
> No dejaré de tomar el café de Mamá Inés.
> Ni renunciaré al verso hecho pregón del Manisero. . . .
> Nadie me va a tumbar nunca. . . .
> Junto a la dicha de compartir con los orishas,
> que soy más cubano en esta fecha.]

These lyrics assert Cuban identity while affirming a deep racial identity. This would flatly contradict the reigning ideology, where race is always sublimated to the building of national identity. Here, the Cuban identity is not mestiza: it is strongly black and proudly exhibits blackness. Being Cuban for them is being more themselves, more "authentically" blacks, at least in their particular optic. Reappropriating the Siguaraya tree of popular legend, whose wood is so strong it cannot be felled, Fabri-K asserts sturdiness and resistance in the face of the social transformations that have made Cuban society. Rappers proclaim a sense of survival passed on through ancestry, predominantly African, and through an indelible marginality. According to this sense, blacks have resisted uprooting, slavery, extermination, and repression; they have survived independence wars and a republican misery, while upholding a culture that those in power tenaciously tried to annihilate, discredit, or ignore. This resistance, furthermore, also runs against the current process of globalization, with "blackness" now held up as a banner against the "loss of values." For many, this is possible through an ancestry that escapes the generalized idea of reason, the official history, but that appears instead as metaphor in traditions, myths, or *orishas*—deities of the Santería pantheon. It traces itself to cultural formations that uphold the timeless unity and strength of black communities throughout the Americas.

As part of this afro-diasporic countercultural genealogy, hip-hop is perceived by its practitioners as a communal activity that leads to a possible identity. For many young rappers in Cuba, blackness and marginality are synonymous with authenticity and integral to a genuine racial or national heritage. Cuban citizens today are confronted with disintegration and miscommunication, products of a new social order, and an accelerated exodus that ruptures traditional family and social mores. Older values are evaporating as marketing and globalization affect even relatively isolated Cuban lives. This is when artists take refuge in the "family" constituted through hip-hop and their community. Thus, these alternative identifications offer the promise of differentiation amid a globalizing world. "Dark is my family today," sings Anónimo Consejo.

When national or ideological identity fails, when the traditional family crumbles, the "tribe" or family remains, oftentimes forged on the basis of racial identity. Many aficionados of hip-hop find a mode of identification in the concept of race (understood more as a historical-cultural concept than an ethnic one). It exists as a shared common experience: African ancestry and alterity within Western contexts.

The art of Juan Roberto Diago also exudes this sense of belonging. The marginalized community is continually incorporated into his work. He sometimes refers to Pogolotti, a suburb of Havana, but his most recent works are set within emblematic centers of urban marginality such as the tenement La California. Identification with the marginal zone comes out, for example, through graffiti. A peculiar stylistic element pervades Diago's work: the recurrence of street slang and random thoughts that appear out of context. These phrases seem to be carelessly placed, but in general express a particular message, in many cases coupled with the demand for the recognition of black culture or space. The apparent decontextualization of such fragments is a move that links Diago's work to the hip-hop aesthetic. It is crucial for the graffiti street artist to leave their mark in the most unexpected places, places that escape their "natural" origin (Chang 2005: 74). Diago's goal is to insert demands for ethnic and sociocultural recognition in the "sacred" sphere of art. His marks, which appear hastily drawn, washed up by time, and incomplete, might not be deemed artistic in any academic sense. But there they are in a painting bound for the museum and exhibition. A popular phrase flies from a casual façade to the gallery wall, from the eyes of the ordinary person to the specialized public, like the trajectory of trains that transport graffiti from one end of the city to the other. However, this is only an impression; in reality Diago's "graffiti" is hardly street art. His experience is not as enmeshed in the real poor neighborhoods as his work

suggests. Seeking cultural recognition for marginalized blacks, Diago cam-
ouflages his technique behind an apparently unfinished, incomplete, and
careless style. But Diago is no primitivist painter.

The marginalized, predominantly black community is a medium through
which to voice the connection with an ancestral Africa, where Diago's essential "tribe" is ultimately located. This tribe is constituted not only by black
Cubans, but also by Africans and all diasporic afro-descendants. In addition
to written signs with graffiti, this community is evoked through the recovery
of African materials (jute sacks, wood from African shipping containers,
etc.). Similar to hip-hop artists, Diago makes do with what's at hand, working
with the waste of a fractured cosmos from abandoned places, as if a junkyard.
This is a practice among the poor and marginalized accustomed to organizing their life around the residue of the same society that excludes them. Blacks
were accustomed to redoing their master's handed-down clothes, working
tools from discarded materials, and inventing music and art out of the left-
behinds of the white world. But in contrast to actual recycling, Cuban hip-hop
or Diago's art is not a simple act of instinctual survival, but the search for a
kind of aesthetic pleasure through the recovery of the old.

Diago makes frequent use of sampling, the process of creating something new out of already existing fragments. Recovering a certain phrase,
making use of African wisdom, respectfully exhibiting his history as a black
man, Diago forms something new out of the old. Within these strategies lies
a subtle and secret link between the creator's discourse and the forms and
spirit of marginality, latent in so much of its corroded, rusted, half-erased,
and dusty material. These samples, discursive as well as material, lend a
particular power and energy to his work. This potency derives from the afro-
diasporic and African experience. As Diago points out, "When I make use of
certain poor or ephemeral materials in my work, I do it only with the intent
of allegorically highlighting the precarious world in which black people have
had to live, what we inherited from slavery, how we live, what our desires are.
It is true that poverty is a widespread condition, but in our case it is particular" (Mateo 2003: 23).

Ruptures, History, and Memory-Time

Another feature of Diago's work is the abruptness of his images: broken,
almost erased. Rupture is one of hip-hop's chief stylistic features. It is suggested aesthetically, by the discourse sustained in the song, as well as di-

rectly sounded. The broken rhythm, ruptured and reconstructed, the drumming as well as the sudden blow of a word are omnipresent in rap music. The violence intrinsic to hip-hop is widespread and a cause for its critics' discomfort. Violence reveals itself from the moment in which the artist deploys a provocative and aesthetically, ethically aggressive style, "a style nobody can deal with—a style that cannot be easily understood or erased, a style that has the reflexivity to create counter-dominant narratives against a mobile and shifting enemy" (Rose 1994: 61). Violence punctuates hip-hop: one finds it in militant hip-hop, in the "gangster" version, as well as in entertaining pop hip-hop. The attempt to disguise the criminal element associated with hip-hop with an activist side is useless. It is also futile to hide its technological and commercial core because hip-hop, as Russell A. Potter and other hip-hop critics note, is about "turning consumption into a production."[11] Though hip-hop was born at the margins of society, the contemporary world is rooted in consumption and hip-hop never intended to adopt an anticonsumerist stance. On the contrary, its ambition is to enter and leave its mark in the world's consumerist sphere, to abruptly penetrate it, flowing, advancing, rupturing its linearity. These are essential characteristics of rap music.[12]

A painting such as Diago's *Yo tengo mi historia* (I have a history) leaves the viewer with a sensation of abrupt shock. One is facing something with missing parts, not nostalgically, but experienced as emptiness or painful rupture. The black face in the painting is barely suggested and has no mouth with which to speak. The subject's neck is mended and has empty spaces for eyes that are nonetheless tremendously piercing and that display an almost ancestral supernatural force. Rising from a mosaic of pieces of wood, this image conveys the incongruence of official narratives that cannot explain the black experience. But blacks exist; they are alive in the background of that history, though in diffuse, ill-defined, and maybe terrifying ways. The title *I Have a History* is an unflinching demand for ethical recognition. As the aggressive affirmation of a silenced voice, it appears rapidly painted, unintelligible, unfinished. One might say that (white) paint is not enough. Nor executed with enough time. Time felt differently by marginal subjects, one at odds with calendars and watches. This is the time in which diasporic blacks have generally lived, one that allows a conceived history and continuity within a world that may cede rights, but not complete equality.

Hip-hop's rhythm has also been depicted as "time out of time." Potter locates hip-hop within a "black diasporic time-zone" (1995: 7), while Tricia

Figure 3. "I have a history." Photo of the painting by Juan Roberto Diago.

Rose equates sampling with a "musical time machine that keeps the time for the body in motion" (1994: 96). This is a metaphor of circularity, an active permanence reminiscent of the time-lag ideas of Homi Bhabha in his analysis of postcolonial thought. Bhabha's optic helps locate the position of hip-hop within, without, against, and alongside modernity. The notion of time-lag encapsulates hip-hop's temporal character. It refers to a process that propels and projects the past, summoning it to offer up its "dead" symbols as the circulatory life "sign" of the present. It is passage of time that quickens the quotidian.[13]

Sampling and versioning offer the possibility of advance, while maintaining a past freed of its obsolescence. This forward movement occurs in circles, taking shortcuts, not in modern linearity. Think of a *cimarrón* (fugitive slave) making his way through the forest; a body in motion that contains the past, the present, and perhaps the future, detached from a fixed route and everyday temporality. The past is no longer deadweight and becomes a part of the present moving body. "Time-lag keeps alive the making of the past" (Bhabha 1994: 364). Through this lag, hip-hop artists wish to incarnate—as a reality, not metaphorically—a marginalized, dark, forgotten past, their own past as subaltern subjects.

For the black subject secularly relegated to the margins of a "real world" that marches toward an exclusive progress, time cannot be identical to the integrated individual's time. Time feels suspended in an eternal present because their situation, at base, is not totally different from that of their ancestors. Those ancestors offer contemporary blacks the possibility of resistance, continuity, of living in a countercurrent. Nevertheless, this other time creates for the person immersed in it an unease of impossibility: the urgent sense that life, in the alleged real time of clocks and calendars, is never enough. This is what Diago's pressing but incomplete images express, especially in *I Have a History*. Just like the materials, time and life reach an end, and the black subject has been unable to express his or her history, only the trace of a hand smeared in white paint remains. When there are no more expressive resources left, only experience remains—the experience, as in the lyrics of Fabri-K, of going to the *rumbas* in the *solares* (tenements), meeting La Negra Mercé, drinking Mamá Inés's coffee, and other "black ways" (*cosas de negros*).

The afro-diasporic tradition is called on by Diago and other hip-hop artists through recourse to the *orishas* of Santería, who, in this way, serve as discursive heroes. Orishas are generally presented as an ethical base, a consoling bedrock amid the disorienting chaos of globalization and exile. They are oppositional, to counteract the persistent racism of Cuban society. The musicians often present themselves as transmitters of the divine word, a wild "voice" that moves above the social narrative because it comes from a superior, more authentic entity: from the "forgotten" history (black heroes) or religious myths. Is this a return to the legendary figure of the griot? The African poet destined to conserve and transmit community tradition across generations? A Pan-Africanist sentiment also accompanies allusions to the deities of Afro-Cuban religion in hip-hop songs. As Anónimo Consejo sings,

> My African language will tell you, boy,
> That these are the spirits
> Who continue to dance the mambo . . .
> I do not do the machete anymore
> We are no longer slaves
> I am no longer in shackles
> Negro Iyalocha goes to the wilderness
> The Babalocha goes to the wilderness
> The fugitive slave passes through plains and hills
> Zimbabwe, Angola, Sierra Leone.
> . . . It is still early, brother,
> Your hand is my hand
> If we join with them we can win . . .
> A united afro will never be defeated.
> [Mi lengua africana te va a decir muchacho
> Que estos son los espíritus
> Que siguen bailando mambo . . .
> No doy machete
> No somos esclavos ya,
> Ya no hay grillete más.
> Negro iyalocha van para los montes,
> que babalochas van para los montes. . . .
> Cimarrón en llano y loma.
> Zimbabwe, Angola, Sierra Leona.
> . . . Aún es temprano hermano.
> Tu mano es mi mano.
> Si las juntamos ganamos . . .
> Lo afro unido jamás será vencido.]

Note the presence of the cimarrón (fugitive slave) in these verses, another form of discursive sampling in Cuban hip-hop. For contemporary artists, the trope of the cimarrón brings identification with the mythic black warriors of past. The cimarrón figure paves the way for expressions of anger that suddenly erupted among Cuban blacks in the nineties. He epitomizes a recognition need within Cuban society. The point is to generate an offensive, warrior-like visibility that, contrary to the place of blacks in traditions maintained by the revolution, no longer accepts his passivity.[14] One is no longer talking about a slave or a selfless combatant who sacrifices everything, especially his or her racial condition, in order to defend the nation, the republic, or revolution. Nor is one speaking of the liberated black "redeemed" from ignorance and segregation. He is no longer a character interpreting an imposed role and reciting imposed ideals. One is now in the presence of a figure retrieved to the present within a time-lag, who offers therefore a vibrant present energy. In "Siguaraya," the Fabri-K collective maintains,

> Revisiting memory still hurts
> History's gift is not precisely flowery
> I am still angry
> And the sharp edge of my machete
> Is and was more powerful than the shackles
> I still keep beating those drums
> In search of the *monte* and leaving the "Yes, sir" behind.
> Climbing each step while I cling to old customs and traditions
> Which is not strange for me
> Because from Cabo de San Antonio to Maisí
> It is African blood which comes from my song . . .
> The *cimarrón* has just arrived.
> [Aún me duele andar en la memoria
> Porque no es precisamente flores el regalo de la historia
> Me queda furia todavía
> Y mucho más poder que aquel grillete
> Tuvo y tiene el filo de mi machete.
> Y yo sigo tocando el tambor,
> Buscando monte y dejando atrás el sí señor.
> Subiendo cada peldaño,
> Atado a costumbres y tradiciones de antaño,

Lo cual no es extraño en mí
Porque desde el Cabo de San Antonio hasta Maisí
Es sangre africana la que emana de mi canto . . .
El cimarrón aquí llegó.]

This positioning contrasts to the invisibility suffered by marginal blacks
during the sixties and seventies. This is understandable, given that those
blacks reflected the revolution's negative image. Marginal blacks were "antisocial" and could not, therefore, be identified with the "new man" (el Hombre
Nuevo) imagined by Che Guevara in his famous essay "Man and Socialism in
Cuba" (1965). It is true that Guevara never specified whether the new man
was white or black. As customary in Cuba, the model subject is raceless. But
it was understood that if the new man were to serve as a shining example for
the rest of society, he could not be someone seen as "primitive" or "ignorant" in the social imaginary. He, since one dealing with a subject that
must exhibit virility, had to be also heroic, ferocious, and atheist, a Marxist-
Leninist figure believing in nothing beyond Che's political doctrines. Under
these circumstances, any allusion to Afro-Cuban religions was immediately
discredited. And, if one could exalt the virile and liberationist character of
cimarrones, their sectarianism, their rebellion without cause, and their rudimentary lifestyle would be questioned—anything incomprehensible within
Marxist terms.

Within this frame, the cimarrón was presented largely as a passive or
sublimated figure, kept in the past like Esteban Montejo, protagonist of the
novel Biografía de un cimarrón (The biography of a runaway slave, 1966) by
Miguel Barnet. This character, an unruly fugitive slave, was "rehabilitated"
by the revolution in the sixties. He was integrated into society and lived
peacefully to a ripe old age. Similarly, a warrior character such as Aristón, as
Antonio Benítez Rojo demonstrates in his short story "La tierra y el cielo"
(Heaven and earth), was condemned to disappear in the revolutionary context. Aristón embodied the divinity of war, Oggún Ferrai, and acted accordingly: he was a ferocious and untamable combatant. His strength was bar-
barian, dictated by divine, irrational plans, not by clear Marxist-Leninist
conviction. For those in power, it became inadmissible for cimarrón behavior to persist.

In Cuba, hip-hop artists, these unrehabilitated cimarrones, know that
their antiestablishment gestures are shocking. They boldly assume this position and continue to bring visibility—physical as well as historical—to

blacks in Cuba. This is what Obsesión embrace in their version of "Drume Negrito."

> I am playing rap following the beat of my *pasa*, my *ñata*, and my *bemba*[15]
> My family tree
> My history, customs, my religion
> And my way of thinking.
> I know the tribunal observes me
> But I also keep an eye on him.
> Granddaddy told me:
> "Son, you can't think twice
> When you're deactivating a bomb."
> That's why I dance the conga
> In the middle of the sentencing, in front of the whole jury.
> [Estoy rapeando al compás de mis pasas,
> mi ñata, mi bemba, mi árbol genealógico,
> mi historia, mis costumbres, mi religión
> y mi forma de pensar.
> Sé que el tribunal me observa
> pero yo también lo miro fijo.
> Abuelo me dijo:
> "Mijo, no se puede titubear
> a la hora de desactivar las bombas."
> Por eso en pleno juicio bailo conga
> frente a todo el jurado.]

Coda: Talking About a Revolution?

There is now an obvious rebelliousness, as well as exhaustion, in the willful protest against enduring inequalities between blacks and whites in Cuba. The rappers of Anónimo Consejo ask, "What's the problem?"[16] This question seems to encapsulate the racial question in contemporary Cuban society. Why does racism persist? Why didn't all Cubans achieve equality after such a prolonged revolutionary experience?

Beginning in the nineties, the defiant gestures of black artists produced an impact, many times upsetting, in Cuban intellectual circles. From an ethical-aesthetic standpoint, hip-hop is identity-making in both Diago's visual art as well as in rap groups like Obsesión, Anónimo Consejo, Hermanos d'Causa, and Fabri-K. The words, the shouting, movements, and images were inscribed within a revolutionary socialist society, and at the same time passing judgment on its racism. These artists transform aesthetically the discrimination suffered for centuries by black Cubans, voice their discontent, and exhibit other forms of "blackness" to revolutionary society.

Note the paradox of their denunciations: they criticize racial policies and norms maintained since 1959 and question the traditional idea of a "raceless Cuba" as well as the revolutionary patriotism that subsumes race to nation, yet they continue to assert that the most authentic form of Cubanness has a revolutionary essence. Thus, in "Drume Negrito," the young musicians highlight the pervading racism of contemporary Cuba while setting their critique in a revolutionary lens:

> I have revolutionary goals.
> Under my arm a diary which does not abandon a guerrilla fighter.
> Its title: Yes, it's me gentlemen . . .
> Immersed within this negritude, I ask:
> Who are you to question my ancestry?
> Who are you to question my decency,
> My integrity, my appearance? . . .
> Many have passed the course on how to be a racist,
> They graduated with honors and parties and to this day
> Remain hiding in the following phrase:
> "All human beings are created equal."
> [Tengo propósitos revolucionarios.
> Bajo mi brazo, un diario que no abandona al guerrillero.
> Su título: Sí, soy yo, caballero . . .
> Sumida en esta negritud pregunto:
> ¿Quién es usted que pone en tela de juicio mi procedencia?
> ¿Quién es usted que cuestiona mi decencia,
> integridad y apariencia? . . .
> y muchos fueron a pasar un curso de como no ser racistas,
> se graduaron con honores y fiestas y hasta el sol de hoy
> permanecen ocultos en la frase esta:
> "Todos los seres humanos somos iguales."]

The authors, as others in hip-hop, see themselves as a brand of "new revolutionaries" and in many cases assume messianic and liberationist stances. They sell themselves as advocates of authenticity against the withering of ethical and moral values in contemporary society. This tendency, found throughout the international hip-hop community, offers a social critique through the idea of confrontation between two identities, two nations, two ethical worlds. On one side, there is a racist dominant society, characterized by a treasonous double morality; opposed to this is the community of blackness, which celebrates a robust, rooted, and honest form of racial identity. The aesthetic of the dispossessed, the result of inequality, becomes a rebellious sword against that same inequality. Its proponents do not accept the inexorability of racial inequality in Cuba. They advocate radical change to subvert the present order. The revolution they voice lives in their works, a social vision captured in lyrics by Hermanos d'Causa.

> For my country and my flag
> Step by step
> Hip-hop revolution
> Up the stairs
> This is my thing
> To unmask
> With my lyrics.
> [Por mi Patria y mi bandera
> De escalón en escalón
> Hip-hop revolución
> Subiendo la escalera trepa
> Esta es mi faceta
> Explotar caretas
> Con mis letras.]

What does this stance mean? Where to place these new bards of progress: inside or outside, in favor or against? Is revolution after The Revolution possible? The gesture of such artists is clearly suggestive, moving, vibrant, as is all revolutionary activity. But it is also utopian. It might evoke some positive changes in Cuban society, as did the revolutionaries of 1959 who banned racial segregation and proclaimed the equality of all Cubans. Under the influence of young black artists, a new movement might again attempt to modify the current relations between blacks and whites in Cuba. But can they come close to the dream of reversing racial inequality? Limited to the social sphere, such actions would not suffice, because the racial problem is not merely a social problem fixable by denunciation, demands of justice and historical recognition, or access to education and decent jobs. Racial inequality survives in Cuba despite sincere attempts to eradicate it. No historical, political, ideological, social, or economic change has succeeded, which makes it seem so inevitable, and so indelible. Through its revolutionary transformation, Cuba became an exemplar of the paradox of persistent inequality: inequality's resistance to even human will and radical historical change.

The revolutionary message of these young black artists, as noted by Sujatha Fernandes, may actually be appealing to Cuban political leaders, similar to how other governments in Latin American and the Caribbean have made alliances with underground rappers. Their revolutionary spirit can be "recycled" by the state, which may use it in order to "bolster the image of Cuba as a mixed-race nation with African roots" (Fernandes 2006: 119). Such practices, historically present in national politics since the nineteenth century, demonstrate how racially centered messages may have lost their original purpose and are being reappropriated within a nationalist ideology that is not especially interested on discussing racial problems in Cuban society today.

Can this outlier case of Cuba convince one, nonetheless, that inequalities in Latin America are neither inevitable nor indelible? When traditional arguments lose force, the search begins for different theories to grasp inequalities in particular national histories. Working within the ambits of history, social systems, politics, and economics no longer suffice. The way forward lies in an analysis capable of taking into account multiple factors at once, as Luis Reygadas argues, without privileging one over another.[17] I have preferred a distinctive ethical-aesthetic approach to racial inequality in Cuba. Artistic expressions of the demand for cultural recognition reproduce the racialized experience through the eye of creation. The ontological is fundamental in artistic creation—or at least more visible compared to other activities—that is, the basic existential mark of human beings, of beings situated over and above their existence as economic, social, political, historical, and ideological beings. Taking this research focus suggests an integration of normally segregated realms. The works of artists presented are a kind of human mixture, not easily distilled, of economic, political, social, sexual, and racial beings. Black artists in Cuba talk about their race, their cultural inheritance, the racism of their society, yet at the same time carry with them, for better or worse, the force of thinkers such as Martí, Guillén, or Ortiz. They create art in a revolutionary context, evince the crisis of the post–Cold War era in Cuba, and are also Latin Americans of the underdeveloped world. The signs of these circumstances and conditions, among others, are palpable in their work. Exploration of their creations thus offers a multidisciplinary vision on the racial problem in contemporary Cuba, which can, in turn, offer a new approximation to the persistent reproduction of inequalities across the region.

A deconstructive will, then, inspires my foray: deconstructing the processes of racial inequality through the works and expressions that denounce and critique it. This is why the political and aesthetic tensions highlighted above—whether Cuban hip-hop finds itself within or outside the revolution —loom central. Adopting a stance suggested by Homi Bhabha for comprehension of contemporary culture going "beyond" fixed categories, I aim to think of the demand for cultural recognition of the nineties beyond a simple polarity, as outside of modernity, afro-diasporic conditions, postindustrialism, or the saga of the socialist revolution. Aesthetic expressions of inequality are indisputable signs of protest against contemporary society and precepts of modernity, while moving nonetheless within their orbit. As critics of Cuban society under socialism, black artists also appropriate some of its ideological moves. A face of defiant opposition to globalization and neoliberalism, they do not escape—if they ever intended to—its commercial and technological apparatus.

Racial inequalities in Cuba have staunchly resisted the egalitarian politics implemented by the revolution since 1959. This situation exemplifies the impossibility of explaining racial inequalities solely through the uneven distribution of economic and educational resources. The existence of "symbolic barriers" (Lamont and Fournier 1992) and "emotional frontiers" between different social groups (Elias 2006; Elias and Scotson 2009) foster the reproduction of inequalities built on binary categories such as black-white, and thus help explain the durability of inequalities in Tilly's sense (1998). Symbolic and cultural barriers compose the ethical-aesthetical framework in which discrimination against blacks operates in Cuba. However, my analysis of artistic expressions critical of racial inequalities on the island augurs new possibilities in alternative aesthetic propositions, like those expressed through the paintings of Juan Roberto Diago or in the rap lyrics of Obsesión, Anónimo Consejo, Hermanos de Causa, and Fabri-K. This shows that the persistence of inequalities throughout Latin America does not exclude the recurring presence of multiple forms of criticism and contestation. The aesthetics of inequality appear above and beyond everyday notions of space and time: todays, tomorrows, and yesterdays; in the time of slavery; in Soviet times; in Berlin Wall–falling time. In the *isla*, on a slave ship, in anticolonial

Africa, in Santería's passion, in prisons, in a boat brimming with exiles. Inequalities exist there, within and outside a particular history, as do their aesthetic expression and protest.

Translated by Celina Bragagnolo

Notes

Paul Gootenberg edited this translation.

1. "Pa'l que no le guste. Pa'l que se moleste. Soy rapero, negro y de La Habana del Este." Habana del Este is a suburban municipality, developed mostly after the revolution, with a concentration of lower- and working-class families. Economic and social stresses are more evident there than in other, less abandoned areas of the city.
2. Cuban Alternative Music "is a music expression that came up in the mid 80's and developed up to our days. It assumes the legacy of the traditional Cuban music, but with a transnational approach according to the present signs of Cuban culture" (Joaquín Borges-Triana, "Música Cubana Alternativa: del margen al epicentro," http://www.hist.puc.cl/iaspm/) or see Borges-Triana (2009: 11).
3. "Hélas! La fin de l'histoire est aussi la fin des poubelles de l'histoire. Même plus de poubelles pour inhumer les vieilles idéologies, les vieux régimes, les vieilles valeurs. Où allons-nous jeter le marxisme, qui avait justement inventé les poubelles de l'histoire?" (Baudrillard 1992: 45).
4. The majority of exiled Cubans live in the United States. The first migratory waves, in the 1960s, were made up largely of wealthy Cubans, who founded the affluent sector of Cuban exiles. Cubans of lower-class status, many of them black, migrated to the United States beginning in the 1980s: the "marielitos" (refugees associated with the Mariel boatlift of 1980) and the "balseros" (boat people). Their economic situation is never solid enough to send large or regular streams of money back to Cuba.
5. Hip-hop media seem to prefer more commercial songs and lately privilege less "offensive" and more "decent" reggeatón. A keen debate about reggeatón and rap has been opened recently in Cuba. See Zurbano-Torres 2007.
6. José Martí, "Mi Raza" in *Patria*, New York, 16 April 1893 (C. B., trans.).
7. Ortiz says, "La *transculturación* expresa mejor las diferentes fases del proceso transitivo de una cultura a otra, porque éste no consiste solamente en adquirir una distinta cultura, que es lo que en rigor indica la voz angloamericana *acculturation*, sino que el proceso implica también necesariamente la pérdida o desarraigo de una cultura precedente, lo que pudiera decirse una parcial *desculturación*, y, además significa la consiguiente creación de nuevos fenómenos culturales que pudieran denominarse de neoculturación" (1983: 90). For Guillén, "Diré final-

mente que estos son versos mulatos. Participan acaso de los mismos elementos que entran en la composición étnica de Cuba. . . . La inyección africana en esta tierra es tan profunda, y se cruzan y entrecruzan en nuestra bien regada hidrografía social tantas corrientes capilares, que sería trabajo de miniaturista desenredar el jeroglífico. . . . Por lo pronto, el espíritu de Cuba es mestizo. Y del espíritu hacia la piel nos vendrá el color definitivo. Algún día se dirá: 'color cubano' " (2002: 92).

8. "Le métissage, qui n'est ni substance, ni essence, ni contenu, ni même contenant, n'est donc pas à proprement parler 'quelque chose.' . . . Mais n'étant pas l'identité, il n'est pas non plus altérité, mais identité et altérité entremêlées, y compris en liaison avec ce qui refuse le mélange et cherche à démêler. Autrement dit, il n'a rien de la certitude du sens ni du désespoir et du non-sens. Il est le sens et le non-sens entrelacés. Enfin, le métissage n'existe pas seulement dans la non-coïncidence, mais dans la non-résolution. Il ne saurait être de l'ordre de la symbiose, ni de la synthèse, c'est-à-dire de l'accomplissement. . . . [I]l est le devenir plus que l'avenir et appelle à être pensé en lui-même dans son inachèvement. Transitoire, imparfait, inachevé, insatisfait, le métissage est toujours dans l'aventure d'une migration, dans les transformations d'une activité de tissage et de tressage qui ne peut s'arrêter. C'est dire combien cette notion est éminemment contradictoire. Elle ne peut être mobilisée comme une réponse, car elle est la question elle-même qui perturbe l'individu, la culture, la langue, la société dans leur tendance à la stabilisation" (Laplantine and Nouss 1997: 82–85).

9. According to the latest census, in 2002 the Cuban population had a total of 7,271,926 whites (65 percent); 1,126,894 blacks (10 percent); and 2,778,923 mestizos (24.9 percent). These results, as compared to those of the preceding census of 1981, have been interpreted by the local press as a tendency toward mestizaje in Cuban society. See *Informe Nacional: Censo de Poblacion y Viviendas: Cuba 2002* (La Habana: Oficina Nacional de Estadísticas, 2005).

10. Orishas are popular deities of the Santería pantheon, an Afro-Cuban religion of Yoruba origin.

11. "Hip-hop's central chronotrope is the turntable, which signifies the ability to 'turn the tables' on previous black traditions, making a future out of fragments from the archive of the past, turning consumption into production. With this mode of turning and re-turning, hip-hop's appropriative art (born of sonic collage and pastiche, reprocessed via digital technology) is the perfect backdrop for an insistent vernacular poetics that both invokes and alters the history of African-American experiences, as well as black music on a global scale" (Potter 1995: 18).

12. "Interpreting these concepts theoretically, one can argue that they create and sustain rhythmic motion, continuity, and circularity via flow; accumulate, reinforce, and embellish this continuity through layering; and manage threats to these narratives by building in ruptures that highlight the continuity as it momentarily challenges it. . . . Let us imagine these hip-hop principles as a blueprint

for social resistance and affirmation: create sustaining narratives, accumulate them, layer, embellish, and transform them. However, be also prepared for rupture, find pleasure in it, in fact, *plan on* social rupture" (Rose 1994: 39).

13. "It is the function of the *lag* to slow down the linear, progressive time of modernity to reveal its 'gesture,' its tempi, 'the pauses and stresses of the whole performance.' . . . When the dialectic of modernity is brought to a standstill, then the temporal action of modernity—its progressive, future drive—is *staged*, revealing 'everything that is involved in the act of staging *per se.*' This slogging down, or lagging, *impels* the 'past,' *projects* it, gives its 'dead' symbols the circulatory life of the 'sign' of the present, of *passage*, the quickening of the quotidian" (Bhabha 1994: 364).

14. A detailed analysis of black roles in post-1959 Cuban literature is Casamayor 2002.

15. *Pasas, ñata,* and *bemba* are pejorative terms describing the hair, nose, and mouth of black people.

16. "Si tu y yo somos iguales, ¿Cual es el problema? . . . Sangre roja hay en las venas ¿Cual es el problema? . . . El que nos divide, ahí esta el problema" (Anónimo Consejo).

17. See Reygadas's essay in this volume.

7

How Latin American Inequality
Becomes Latino Inequality

A Case Study of Hudson Valley Farmworkers

MARGARET GRAY

"I'm afraid I won't see my family again. I don't want to die in this country." These are the words of Arturo, a thirty-year-old from Mexico, who, when I met him, was working as a fruit packer at an orchard in Columbia County, about two hours north of New York City.[1] He was housed in a trailer on the farm, amid apple trees. During our interview he was seated on a pile of bare, soiled mattresses in the middle of his livingroom. The housing was poor, he explained. I could see that for myself. Arturo had only been in the United States—having traveled directly to this farm—for one month. He told me, "I came out of necessity. There was no work at home." As a fruit packer, he worked six 8-hour days a week and was paid $6 an hour, around $200 a week after his employer-deducted taxes. He had just sent $450 to his wife and mother in Mexico; he planned to do the same the following month. Although he thought he should be paid $8.50 an hour (that would raise his weekly earnings by about $80), he told me, "I know it is not possible to earn more." He acknowledged that he didn't know the laws for farmworkers and understood his paycheck only "a little." Agriculture was not Arturo's preferred pursuit. He wanted to be a mechanic, but realized he could not do this: "I'm just trying to survive. I need English. I have no support. There are too many requirements here to be a mechanic, you need a diploma." At home, back in Mexico, he had been an artisan and a farmworker. With only a second-grade formal education and no English-language skills, his opportunities were severely limited. He hoped things would be different for his children: "I want them to work hard to have what I can't get—a better future."

Arturo's situation epitomizes that of many low-wage, immigrant laborers, particularly in the expanding service sector in the United States at the start of the twenty-first century: isolated and lonely (despite living and working with kin and community members from home), poor, lacking skills to advance, ignorant of labor laws, with little expectation of improving his circumstances, but willing nonetheless to make extreme sacrifices for the sake of his children. Moreover, his predicament is not appreciatively different from that of U.S. farmworkers at the end of the nineteenth century. He and his peers are as exploited today as their counterparts were then, before the enactment of New Deal legislation, which was intended to protect workers and their rights, but which nonetheless excluded the agriculture industry.[2]

The predicament of marginalized New York farmworkers like Arturo is the result of several overlapping constraints. As Luis Reygadas argues, the accumulation of multiple processes—rather than any historical monocausal factor—is usually at the root of inequality.[3] In that vein, I propose that four broad processes have led to the marginalization of Latino farmworkers: inequality in their home countries, with its resulting poverty and minimal formal education, limits their opportunities for work; established hierarchies in the United States around race, ethnicity, and class facilitate their exploitation; the "farmworker" as a job category signals powerlessness due to agricultural exclusions from protective labor laws; and the majority of Latino farmworkers in the United States and in New York are undocumented, which causes them to live in a constant climate of fear. The story of U.S. farmworkers is thus one of overdetermined marginalization and powerlessness, given their systematic exclusion, for multiple reasons, from social, political, and economic opportunities. Despite such odds, workers like Arturo —both historically and in other regions today—have engaged in individual and collective action to contest inequalities and change their situations.

Several processes intersect to form Latino inequality out of Latin American inequality. After presenting a theoretical framework for examining the reproduction of this inequality, I share migration stories from my respondents to detail their firsthand experiences during this process. In the third section of this essay, I step back from the personal to analyze the emigration-immigration process from a broader perspective. Finally, I argue that—despite their marginality—the farmworkers I interviewed are poised to develop a social movement to contest their condition of inequalities.[4]

To study New York farmworkers, I conducted 113 ethnographic interviews with farmworkers in upstate New York's Hudson Valley, with the help of Bard College student interns (2002). To locate subjects, I identified high-acreage farms in the Hudson Valley with crops ready for fall harvest. Using a classic snowball technique, I asked those I met on these farms in turn to identify additional workers for me to interview. I also received introductions to interviewees from staff at farmworker-advocacy organizations. Furthermore, I engaged in participant observation (2001–2003) and interviews (2003) with farmworker advocates, service providers, and others.

The Reproduction of Inequality

The question of how inequality is reproduced intersects with the debate about why immigration increases.[5] One answer can be found in the theory of "migration networks" (Portes and Bach 1985; Massey et al. 1987; Massey, Durand, and Malone 2002; Zabin et al. 1993). The main tenet of this theory is that reciprocal social relationships rooted in the sending country's hometowns promote migration to receiving countries. Pioneering immigrants to a regional economy not only serve as recruiting agents for others in their hometowns, but also provide a necessary social and economic bridge to new immigrants. Another answer has been identified by the dual-labor-market theory, which divides jobs in industrialized economies into primary and secondary sectors (Piore 1979; Reich, Gordon, and Edwards 1973). The former offer well-paid, stable jobs, with opportunity for advancement and well-established work rules, while the latter offer none of those and have inconsistent work rules and poor working conditions. Dual-labor-market theory describes international migrants as uniquely motivated for secondary-sector jobs since they are target earners (looking to fund specific projects such as home construction or children's education) and do not require the social status that comes from primary-sector jobs (Piore 1979). Moreover, the conversion of receiving-country wages to home-country economies allows international migrants to improve their families' quality of life, sometimes in a dramatic manner.

In this case study I do not seek to contradict the supply-side analysis of network migration theory or refute the demand-side inquiry of the dual-labor-market theory. Rather, my work should be understood as complementary by uncovering the contemporary mechanisms through which Latino immigrant workers are positioned at the bottom of the economic hierarchy. I draw on Charles Tilly's theory of durable inequality to show why Latino workers are sought by employers, which represents a process of the reproduction of inequality. Furthermore, this study adds to the field of "new destination" studies by examining a newly transformed regional economy

(Zúñiga and Hernández-León 2005; Murphy, Blanchard, and Hill 2001). While Latinos were certainly important in U.S. agriculture throughout the twentieth century, the same is not true for New York farms, which until the end of that century relied predominantly on African American and Caribbean workers. Between 1989 and 2000, Latino farmworkers quickly increased from one-third to two-thirds of the New York farm workforce, while black workers decreased from two-thirds to one-third (Pfeffer and Parra 2004). The replacement of black workers with Latinos is due in part to the fact that the "hard-won social-welfare policies" to which Paul Gootenberg refers put black U.S. workers in a position to demand more from employers (Gray 2007).[6] Moreover, in the 1970s and 1980s, New York agriculture saw declines in both wages and working conditions (Barr 1988). The growing leverage of those black workers, some of it due to the civil-rights movement, helped them challenge their inequality. But in New York agriculture, they were not given a chance to pursue their challenges; rather, they were replaced by a more vulnerable population of immigrant workers.

The interviews I conducted lend support to Tilly's theory about how inequality becomes institutionalized as a durable condition. In *Durable Inequality* (1998), Tilly argues that elites, who are active in amplifying inequality, usually do so "to solve other organizational problems." In this sense, an employer's primary goal is to maximize profits, and not intentionally to create inequality between management and workers. Tilly argues that when employers rely on existing inequalities, it is much less expensive than creating new inequality on the job. Socially recognized inequalities—what Tilly calls "categorical inequalities"—produce disparities in resources. Such categories include already identified social pairings, such as citizen-noncitizen, male-female, and white-black. These categorical inequalities are adopted by organizational arrangements, such as workplaces, to control employees. In his work on the lettuce industry in California, Robert Thomas advances a similar argument, contending that agribusiness does not create the inequity between citizenship and race categories, but rather exploits these status hierarchies for profit (1985: 27).

Categorical inequalities set the stage for management-worker relations, since the owners and managers usually represent the powerful half of social pairs. Tilly argues that social practices then emerge to reinforce the inequality. One of Tilly's examples is the family setting: men eat more than women, and women reinforce men's appetites by giving up their food for men. At the national level, categorical inequalities are reinforced when citizens vocalize their privilege by disparaging noncitizens, who are thus made to feel inferior. Such social practices develop over time, are reproduced in the work setting, and facilitate the control of employees. Accordingly, there is inevitably a deep inequality when an undocumented, Latino, non-English-speaking, uneducated worker is employed by a white, educated citizen. The relational disparity in legal status, race, ethnicity, language, education, and class underpin, for both employee and employer, a dynamic in which the boss has power over the worker. This is true politically, socially, and economically, but it most prominently affects workplace relationships. The employer's authority as a boss and the worker's due respect to this authority replicate existing status hierarchies and reinforce the employer's ability to secure farmworkers' compliance. When they hire immigrant workers, employers take advantage of preexisting social categories that make workers vulnerable to exploitation. Moreover, the migration process itself creates inequality.

Familiarity with the historical use of agricultural labor in California is also vital for understanding the plight of modern-day farmworkers, since California has long been the largest farming state in the country in employment, production, and the size of farms. Over the twentieth century, California farmers resorted to "ethnic succession" and ethnic segmentation to pit workers against each other, maintain a tractable workforce, and prevent worker organizing. This model proved highly profitable and justifiable, given that, for the most part, these workers had been isolated from mainstream society. California's agricultural employers hired successive groups of marginalized workers, including Chinese, Japanese, Mexican, South Asian Hindu (who arrived through Canada), Armenian (coming from industrial jobs on the East Coast), and Filipino workers. American protectorates such as Hawaii and the Philippines were important sites for identifying potential immigrant workers (Majka and Majka 1982; McWilliams 1939). Each successive wave replaced a previously controllable group, because the new group had vulnerabilities that allowed more profit, until, that is, they began to organize, at which point the cycle of replacement—ethnic succession—began anew.[7] The ethnic succession and segmentation honed in California was repeated throughout the country over the course of the twentieth century and into the twenty-first century, arriving more recently in New York State.

The use of immigrant and noncitizen workers in agriculture is well documented and fits with Tilly's notion that employers capitalize on categorical inequality, a process he calls "reinforced inequality." Moreover, many citizens who were hired as farmworkers were often so powerless that they seemed closer to being noncitizens than citizens.[8] In addition, twentieth-century labor laws and other progressive social legislation, which greatly improved working and living conditions for industrial workers, excluded agricultural workers. While the New Deal gave rise, in the 1930s, to sweeping social legislation that changed the landscape of work for white workers in the United States, black workers remained systematically excluded from most of these policies.[9] Most significantly, farmworkers were excluded from the minimum-wage, overtime-pay, and collective-bargaining laws.[10] Therefore, farmers were held to lower labor standards than were other employers. Federal and state legislation after the New Deal largely perpetuated the pattern of excluding farmworkers.[11] The accumulation of mutually reinforcing factors has been a long process and has created advantages and disadvantages.[12] These factors have coalesced to create a job category—farmworker—that in and of itself has the traits of categorical inequality. It is, furthermore, a fluid category, tailored to different types of workers through ethnic succession in the workplace.

Migration Stories

Arturo came from a semi-arid, mountainous region in southern Mexico where agriculture is the primary activity and where only a small portion of the population works in manufacturing. He has a second-grade education, having left school at the age of eight, and can barely read and write in Spanish. He used to work the land in Mexico, but was more recently employed as an artisan who crafted such objects as *tortilleros*, woven tortilla holders. In Mexico, he earned a little more than four U.S. dollars a day; since this was not enough to sustain himself, his wife, and two children, for economic reasons he came to New York State. He joined a brother who had arrived a few months earlier. Like most of the undocumented workers I met, Arturo crossed the border illegally, paying a "coyote" to help him navigate the difficult terrain with only the clothes on his back and little food or drink. From there, he came directly to the Hudson Valley region, where he found little similarity to his home in Mexico. In the United States, he did not have his family, and the loneliness was difficult to cope with. He was unsure about his future, saying, "only God knows" and that maybe he would return to Mexico. Arturo felt that he had little choice but to accept the conditions and pay of his job. It was a "necessity," and he was acutely aware of his limitations for finding better employment.

María, a twenty-two-year-old whose first language was not Spanish, identified herself as indigenous. She was from a rural area in southern Mexico and had a sixth-grade education; she was a produce packer on a farm in Mexico. Her husband, Carlos, who was thirty years old, was born in Mexico City, but his family was from the same town as María. He also identified as indigenous yet learned Spanish as his first language. Carlos had only a first-grade education; he left school at age ten. With few prospects in Mexico, and friends every year offering to get them jobs in the United States, María and Carlos finally decided to leave Mexico and placed their oldest child in the care of extended family. For four years and through the births of three more children, María and Carlos worked on farms along the East Coast. At the time of the interview, they were employed by a contractor who finds jobs for them in Florida, New Jersey, and New York.

They liked their jobs, but explained they would basically do anything and would clock as many hours as they could. They were fearful of being deported and worried about what would happen to their children if that were to occur. A few weeks before I met them, on their way from Florida to New Jersey, their work crew stopped at a motel for the night. Looking to save cash, the crew leader rented only a few rooms for the mostly male crew, and María's family, with three small children, was not allowed to sleep in the motel, where, according to María, the crew leader said they would take up too much space. Instead, they were forced to spend the night in a van, among the farmworkers' belongings. In the middle of the night motel security showed up in the parking lot with flashlights, and the family had to huddle in the van to hide from sight—a frightening experience that made their vulnerability palpable. Despite their fears, however, María and Carlos were hopeful for the future. They intended to build a house back in Mexico and to pay for their children's educations. At the same time, they wanted to be U.S. citizens and live here permanently for the sake of their children, "so they aren't like us."

These are only two stories, but they faithfully reflect what the farmworkers I interviewed said again and again: their economic circumstances drove them to migrate; their border crossings were difficult and often costly; while the money from their U.S. jobs served them well, they wished they could earn more and hoped their children would not repeat the same difficult life; they were unsure about their futures and were instinctively attracted to returning home, but understood that the United States offered more opportunities.

Almost all those interviewed reported an economic rationale for coming to the United States. Home employment reflected workers' generally low level of job skills. Eighty percent of those interviewed indicated that they performed farm labor in their home countries. Of this group, almost half reported they were engaged in subsistence farming. The high rate of workers who had engaged in farmwork in their home countries indicates a population that was mostly from rural areas, where, as Reygadas discusses, poverty is more pronounced and opportunities are more limited.[13] Workers made comments like "I used to have my own potato farm, but there is no water. Nothing happens with land that is dead," and "I make little earnings because I spend the profits on maintaining my farm." Those hailing from urban areas also gave testimony of limited opportunities. A former garment worker from Mexico told me she was fired when she turned fifty: "I worked in a factory, but after a certain age they don't let you work."

Eighty-five percent of the undocumented workers interviewed reported that they heard about their jobs through family or friends. But to secure those jobs they had to get across the border. Some paid for tourist visas; one worker reported paying $4,000 to a "coyote" for a tourist visa after her first attempt to surreptitiously cross the border failed. One interviewee reported that he bought a map and just walked across, but very few crossed without paying a coyote. For those who paid to cross the Mexican-U.S. border, prices ranged from $150 for a ride in a car to $2,000 for a coyote escort on foot. Many described their journey on foot across the Mexican-U.S. border. One reported, "I crossed with twenty-six Guatemalans and walked through the desert for thirty-six hours. I slept only one hour. I had no food and only drank some water. One girl could not walk anymore and got caught by immigration. We hid behind the hills." Several reported running across the border. Others reported walking with a coyote through the desert for hours or days. One said that he only remembered "walking and suffering of hunger and thirst." Many did not make it on the first attempt. I heard from workers who tried three or four times, having spent one month or more near the border waiting for the right opportunity. One respondent from Guatemala said he was caught by immigration officials on the United States side of the border who accepted a bribe to let him go. Some had to cross more than one border. A young woman from El Salvador who was joining her husband reported paying $10,000 for the forty-five-day trip that brought her to the

Hudson Valley. A worker from Guatemala said he was crammed into the back of a truck with two hundred others for twenty-four hours to get to Mexico, and that it took him a total of thirty-five days to reach New York.

Farmwork is a relatively easy job for new arrivals to acquire; it is a bottom-rung position. Not only are farmworker wages low, with few benefits, but the vast majority of agricultural jobs in the Hudson Valley are also seasonal and provide only temporary employment. The average hourly pay reported by those interviewed was $6.92 in 2002. Annual incomes from farmwork in the Hudson Valley, reported by workers, averaged $6,643 in 2002 and $7,345 in 2001. Nonetheless, this income is significant both in New York and at home. For most new arrivals, U.S. jobs are secured in New York with the primary goal of improving conditions for themselves and their families in their home countries, rather than with the intent to settle in the United States permanently (Piore 1979; Massey, Durand, and Malone 2002).

Low-paying jobs in the fast-food industry or in retail stores were generally not available to these workers. Their lack of English-language skills inhibited their ability to find and advance in jobs, prevented them from communicating effectively with their colleagues, managers, and employers, and, in general, excluded them from communities outside of their kin networks. Overall, the interviewees had very low literacy levels (few could read even in their native languages). For those with English as a second language, their self-reported proficiency was an average of 1.2 on a scale of 0 to 5. Many of these obstacles were related to their poverty and a lack of resources to acquire skills at home; they were also related to the difficulties the workers faced with regard to finding the time to acquire these skills while in the United States. For them, free time was a rare luxury.

The workers I interviewed were well aware of the barriers that prevented them from pursuing better work. Chief among reported obstacles were lack of opportunity (21 percent), poor English-language skills (19 percent), legal status (10 percent), skill level (10 percent), and transportation (6.4 percent). Workers elaborated: "No skills, no education. I can't read well, I can't do better"; "I have no documents, no English, no transportation. It can't happen"; "I need English. I have no education. One needs connections to be able to get a job here or in Mexico"; and "I can't do better. I don't have an education. I can't read well." Low levels of education and literacy severely restricted workers' ability to find better jobs. The data indicate a low level of formal education for all interviewees. Twelfth grade was the highest completed, while the average worker had not advanced beyond the sixth grade.

The generally low level of education among the group interviewed suggests that most of these farmworkers came from a background of dire economic necessity, with few chances for educational or career advancement.

Given such limited prospects, many of those I interviewed reported feeling restricted to their current job, including poor working conditions. Their words reflected this: "I have no social security number and was fired from my restaurant job, but I can work on a farm"; "It is difficult for an undocumented worker. It's hard to find work"; "I go home to Mexico and this job waits for me"; and "I got laid off construction work and the employer called me. I'll try again." For those in the formal guestworker program, there are no options for job mobility, except perhaps to change farms. One guestworker told me, "You do not have opportunities with the [guestworker] system. You come here, work and go back." While job mobility on farms was limited, acquiring jobs outside of agriculture seemed almost impossible. When one young male told me that he wanted to be a lawyer, he and his coworker broke out in loud laughter. Similarly, a young female responded that she desired an office job, and then she and her sister laughed out loud. The laughter was clearly in response to the ludicrous reference to finding professional employment. The sole interviewee born in the United States gave a biting response when asked about his future plans: he said he wanted to be president because "the poor do not help the poor."

The Migratory Process

My informants carried the burdens of categorical inequalities with them from their home countries, which exacerbated their weak position in the United States. Primarily, workers' low levels of formal education and literacy, their poor English-language skills, and their lack of job skills intersected with race, ethnicity, and class to prevent them from accessing higher paying work in the United States. However, to focus on the specific inequalities of workers overlooks the macrostructures that have influenced not only the conditions of these workers' lives in their home countries, but also their decisions to emigrate and their situations once they arrive. Constraints on workers' ability to improve their working and living conditions, both at home and in the United States, and to contest their inequality (in both places) were shaped by powerful, social, economic, and political factors. The strictly relational sides of inequality described by Tilly should be articulated with an analysis of macroeconomic, political, and global structures that exacerbate this asymmetric distribution of advantage and disadvantage.

To fully understand a migration process, one must look not just at immigration to and integration in the receiving country, but also at emigration and conditions in the home country. For example, Abdelmalek Sayad, in his writings on Algerians in France, argues that emigration and immigration are inseparable and reflect a dynamic, reciprocal, and shared history between receiving and home countries, and between emigrants and immigrants (2004: 29). Similarly, Douglas Massey, Jorge Durand, and Nolan Malone, in their research on the history of Mexican migration to the United States, dissent from the generic assumption that individuals engage in a simple cost-benefit analysis of their material well-being before migrating. Explanations of migration patterns, they posit, must take into account immigrants' incentives in both home country and receiving country (2002: 9). Relating these incentives to personal experiences allows one to see how inequality is reproduced through the emigration-immigration process.

Emigration is often the result of the upheaval—in part instigated by forces in wealthier countries—of traditional economic processes and markets. Free-trade-inspired economic development has radically changed traditional agricultural practices that once maintained rural poverty, yet assured stability. The North American Free Trade Agreement (NAFTA) of 1994, which served to facilitate the free movement of capital and goods between North American nations, also increased out-migration to the United States. In the Mexican countryside, the results include diminished labor demands and the squeezing out of small landholders (Massey, Durand, and Malone 2002). Instead of creating a new egalitarian category that would allow the citizens of greater North America to move freely for work between both countries, NAFTA re-emphasized categories of citizen-noncitizen and legal worker–undocumented immigrant, which benefit the employers. Understanding these larger forces lends meaning to workers' testimony about "dead land," "no water," and "all profits going to maintain the farm." These vague and individually posed phrases capture the ill effects of the loss of crop subsidies, the end of farm credit programs, and the scarcity of markets for small farmers' produce.

Home conditions are also telling when one considers how the lack of institutional protections for the rural poor in Latin America shapes inequality and immigrants' expectations of labor law coverage in the United States.

As Christina Ewig points out through her examination of state healthcare policy in Peru, one does not have to cross a national border to find oneself on the oppressed side of a national economic hierarchy.[14] Her examination of internal "colonization" in Peru shows how categorical inequalities along lines of class, gender, and race led to the exclusion many Peruvians— mostly the indigenous, rural dwellers, women, and urban poor—from receiving health benefits and the advantages of citizenship. This is also the case in labor law, despite the importance of agriculture throughout Latin America. Rural workers have not shared in the labor gains won by their urban working-class counterparts in the course of the last century (Roxborough 1994: 310). The marginalization of agricultural workers from the greater society in the United States is mirrored in Latin America, although in the latter the gap may be considerably wider. Many rural Latin Americans are devoted to subsistence farming (self-employment) rather than to wage labor. Those who are hired as agricultural wage laborers are rarely retained on a steady basis and are often employed informally. As such, farmworkers in Latin America are rarely covered by labor laws (Roxborough 1994: 308).

Immigration policies in the United States also perpetuate the vulnerability of immigrant workers. They are often symbolic and self-contradictory (Andreas 2001; Massey, Durand, and Malone 2002). For example, the 1986 Immigration Reform and Control Act (IRCA), which was promoted as a response to immigration dilemmas, in fact increased the number of immigrants arriving in the United States by granting resident status to several million undocumented persons. Those who secured a green card through IRCA's provisions were also able to secure better jobs in the formal economy and bring their families over, while several million undocumented workers filled the jobs they left. The IRCA was also designed to deter further immigration by setting penalties for employers who knowingly hire undocumented individuals. The result was not a crackdown on employers but rather the "illegalization" of workers. While failing to curb the inflow of newcomers, these policies have contributed to the creation of an unprotected class of laborers and spurred a drop in labor-law compliance in the workplace. There has also been a decline in U.S. wages, soaring domestic-income inequality, and worsening labor conditions (Massey, Durand, and Malone 2002: 2–3).

Considering immigration alongside emigration, as Sayad does, reveals how immigrants' lives are characterized by a "double absence." They are no longer present in their home communities, yet as undocumented persons in receiving countries, they become non-nationals and are excluded from the political sphere even as they toil in the economic sphere. Typically, immigrant economic inclusion leads to political incorporation, but for the undocumented worker the opposite is true. Sayad asks how one can reconcile the idea that such an immigrant is "only partly present, and therefore, in a way, being (morally) absent from the place in which one is physically present" (2004: 297). In answer to his own question, Sayad stresses the state's rationale: by creating hierarchies among immigrants, the state and its nationals can justify the denial of benefits to certain groups. The categorical divide between citizen-noncitizen (92 percent of those interviewed were undocumented workers and guestworkers) affects a range of opportunities for pursuing social, economic, and political incorporation, and employers profit from it. As a result, undocumented workers live in constant fear of being fired, incarcerated, and deported (Chávez 1992). Guestworkers are afraid they will not be invited to continue to participate in the contracted-farmworker program, which is dependent on an employer's reference and the home government's approval. In order to minimize the chances of having their fears realized, both undocumented workers and guestworkers tend not to complain about their situations and, in general, are regarded as a docile workforce. The boss does not have to explicitly threaten to expose legal status; it is an unspoken understanding.

When interviewees spoke to me about their fears, immigration authorities or "la migra" was by far the most common issue. Fifty-one-year-old Alejandro from Mexico told me how difficult it was to be without his family, his people, who were in Mexico. Expressing his fear that immigration officials would take him away, he told me, "We are treated like unknown people. We are not fugitives. We come here to do farmwork because we do not have jobs at home." Alejandro was nevertheless made to feel like a fugitive: he had illegally crossed the U.S.-Mexican border three times and planned to do so again. For three years, he had been working in the East Coast migrant stream—first in New Jersey, then in New York, followed by Florida, before returning home for an annual visit. As for improving his situation in the United States, he told me, "We are not paid well and cannot ask for more." It is worth noting that employers, too, fear "la migra."

Additional funding from Congress for tighter border security after 9/11, for increasing the number of immigration officers, and for the expansion of detention centers has been spent not only at the southern border of the United States, but also at the northern border, which is near prime farming areas in New York State. Knowing that so many farmworkers are undocumented and with a spike in deportations in western New York, farmers themselves fear a labor shortage and that their workforce will disappear at a critical moment in the growing or harvest season.[15] Moreover, employers' fear, like that of workers, is reinforced by rumors about deportations as well as by actual occurrences. Growers have complained about the recent deportations and lobbied Congress to pass immigration legislation that would help them secure legal guestworkers. At the same time, employers dread speaking to the press about the situations out of concern that the visibility will make their businesses targets of immigration enforcement.[16] This scenario reveals that despite the power that employers have over their workers, other factors limit employer power when it comes to workplace relations. It also shows how the growers themselves are, at times, compromised in their ability to wield their power—in this case to argue against the national government's strategy to target employers who hire the undocumented. As a result, farmers warn their workers to be very careful about traveling around local towns. An unfortunate consequence has been to further isolate workers from local communities.

Workers' drive for material benefits to support their families was clearly evidenced by many comments: "I want to be in Guatemala with my family, but I don't know if I will find work there"; "I keep working so my children can have an education"; "I dedicate myself to my children"; "I want to be with my family, I will work in any job"; "I don't want to worry about not having enough money to help my children"; and "I work so my children will have professions." But migration must also be understood as a household or community decision to minimize risk by diversifying resources. In Latin America, economic risk for the poor cannot be minimized through institutional cushions such as insurance or credit (Massey, Durand, and Malone 2002). Rather, labor migration is one of the few options; even a sole family member's U.S. wages help sustain families left behind. Here, however, one confronts the paradox of international migration: on the one hand, workers are often fully aware that they are being exploited, and they would improve their plight if they could; on the other hand, their remittances change their families' lives at homes, often from mere survival to well-being. Jeannine Anderson's examination of transcendence helps shed light on this paradox.[17] The poor, she explains, often do not focus excessively on their oppression. With this in mind, one can understand how an immigrant may complain to an advocate about mistreatment, fear, and regret, yet explain to her employer how the U.S. dollars earned on the job have transformed life back home.

Furthermore, the migration experience reveals that while immigrant workers easily imagine sending money home, they don't always have a good grasp of the sums they need to earn to accomplish this. Dreams of overcoming poverty by traveling to the United States are often dashed when new arrivals discover its cost of living and other unexpected expenses. Immigrants are burdened with the need to generate more income than that required just to cover their subsistence. In her research on Long Island's Central American newcomers, Sarah Mahler found that immigrants must earn surplus income to cover the debts they incurred from traveling to the United States. Moreover, they need to send money to family in their home countries, to provide for their own well-being in the United States, and to amass some savings to bring with them on their return to their home countries (Mahler 1995). This was certainly true for the farmworkers I interviewed. Almost all the workers interviewed reported sending remittances home, usually through a wire transfer via Western Union. The sum varied from $200 a year (to parents) to almost all an interviewee's income (to his wife and children). Those who sent money home on a monthly basis, or even more frequently (two-thirds of workers interviewed), averaged $513 in remittances per month, which represents about half of an average interviewee's monthly take-home pay.

While their poverty hobbled them at home, in the United States it led to outright exploitation, since employers who hire low-skill immigrants know that such workers have few job options and are often desperate for income. In this way, employers have converted home-country poverty to their advantage and reinforced this dynamic by paying poverty-level wages. Workers, particularly new arrivals, further reinforce this practice. While often aware of their plight, they tend to evaluate their hourly pay and social status by measures more appropriate at home (Piore 1979; Massey, Durand, and Malone 2002: 16). Immigrants strive to overcome the negative consequences of inequality in their countries of origin, but when they arrive in the United States they confront another set of categorical inequalities that push them to the bottom of the job ladder. Migration also can enhance inequality in home countries, as a disparity is created between families at home who receive U.S. dollars and those who do not. At the same time, in the receiving regions, new relations of inequality are created as home-country inequality merges with the disadvantages of low-wage U.S. work. In this last sense, one can see that the reproduction of inequality is not only about how employers exploit inequality to make a profit, but also about how new communities of under-paid U.S. workers (after all, they work and live in the United States) struggle to establish themselves in rural areas, poor urban neighborhoods, and the business districts of working-class suburbs.

Potential for Contesting Inequalities

Thus far I have painted a rather bleak picture of the situation of the Hudson Valley farmworkers I interviewed. They seem desperate, resigned to their situations, and fearful of retaliation from employers and authorities if they speak out against their exploitation. They are an excluded group that has not been able to press concerns against institutional elites. While it may be easy to depict an extreme marginalization of such workers, the fact that members of an excluded group are not using their power does not mean they have none; rather, their power is inhibited by powerful constraints. Other U.S. workers in arguably similar positions have attempted to change their situations through collective action: late-nineteenth-century railroad, steel, and iron workers; early-twentieth-century immigrant women sweatshop workers; and 1970s California farmworkers. More recently, small successes have been achieved by immigrant workers in the Los Angeles service sector (Milkman 2006). How can social-movement theory be applied to evaluate the potential for noncitizen workers to contest their inequality? Or, in the specific case at hand, can one predict how Hudson Valley or New York farm-worker collective action might emerge?

In his study of mid-twentieth-century black insurgency in the southern United States, Doug McAdam (1982) proposes that collective action emerges in response to changes occurring in three circumstances. The first factor he introduces, borrowing from Peter Eisinger (1973), is "the structure of politi-cal opportunities," which describes the power relationship between the ex-cluded group and institutionalized politics (which represent concentrated wealth and power, i.e., employers or the state). Change registers either when the excluded group gains leverage or when institutionalized political actors and systems lose legitimacy. Such shifts, even symbolic ones, alter power relations to the advantage of the excluded group (McAdam 1982: 43). The second factor is "readiness" or the level of organizational infrastructure within the excluded group that links members of the group to an organized political effort (McAdam 1982: 44). Finally, McAdam notes "insurgent consciousness," which is understood as the excluded groups' shared opinion that their political efforts are important and likely to yield success.

Changes in the structure of political opportunity (McAdam's first factor) for New York farmworkers have occurred in two arenas. The first is around the recent national policy quagmire over immigration, where post-9/11 nativist rhetoric pervades the public debate on national border and immigration issues. This imagery is repeated at the state and local level as law-enforcement officials, service administrators, shopkeepers, and even neighbors target those who appear "illegal." Though largely in response to the seemingly inadequate and unfair federal policies on borders and immigration, these perceptions are held by opposing sides. On one hand are immigrants and their supporters pushing for enhanced opportunities and rights for immigrants; on the other hand are those who would like the federal government to take a stronger stance to stem illegal border crossings and lower incentives for the undocumented. Both sides are unhappy with the response of the federal government. One result is the myriad conflicting local and state policies to ameliorate the shortcomings of federal decisions. For example, in New York State, the attorney general set up a task force to aggressively protect immigrant rights, whereas small towns in New Hampshire and elsewhere have attempted to use trespassing laws to rid their towns of undocumented individuals. Denying drivers' licenses to the undocumented is a striking example of a policy that has significantly affected the quotidian experiences of many undocumented individuals: they are now afraid to drive, have lost jobs that required driving, and fear that a minor traffic infraction will reveal their legal status and lead to deportation. In the current political climate, immigrants, both with proper documents and without, are constantly reminded that surveillance and suspicion follow them well past the official border.

Each recent additional layer of legal protection for, or legal attack on, immigrants carries with it a critique of the reigning policy. Moreover, inherent in this ongoing tangle of policies is the declining credibility of government with regard to immigration issues, which undercuts the legitimacy of the government and the policies themselves. In the spring of 2006, unprecedented numbers of immigrants took to the streets in cities and towns across the United States, calling for immigration reform. Both the succession of inadequate policies and this national outcry of protest are portrayed prominently in the Spanish-language media. This highly publicized combination of perceived loss of government legitimacy and the rising leverage of the immigrants is likely to have a ripple effect on movements of smaller scope, including that of Hudson Valley farmworkers.

Second, at the state level New York has seen an active research and advocacy campaign to promote farmworker rights. This structural shift in political opportunity, which spans approximately fifteen years, is very different from the current national campaign. A targeted research campaign has worked to undermine the position of employers and the state government vis-à-vis farmworker rights. Farmworkers in New York, as in most states, are denied the right to overtime pay, rest days, and collective-bargaining protections, among other rights. In 1991, a Cornell University academic taskforce, commissioned by then New York Governor Mario Cuomo, conducted an extensive study on farmworker rights and called for New York State to extend agricultural laborers the same rights as other workers, particularly in regard to collective-bargaining protections (Task Force Report 1991). Soon after, in 1992, farmworker advocates in eastern New York engaged in a campaign against sanitation-code violations in farm labor camps. State senate hearings on agricultural labor issues followed in 1994, and the corresponding report, published in 1995, also called for an extension of rights to farmworkers (New York State Senate-Assembly Puerto Rican/Hispanic Task Force 1995). The sanitation exposé and senate hearings laid the groundwork for public events, most notably Farmworker Advocacy Day, an annual spring event for agricultural workers and their supporters to garner public attention and approach state legislators about farmworkers' unequal treatment under the law.

Apart from research visibility, New York farmworkers have had success in organizing, legal casework, and legislative campaigns. A farmworker-directed organization, El Centro Independiente de Trabajadores Agrícolas/Independent Farmworker Center (CITA), has helped hundreds of workers, for example, supporting them in negotiating contracts with employers. Moreover, farmworkers and their advocates take pride in claiming success for three pro-farmworker laws that have passed in the New York state legislature and that set the foundation, in terms of support, rationale, and precedent, for wider laws. Advocacy successes include material benefits such as winning backwages and securing a raise in the farmworker minimum wage. Other benefits are less tangible, such as worker empowerment through leadership training, media exposure, and relationships forged with powerful allies. Yet all these efforts in New York have upset the power balance between farmers and the state on one hand and the farmworkers on the other, leading to a backlash against the New York farmworker movement. Employers and other agricultural actors have used multiple strategies to undermine farmworker advocates, trying to influence public opinion and policy, exposing or challenging funders of the advocacy organizations, and promoting audits of advocacy organizations' activities. Even those attempting to document the movement (such as academics) have been targeted.

Such shifts in political opportunity account for naught without an organizational infrastructure (McAdam's second factor) to plug farmworkers into a movement. Coordinated advocacy efforts for New York farmworkers by nonprofits and others have gained speed in the past two decades. Advocates have responded with righteous fervor to farmworkers' lack of political power, vulnerability to exploitation, cases of substandard living and working conditions, and lack of labor rights. In 1988, a coalition of nonprofit, religious, and educational organizations was formed in western New York to address agricultural workers' living and working conditions. Two years later, a similar coalition formed in eastern New York, in the Hudson Valley. In the mid-1990s, the Justice for Farmworkers Coalition (JFW), a statewide umbrella group, came together. The JFW encompasses several organized groups of actors and coordinates independent advocacy efforts, through, for example, its Justice for Farmworkers Campaign, a legislative crusade to ensure farmworker equality under New York's labor laws. The movement's main strategies are legal cases, a legislative campaign, and organizing. To date, organizing has been the weakest of the three, though not for lack of coordination on the organizers' side. In fact, organizers may have already laid a strong groundwork for a movement to take off when the other factors align.

The final factor, insurgent consciousness, requires, in addition to increased leverage, that the excluded group stop accepting the status quo and challenge their situations, usually by an assertion of rights (Piven and Cloward 1979: 3–4). Time will tell if this factor aligns with the others. However, it is clear that immigrant agricultural workers are not merely passive victims of inequality. The simple fact that they left their countries of origin indicates a considerable will and capacity to change their situations. In this case, individuals or families have taken advantage of the possibility of obtaining, in the United States, a better-paying job than otherwise available at home. Under certain structures of opportunity and through established processes of organization and emerging identities, this individual agency can turn into a collective agency to act politically in the face of their shared disadvantages as a group.

Another perspective on insurgent consciousness is offered by the anthropologist Jeanine Anderson, who argues that the poor do not necessarily focus their daily attention on their poverty.[18] Rather, like most people, they cultivate dreams of a good life. The actions that outsiders and academics might categorize as poor people's survival mechanisms or desperation may in fact be the manifestation of their dreams for the achievement of a better life, what Anderson calls "transcendence projects." Examining the poor in the light of such projects helps to counter outsider narratives, imposed on the poor, of their consciousness or action. Personal and community transcendence projects may be antipoverty projects, such as migrating or outright displays of resistance to the status quo. And while many do achieve some level of transcendence, it is important to note, as Anderson does, that this usually occurs in relation to other poor people. It is rare for the poor, no matter how successful their own investments, to rise above the structural hierarchies they live under, particularly with respect to class.

Conclusion

The discussion of how inequality crosses borders is not a new one and certainly the stories of those I interviewed are often reminiscent of Piore's classic Birds of Passage. Yet, while Piore is correct, these immigrants maintain the social status of home and are what Alejandro Portes has called "economic heroes at home." Portes also notes that this does not alter the fact that they are blatantly exploited in the United States.[19] Moreover, as Piore has argued, the ideal migrant worker is the temporary one, but that scenario is increasingly changing, particularly as the Mexican-U.S. border continues to tighten. One would be doing oneself a disservice by imagining such workers simply as international migrants (including those who only plan to stay a short time). Instead, one needs to conceive of them as what they truly become when they cross the border—U.S. workers. To such a degree one accepts that the reproduction of inequality is twofold: first, the individual immigrant is taken advantage of due to his or her categorical inequalities; and second, communities of immigrants find themselves struggling in poverty in the United States. In regard to the latter, one sees the reproduction of the painful elements of the American dream—sacrifice, adverse working conditions, low pay, overcrowded housing, and separated families—but unlike those who were part of the midcentury "ethnic miracle," today's low-wage immigrant workers will have little opportunity to assimilate and pull themselves up into the primary sector. With the increasing gap between the wealthy and the poor in the United States (and globally), it is incumbent on our political system to take notice of those on the bottom and their future direction.

The history of farmworker exploitation helps one understand that the categorical inequality of employer-farmworker stems from the persistent use of flexible categories of vulnerabilities. The categories themselves (such as race) may change over time, and even shift across borders, but they continue to replicate indelible inequality. The contemporary subjects of this essay have their own specificities, but in a historical light the constraints they face resonate with powerful legacies from U.S. history. In that long analysis, the factors that maintain inequality and constrain farmworkers' access to power—to voice complaints, to better their working and living conditions, and to collectively organize—are structurally tied to the conditions necessary for employers' continual accumulation of profit. These factors are also tied to historical categorical inequalities: master/slave, landowner/worker, citizen/noncitizen, native born/immigrant, and racial majority/minority. African slaves, of course, toiled without wages and were confined to specific areas under the control of their masters. The unfortunate legacy of this model of labor control and its bearing on management-worker relations in agriculture cannot be overstated. The class and race relations that flourished in the rural South as a result of slavery have significantly influenced the legal rights of twenty-first-century farmworkers (Linder 1992).

At its root, Tilly's theory of durable inequality is about power differentials that are constantly shifting. One might reconfigure Tilly's ideas to this case and argue that the employer-farmworker category itself is a categorical inequality in the United States that encompasses such categorical inequalities as citizen, non-citizen, or native born immigrant. Because of their fluid nature, the categories of inequality themselves are not the most prominent aspect of farmworkers' marginalization, as they have shifted over time. In this sense, racial categorical pairs such as white/black and white/Latino, and hierarchy pairs such as master/slave, farmer/migrant, and citizen/ undocumented help one to understand the development of employer-farmworker. This represents employers' incessant drive to find workers they can profit from by adopting reigning categorical pairs to their advantage.

Farmwork inequalities as they currently exist may help explain why New

York has witnessed few farmworker protests, strikes, or organizings. Workers' quiescence is no indication of satisfaction with their jobs; it is a result of workers' fear of speaking out and their willingness to accept dismal working conditions because of their weak political power. The high concentration of undocumented workers and guestworkers—92 percent of workers interviewed—shapes their chronic vulnerability, as the risk of deportation underlies workers' fear of voicing complaints. They are willing to endure substandard working and living conditions and are disinclined to engage in actions that put their jobs at risk, including those to improve their working conditions. Guestworkers also fear they will not be able to return to the United States. To minimize risks, both undocumented workers and guestworkers tend to stay quiet about their situations. According to Mahler, this pressure on workers, coupled with their need to earn, results in workaholic workers, rather than complaining ones (Mahler 1995: 92).

Yet what is diminished is the exercise of worker power, not its potential—for example workers' potential to strike or otherwise disrupt production and negotiate with the boss. Employers, after all, are utterly dependent on their workers. How is this related to the development of collective action? Real social movements do not comprise disparate protests epitomized by intense drama (as they are often portrayed). Rather, social movements, as McAdam has shown, are cumulative and develop slowly over time. This case study also suggests that among New York immigrant farmworkers, structures of political opportunity are changing, organizational networks for promoting organizing and membership are active, and the rise of an insurgent consciousness appears possible. It is now a matter of time to see if and when this movement erupts and how far it can go in terms of meeting its goals and redressing social inequalities.

Notes

The author expresses her gratitude to the International Ladies Garment Workers Union Twenty-First Century Heritage Fund for funding her research on Hudson Valley farmworkers and to Bard College for supporting the Migrant Labor Project under whose auspices this research was conducted.

1. I use pseudonyms in place of farmworkers' real names.
2. Many studies of farmworkers point out that the conditions of contemporary farmworkers are remarkably similar to those of the turn of the last century (Barr 1988: 41; Mooney and Majka 1995; Nelkin 1970: 1; Oxfam America 2004: 2).

3. See Reygadas's essay in this volume.
4. As a case study, this essay does not seek to represent the farmworkers throughout the region, let alone all those in New York. Rather, I analyze how, for the workers I interviewed, inequality is reinforced and mutated. When inequality crosses borders from Latin America to the United States, it becomes magnified. My intention is also to expose the situations of a highly marginalized group. Farmworkers have long suffered structural and institutional conditions that have more recently become prevalent in other sectors of our society. In addition, the late-twentieth-century shift in New York agriculture from domestic to immigrant labor is emblematic of the changing demographic of workers in other areas of work. Consequently, my research elucidates working conditions seen in low-wage working arrangements that encompass more than upstate agriculture.
5. Classical economic interpretations of international migration (for example, Galbraith 1979; Todaro 1976; Greenwood 1975; and Sjaastad 1962) have been largely criticized for assuming rational motivation on the part of immigrants, ignoring large-scale migration that contradicts the theory's main tenets, and not considering sociological variables (for example Papademetriou and Hopple 1982; Arizpe 1981; Portes and Walton 1981). This case study points to one major contradiction in conventional theory. Classical economic theory posits that labor migration from poorer countries to richer ones will cause equilibrium in wages: immigrants will lower wages in the host country, and the sending country will experience a labor shortage that will result in higher wages. However, an alternative dynamic seems to be at work instead: lowered wages precede the majority of immigrant workers. New York agriculture saw declining wages and worsening labor conditions in the 1970s and 1980s (Barr 1988), which gave rise to disgruntled native U.S. workers, who employers sought to replace. New York farm jobs then attracted a stream of immigrant workers, who, using Piore's (1979) logic, were willing to do the work. Space limits the full investigation of this point in reference to this case study.
6. See Gootenberg's essay in this volume.
7. The use of successive groups of immigrant labor in California in the late 1800s and early 1900s is detailed in Carey McWilliams's exposé of U.S. farmworker conditions (1939). For the role of local, state, and federal government in regulating the immigration and exploitation of farmworkers, see Daniel 1981; Majka and Majka 1982.
8. These workers did not have the full rights of other citizens, including voting rights, freedom of movement, freedom from forced labor, and labor rights. Residency requirements, for instance, excluded citizen migrants from voting. Vagrancy laws allowed for forced labor or the imprisonment of workers who refused to work (Grossardt 1996; Hahamovitch 1997; also Friedland and Nelkin 1971).
9. In probably the most well-documented work on the exploitation of U.S. farm

labor from a legal perspective, Marc Linder explains that institutionalized racism was the backbone of southern politics and economics and the main factor influencing state policies on agricultural labor (Linder 1992, chap. 4; also Hahamovitch 1997, chap. 6).

10. The National Labor Relations Act of 1935, which established certain collective bargaining protections (fostering workers' ability to help themselves), yet does not cover farmworkers, is often the main point of departure for a discussion of this exclusion (Edid 1994; Linder 1992; Rothenberg 2000).

11. New York's 1937 Labor Relations Act established in law that farmworkers are not considered "employees," and the 1938 New York State Constitution thus excludes them from rights enjoyed by other workers in the state, including overtime pay, a day of rest, and collective bargaining protections.

12. See Reygadas's essay in this volume.

13. See Reygadas's essay in this volume.

14. See Ewig's essay in this volume.

15. Lisa W. Foderaro, "Plenty of Apples, but Possibly a Shortage of Immigrant Pickers," *New York Times*, 21 August 2007.

16. Nina Bernstein, "Immigration Raids Cause Fear on New York Farms," *New York Times*, 24 December 2006.

17. See Anderson's essay in this volume.

18. See Anderson's essay in this volume.

19. Portes used this comparison at a presentation during the Second Cumbre of the Great Plains: Re-visioning Latino America—New Perspectives on Migration, Transnationalism and Integration, University of Omaha, 22–24 April 2005.

Funes and the Toolbox of Inequality

JAVIER AUYERO

"With one quick look," writes Jorge Luis Borges in his tale "Funes, His Memory," "you and I perceive three wineglasses on a table. Funes perceived every grape that had been pressed into the wine and all the stalks and tendrils of its vineyard. He knew the forms of the clouds in the southern sky on the morning of April 30, 1882, and he could compare them in his memory with the veins in the marbled binding of a book he had seen only once, or with the feathers of spray lifted by an oar on the Río Negro on the eve of the Battle of Quebracho" (Borges 1999: 135). Ireneo Funes had a prodigious memory; he "remembered not only every leaf of every tree in every patch of forest, but every time he had perceived or imagined that leaf." He was incapable of general ideas: "Not only was it difficult for him to see that the generic symbol 'dog' took in all the dissimilar individuals of all shapes and sizes, it irritated him that the 'dog' of three-fourteen in the afternoon, seen in profile, should be indicated by the same noun as the dog of three-fifteen, seen frontally." Funes, who died young, in 1889 was, Borges writes, "the solitary, lucid spectator of a multiform, momentaneous, and almost unbearably precise world" (136). But, despite all his meticulous memory, he was "not very good at thinking." Thinking, Borges suggests, "is to ignore (or forget) differences, to generalize, to abstract. In the teeming world of Ireneo Funes there was nothing but particulars—and they were virtually *immediate* particulars" (137).

   An observer of Latin America's contemporary social, political, economic, and cultural realities faces a dilemma similar to Funes. Too many particulars, too many immediate concerns bombard the onlooker and obfuscate his or her vision. How to make sense of the region's present condition? Let's perhaps imagine a curious citizen of the "advanced" North traveling through the region. Let's imagine she is a college student on some "study-abroad" program. Picture her in Quito, Buenos Aires, or Mexico City. She starts her day perusing the pages of El *Comercio*, *Clarín*, or *La Jornada* (to take three politically diverse newspapers from Ecuador, Argentina, and Mexico). After even a superficial glance at the press, she will be taken aback by the impressive number of seemingly contradictory developments. She will certainly be impressed by the striking variety of social movements (land squatters, occupation of factories, demands for better working conditions, resisting police brutality, road blockades to protest against the environmental waste left by transnational companies, etc.). And these dramatic actions clearly coexist with the practices of traditional political parties, which have little interest in popular mobilization and are heavily invested in their seemingly perennial routines of patronage politics. Let her stay just a couple of weeks in any of these cities (or in Caracas, Bogotá, Lima, or Santiago) and she will soon learn that entrenched elites (old money and new) live more or less peacefully side by side with more or less progressive, more or less left-leaning governments that indulge in occasional outbursts of more or less radical anti-oligarchic rhetoric. Our traveler will read about recently approved "civil unions" and soon gather that sexual, ethnic, and racial "minorities" are increasingly active in their claims for civic rights, sometimes making dramatic gains. Agnostic as she is, she will not fail to note that when women's reproductive rights are involved, some of these claims will be met with ultraconservative reactions (usually led by the Catholic Church); as a product of an elite college in the North, she will probably be amused by the defense of "family values" used by right-wing groups, as recently as July 2006, to oppose a law allowing Argentine men to have vasectomies. She will also learn about the continuing waves of emigration in many of the countries of the region, which are witnessing substantial numbers of their most young and active citizens leave for Europe or the United States in search of better futures (she will vaguely recall the Spanish-speaking cleaning personnel at her university and the landscapers at her parents' summer house). In the newspaper "police blotter," she is likely to find news about drug smuggling, with comments about the apparently intractable spread of drug production, consumption, and trafficking, now moving from peripheral areas into the big cities, with the attendant explosion of violence and crime. As a foreigner, she will be warned not to leave her hotel; Latin American cities are—so she is told—extremely dangerous.

Being curious, our trekker will disregard these words of caution and venture outside. She will take cabs or public transportation and will soon encounter another distinctive feature of any Latin American metropolis: its dramatic contrasts. The luxurious wealth of cosmopolitan bourgeoisies will make her wonder whether she is in Mexico City or Buenos Aires or some other First World global city—such is the cornucopia of pricey restaurants offering all kinds of international delicacies, gourmet shops, exclusive boutiques, and French hand laundries, and such luxurious new developments and shopping malls in certain urban zones. Not too far from there, she will also come upon the vast territories of urban refuse: enclaves of misery that with different names and histories characterize every single city in contemporary Latin America. If she is in Buenos Aires, she might be able to join one of the "villa tours" that are now offered to foreign tourists. Corridors of modernity and wealth (gated communities that house the upper and upper-middle classes, heavily guarded and walled barrios connected to wealthy areas of the city center via express highways) boom alongside villas, *asentamientos precarios, comunas,* and *colonias populares.* She might now recall a 2001 UN-HABITAT report she once read for a sociology class, which states that a third of the population of Latin America still lives in slums.

Our visitor will be in awe, and although able to recount all the details of her visit in precise detail, she will probably be unable to make sense of the booming and buzzing present condition of Latin America. Much like Borges's Ireneo Funes, she needs categories, classificatory schemes, to understand and explain what is right in front of her eyes. Only categories can help her to organize (and to abstract from) the "multiform, momentaneous, and almost unbearably precise world." Only with categories will she be able to disregard some things and to focus attention on the ones that matter.

The contributors to this volume should be able to help visitors such as our college student as well as the many scholars interested in and concerned about the past, present, and future of Latin America. They provide a useful set of tools to scrutinize the region's social, political, cultural, and economic landscape. Call that set the Inequality Toolbox. As in every toolbox, there is practical diversity. Some tools are good for looking macroscopically at the region as a whole and for extracting the mechanisms and processes that perpetuate or challenge existing arrangements (Reygadas). Others serve to zoom in and dissect a primary causal factor (e.g., state policies) in the construction and reproduction of inequality along race and gender lines (Ewig). Some tools, as Paul Gootenberg rightly notes, are more sensitive to the past (and echoes of the past living in present arrangements) than others. Smaller but equally powerful tools serve to inspect the crucial role of invisible political information in the perpetuation of inequities (Renno) and the role of precariousness in the potential of and obstacles to collective action to challenge asymmetrical relations (Gray). Instruments attentive to the power of culture (understood here as systems of meanings, but also as sets of practices) are put to good use to examine poor people's aspirations and projects (Anderson), and creative black representations of their own plight and exclusion (Casamayor). The Inequality Toolbox contains more instruments than the ones deployed so skillfully in this volume. Some tools, for example, are quite handy at illuminating disparities in education and can be called the "cultural capital" kit; others are helpful in making sense of the unequal distribution of healthy habitats and can be called the "environmental justice" toolkit. The toolbox metaphor resonates well with this volume's emphasis on "constructed" inequalities: analyses that look at the making of social arrangements and that as tools might also help suggest the ways that unequal relations can one day be "de-constructed" as well.

Most if not all of the essays herein explicitly or implicitly take heed of Charles Tilly's mechanism-based approach to durable inequality and to critically translate its insights into new and different contexts (1998). According to Tilly, categorical distinctions and inequities (whether by race, class, gender, ethnicity, citizenship, age, etc.) are caused by two main mechanisms ("exploitation" and "opportunity hoarding") and strengthened by two others ("emulation" and "adaptation"). One of the challenges for those trying to put Tilly's toolbox to good use is to see how these mechanisms operate across national contexts and across categorical distinctions. Another challenge this volume's contributors appear to agree on is to push what Paul Gootenberg calls Tilly's "structuralism" into more culturally and historically sensitive directions. In fact, an invisible link running through the essays is a kind of cultural critique of Tilly's mechanism- and process-based perspective.

Conceptual tools developed by the French sociologist Pierre Bourdieu's "genetic structuralism" (1977; 1991; 1998; 2000) should come in handy for such a scholarly project. His working concepts, interrogating arrows pointing to the social world—such as "habitus" (which highlights the incorporation of resilient divisions into the schemes of perception and the value that agents use to think, feel—and act on—those divisions); "symbolic violence" (which points to the possible convergence of dominant and dominated classificatory schemes); and "doxa" (which calls attention to the potential taken-for-granted character of the dominant social order)—could work well in tandem with a mechanism- and processed-based approach. In fact, Bourdieu's exploration of the dynamics of fields resembles Tilly's relational approach to inequality reproduction in ways that could be fruitfully exploited both theoretically and empirically.

In drawing on Tilly while seeking to extend his framework into more symbolic dimensions of social inequalities, the essays in this volume indeed add to a more heterogeneous but at the same time more useful and productive toolbox. Scholars whose main craft is to understand and explain the resilient and also contested character of privilege, difference, and exclusion can now borrow these tools.

Even if no book can focus on every tool at one's disposal, one should acknowledge this crafty group of scholars for helping the many Funeses and traveling students enchanted by and worried about contemporary Latin America. These tools help construct a coherent and illuminating story about the present state of the hemisphere—a story that would marvel interlocutors by its interdisciplinary core, a feature rarely seen in narratives of inequality in this or any other corner of world. These essays provide a truly provocative set of analytical instruments and empirical analyses that serve to get a better grip on the region's troublesome predicaments, in both their objective and subjective dimensions. Inequality in Latin America, one learns, is not simply about the objective unequal distribution of material resources. It is also about the intricate subjective representations and lived experiences that often help to perpetuate inequalities and that other times contain the seeds to contest this seemingly indelible underside of Latin America.

Abel, Christopher, and Colin Lewis, eds. 2001. *Exclusion and Engagement: Social Policy in Latin America*. London: Institute of Latin America Studies.

Abers, Rebecca. 1998. "From Clientelism to Cooperation: Local Government, Participatory Policy, and Civic Organizing in Porto Alegre, Brasil." *Politics and Society* 26, no. 4: 511–39.

Adelman, Jeremy, ed. 1999. *Colonial Legacies: The Problem of Persistence in Latin American History*. New York: Routledge.

Aguirre, Rosario. 2005. "Trabajo no remunerado y uso del tiempo: Fundamentos conceptuales y avances empíricos: La encuesta Montevideo 2003." *El tiempo, los tiempos, una vara de desigualdad*, by Rosario Aguirre, Cristina García Saínz, and Cristina Carrasco, 9–34. Santiago: ECLAC, Women and Development Unit.

Ahmad, Ehtisham, Jean Dréze, John Hills, and Amartya Sen, eds. 1991. *Social Security in Developing Countries*. Oxford: Clarendon.

Aliaga Linares, Lissette. 2002. *Sumas y restas: El capital social como recurso en la informalidad*. Lima: Alternativa / Fondo Editorial de la UNMSM.

Allen, Catherine J. 1988. *The Hold Life Has: Coca and Cultural Identity in an Andean Community*. Washington: Smithsonian Institution Press.

Altimir, Óscar. 1999. "Desigualdad, empleo y pobreza en América Latina: Efectos del ajuste y del cambio en el estilo de desarrollo." *Pobreza y desigualdad en América Latina: Temas y nuevos desafíos*, comp. Víctor Tokman and Guillermo O'Donnell, 23–54. Buenos Aires: Paidós.

Alvarez, Michael, and John Brehm. 2002. *Hard Choices, Easy Answers: Values, Information and American Public Opinion*. Princeton: Princeton University Press.

Alvarez, Sonia, and Alberto Escobar, eds. 1992. *The Making of Social Movements in Latin America*. Boulder: Westview.

Amsden, Alice. 2001. *The Rise of the "Rest": Challenges to the West from Late-Industrializing Economies*. New York: Oxford University Press.

Anderson, Benedict. [1983] 1995. *Imagined Communities: Reflections on the Origins and Spread of Nationalism*. London: Verso.

Anderson, Jeanine. 1992. "Estrategias de sobrevivencia revisitadas." *Las mujeres y la vida de las ciudades*, ed. María del Carmen Feijóo and Hilda María Herzer, 33–62. Buenos Aires: Instituto Internacional de Medio Ambiente y Desarrollo.

——. 2007. "Urban Poverty Reborn: A Gender and Generational Analysis." *Developing Societies* 23, nos. 1–2: 221–41.

Andreas, Peter. 2001. *Border Games: Policing the U.S.–Mexico Divide.* Ithaca: Cornell University Press.

Andrews, George Reid. 1996. "Brazilian Racial Democracy, 1900–90: An American Counterpoint." *Contemporary History* 31, no. 3: 483–507.

Appadurai, Arjun. 1996. *Modernity at Large: Cultural Dimensions of Globalization.* Minneapolis: University of Minnesota Press.

Archer, Ronald. 1990. "The Transition from Traditional to Broker Clientelism in Colombia: Political Stability and Social Unrest." Working Paper no. 140. Notre Dame: Helen Kellogg Institute for International Studies.

Arizpe, Lourdes. 1982. "The Rural Exodus in Mexico and Mexican Migration to the United States." *International Migration Review* 15: 626–49.

Arnold, Denise. 1997. "Making Men in Her Own Image: Gender, Text, and Textile in Qaqachaka." *Creating Context in Andean Cultures,* ed. Rosaleen Howard-Malverde, 99–131. New York: Oxford University Press.

Arroyo Laguna, Juan. 2000. *Salud: La reforma silenciosa.* Lima: Universidad Peruana Cayetano Heredia, Facultad de Salud Pública y Administración.

Ascher, William. 1984. *Scheming for the Poor: The Politics of Redistribution in Latin America.* Cambridge: Harvard University Press.

Assadourian, Carlos. 1982. *El sistema de la economía colonial: Mercado interno, regiones y espacio económico.* Lima: Instituto de Estudios Peruanos.

Auyero, Javier. 2000. "The Logic of Clientelism in Argentina: An Ethnographic Account." *Latin American Research Review* 35, no. 3: 55–81.

——. 2001a. *Poor People's Politics: Peronist Survival Networks and the Legacy of Evita.* Durham: Duke University Press.

——. 2001b. *La política de los pobres: Las prácticas clientelistas del peronismo.* Buenos Aires: Manantial.

——, comp. 1997. *¿Favores por votos? Estudios sobre clientelismo político contemporáneo.* Buenos Aires: Losada.

Avritzer, Leonardo. 2002. *Democracy and the Public Sphere in Latin America.* Princeton: Princeton University Press.

Banck, Geert A. 1999. "Clientelism and Brazilian Political Process: Production and Consumption of a Problematic Concept." *Modernization, Leadership, and Participation: Theoretical Issues in Development Sociology,* ed. Peter J. M. Nas and Patricio Silva. Leiden: Leiden University Press.

Barnet, Miguel. 1996. *Biografía de un cimarrón.* Havana: Instituto de Etnología y Folklore.

Barr, Donald. 1988. *Liberalism to the Test: African-American Migrant Farmworkers and the State of New York.* Albany: State University of New York, New York State African American Institute. Institute Document no. 88-2.

Barrig, Maruja. 1989. "The Difficult Equilibrium between Bread and Roses: Women's Organizations and the Transition from Dictatorship to Democracy in Peru." *The*

Women's Movement in Latin America: Feminism and the Transition to Democracy, ed. Jane Jaquette, 151–76. Boston: Unwin Hyman.

———. 1992. "Nos habíamos amado tanto: Crisis del estado y organización feminina." La emergencia social en el Perú, ed. Maruja Barrig, Lidia Elías, and Lisbeth Guillén, 7–17. Lima: ADEC-ATC.

Bartels, Larry M. 1988. Presidential Primaries and the Dynamics of Public Choice. Princeton: Princeton University Press.

———. 1993. "Messages Received: The Political Impact of Media Exposure." American Political Science Review 30: 709–23.

———. 1999. "Panel Effects in the American National Election Studies." Political Analysis 8, no. 1: 1–19.

———. 2005. "Homer Gets a Tax Cut: Inequality and Public Policy in the American Mind." Perspectives on Politics 3, no. 1: 15–32.

Bartra, Roger. 1987. La jaula de la melancolía: Identidad y metamórfosis del mexicano. Mexico City: Grijalba.

Baudrillard, Jean. 1992. L'illusion de la fin ou la grève des événements. Paris: Galilée.

Benítez Rojo, Antonio. 1968. "La tierra y el cielo." El escudo de hojas secas, 9–30. Havana: Unión de Escritores y Artistas de Cuba.

Bhabha, Homi. 1994. The Location of Culture. London: Routledge.

Birdsall, Nancy, Carol Graham, and Richard Sabot, eds. 1998. Beyond Tradeoffs: Market Reforms and Equitable Growth in Latin America. Washington: Inter-American Development Bank / Brookings Institution Press.

Blondet, Cecilia, and Carmen Montero. 1995. "La situación de la mujer en el Perú 1980–1994." Working Paper no. 68. Lima: Instituto de Estudios Peruanos.

Bock, Gisela and Pat Thane, eds. 1991. Maternity and Gender Policies: Women and the Rise of the European Welfare States, 1880s–1950s. New York: Routledge.

Boloña, Carlos. 1994. Políticas arancelarias en el Perú, 1880–1980. Lima: Instituto de Economía de Libre Mercado.

Bonfil, Guillermo. 1989. México profundo: Una civilización negada. Mexico City: Consejo Nacional para la Cultura y las Artes / Alianza.

Borges, Jorge Luis. 1999. "Funes, His Memory." Collected Fictions, trans. Andrew Hurley, 131–37. New York: Penguin.

Bourdieu, Pierre. 1977. Outline of a Theory of Practice. Cambridge: Cambridge University Press.

———. 1991. Language and Symbolic Power. Cambridge: Harvard University Press.

———. 1998. Practical Reason. Stanford: Stanford University Press.

———. 2000. Pascalian Meditations. Stanford: Stanford University Press.

Bourdieu, Pierre, and Loic Wacquant. 1992. An Invitation to Reflexive Sociology. Chicago: University of Chicago Press.

Bravo Castillo, Elsi. 1980. "Un enfoque sobre la política de salud en el Perú." La salud en el Perú. Cuaderno no. 28. Lima: Centro Latinoamericano de Trabajo Social.

Brehm, John. 1993. *The Phantom Respondents.* Ann Arbor: University of Michigan Press.

Brubaker, Rogers, and Frederick Cooper. 2000. "Beyond Identity." *Theory and Society* 29: 1–47.

Brunner, José Joaquín. 1978. "Apuntes sobre la figura cultural del pobre." Working Paper no. 69/78. Santiago: Facultad Latinoamericana de Ciencias Sociales.

Brusco, Valeria, Marcelo Nazareno, and Susan Stokes. 2004. "Vote Buying in Argentina." *Latin American Research Review* 39, no. 2: 66–88.

Burgwal, Gerrit. 1995. *Struggle of the Poor: Neighborhood Organization and Clientelist Practice in a Quito Squatter Settlement.* Amsterdam: CEDLA Thesis Publishers.

Burns, E. Bradford. 1983. *The Poverty of Progress: Latin America in the Nineteenth Century.* Berkeley: University of California Press.

Calavita, Kitty. 1992. *Inside the State: The Bracero Program, Immigration and the I.N.S.* New York: Routledge.

Caldeira, Teresa. 2000. *City of Walls: Crime, Segregation, and Citizenship in São Paulo.* Berkeley: University of California Press.

Campbell, Angus, Phillip Converse, Warren Miller, and Donald Stokes. 1960. *The American Voter.* New York: John Wiley and Sons.

Cancino, Ignacio. 1995. *Vendedores ambulantes en Ate-Vitarte: Formas de trabajo y reproducción.* Lima: EDAPROSPO.

Carbajal, Juan Carlos, and Pedro Francke. 2003. "La Seguridad Social en salud: Situación y posibilidades." *La salud como derecho ciudadano: Perspectivas y propuestas desde América Latina,* ed. Carlos Cáceres et al., 509–25. Lima: Universidad Peruana Cayetano Heredia.

Carsten, Janet, and Stephen Hugh-Jones. 1995. Introduction to *About the House: Lévi-Strauss and Beyond,* ed. Janet Carsten and Stephen Hugh-Jones, 1–46. Cambridge: Cambridge University Press.

Casamayor, Odette. 2002. "Les masques du Noir: Quelques approximations sur la présence du Noir cubain dans le récit cubain contemporain." *Cahiers d'études africaines* 62, no. 1: 7–29.

Castañeda, Jorge. 1993. *Utopia Unarmed: The Latin American Left after the Cold War.* New York: Alfred A. Knopf.

Castellanos, Alicia, coord. 2004. *Etnografía del prejuicio y la discriminación: Estudios de caso.* Mexico City: Universidad Autónoma Metropolitana.

Centeno, Miguel, and Fernando López-Alves, eds. 2001. *The Other Mirror: Grand Theory through the Lens of Latin America.* Princeton: Princeton University Press.

Chalmers, Douglas, Scott Martin, and Kerianne Piester. 1997. "Associative Networks: New Structures of Representation for the Popular Sector?" *The New Politics of Inequality in Latin America: Rethinking Participation and Representation,* ed. Carlos M. Vilas, Katherine Hite, Scott B. Martin, Kerianne Piester, and Monique Segarra, 542–82. Oxford: Oxford University Press.

Chalmers, Douglas, Carlos M. Vilas, Katherine Hite, Scott B. Martin, Kerianne Piester, and Monique Segarra, eds. 1997. *The New Politics of Inequality in Latin America: Rethinking Participation and Representation.* Oxford: Oxford University Press.

Chang, Jeff. 2005. *Can't Stop. Won't Stop: A History of the Hip-Hop Generation.* New York: St. Martin's.

Chávez, Leo R. 1992. *Shadowed Lives: Undocumented Immigrants in American Society.* New York: Hartcourt Brace.

Chiriboga, Manuel. 2004. "Desigualdad, exclusión étnica y participación política: El caso de CONAIE y Pachakutik en Ecuador." *Alteridades* 14, no. 28: 51–64.

Coatsworth, John H. 2005. "Structures, Endowments, and Institutions in the Economic History of Latin America." *Latin American Research Review* 40, no. 3: 126–44.

——. 2008. "Inequality, Institutions, and Economic Growth in Latin America." *Latin American Studies* 40: 545–69.

Coatsworth, John H., and Alan Taylor, eds. 1998. *Latin America and the World Economy since 1800.* Cambridge: Harvard University Press / David Rockefeller Center for Latin American Studies.

Collier, David, ed. 1979. *The New Authoritarianism in Latin America.* Princeton: Princeton University Press.

Contreras, Carlos. 2004. *El aprendizaje del capitalismo: Estudios de historia económica y social del Perú republicano.* Lima: Instituto de Estudios Peruanos.

Cope, Douglas. 1994. *The Limits of Racial Domination: Plebeian Society in Colonial Mexico City, 1660–1720.* Madison: University of Wisconsin Press.

Cotler, Julio. 1978. *Clases, estado y nación en el Perú.* Lima: Instituto de Estudios Peruanos.

Coubés, Marie-Laure, María Eugenia Zavala de Cosío, and René Zenteno, compilers. 2005. *Cambio demográfico y social en el México del siglo XX: Una perspectiva de historias de vida.* Tijuana: El Colegio de la Frontera Norte.

Cueto, Marcos. 1992. "Sanitation from Above: Yellow Fever and Foreign Intervention in Peru, 1919–1922." *Hispanic American Historical Review* 72, no. 1: 1–22.

——. 1994. *Missionaries of Science: The Rockefeller Foundation and Latin America.* Bloomington: Indiana University Press.

——. 1997. *El regreso de las epidemias: Salud y sociedad en el Perú del siglo xx.* Lima: Instituto de Estudios Peruanos.

——. 2001. *Culpa y coraje: Historia de las políticas sobre el VIH/sida en el Perú.* Lima: Universidad Peruana Cayetano Heredia.

——. 2002. "Social Medicine in the Andes, 1920–50." *The Politics of the Healthy Life: An International Perspective,* ed. Esteban Rodríguez-Ocaña, 181–96. Sheffield, England: European Association of the History of Medicine and Health Publications.

——. 2004. "The Origins of Primary Health Care and Selective Primary Health Care." *American Journal of Public Health* 94, no. 11: 1864–74.

——. n.d. "Visiones de medicina y exclusión en los Andes y los Amazonas peruanos en la década de los cuarenta." Lima, unpublished manuscript.

Daniel, Cletus E. 1981. *Bitter Harvest: A History of California Farmworkers, 1870–1941*. Ithaca: Cornell University Press.

Davidson, Judith R., and Steve Stein. 1988. "Economic Crisis, Social Polarization and Community Participation in Health Care." *Health Care in Peru: Resources and Policy*, ed. Dieter K. Zschock, 53–77. Boulder: Westview.

Davis, Shelton. 2002. "Indigenous Peoples, Poverty and Participatory Development: The Experience of the World Bank in Latin America." *Multiculturalism in Latin America: Indigenous Rights, Diversity and Democracy*, ed. R. Sieder, 227–51. Houndmills, United Kingdom: Palgrave Macmillan.

de Ferranti, David M., Guillermo E. Perry, Francisco H. G. Ferreira, and Michael Walton. 2004. *Inequality in Latin America: Breaking with History?* Washington: World Bank / Latin America and Caribbean Studies.

de la Cadena, Marisol. 2000. *Indigenous Mestizos: The Politics of Race and Culture in Cuzco, Peru 1919–1991*. Durham: Duke University Press.

Delli Carpini, Michael X., and Scott Keeter. 1996. *What Americans Know about Politics and Why It Matters*. New Haven: Yale University Press.

DESAL (Centro de Investigación y Acción Social para el Desarrollo Social en América Latina). 1969. *Marginalidad en América Latina: Un ensayo de diagnóstico*. Barcelona: Herder.

De Soto, Hernando. 1986. *El otro sendero*. Lima: Instituto de Libertad y Democracia.

Devisch, René. 1995. "Frenzy, Violence, and Ethical Renewal in Kinshasa." *Public Culture* 17: 593–629.

Dore, Elizabeth, and Maxine Molyneux, eds. 2000. *Hidden Histories of Gender and the State in Latin America*. Durham: Duke University Press.

Douglas, Mary, and S. Ney. 1998. *Missing Persons: A Critique of Personhood in the Social Sciences*. Berkeley: University of California Press / Russell Sage Foundation.

Drake, Paul W., and Eric Hershberg, eds. 2006. *State and Society in Conflict: Comparative Perspectives on Andean Crises*. Pittsburgh: University of Pittsburgh Press.

Duncan, Kenneth, and Ian Routledge, eds. 1977. *Land and Labour in Latin America*. Cambridge: Cambridge University Press.

Dussel, Enrique. 1998. *Ética de la liberación en la edad de globalización y la exclusión*. Madrid: Trotta.

Eckstein, Susan. [1977] 1988. *The Poverty of Revolution: The State and the Urban Poor in Mexico*. Princeton: Princeton University Press.

Eckstein, Susan, and Timothy Wickham-Crowley, eds. 2003. *Struggles for Social Rights in Latin America*. New York: Routledge.

Edelman, Marc. 1999. *Peasants against Globalization: Rural Movements in Costa Rica*. Stanford: Stanford University Press.

Edid, Maralyn. 1994. *Farm Labor Organizing: Trends and Prospects*. ILR paperback, no. 21. Ithaca, N.Y.: ILR Press.

Ehrick, Christine. 2005. *The Shield of the Weak: Feminism and the State in Uruguay, 1903–1933*. Albuquerque: University of New Mexico Press.

Eisinger, Peter K. 1973. "The Conditions of Protest Behavior in American Cities." *American Political Science Review* 67: 11–28.

Elias, Norbert. 2006. "Ensayo acerca de las relaciones entre establecidos y foras-teros," *Revista Española de Investigaciones Sociológicas*, 104, no. 3: 219–51.

Elias, Norbert, and John L. Scotson. 2009. *The Established and the Outsiders.* Dublin: University College of Dublin Press.

Engerman, Stanley, and Kenneth Sokoloff. 1997. "Factor Endowments, Institutions and Differential Paths of Growth among New World Economies." *How Latin America Fell Behind*, ed. Stephen Haber, 260–306. Stanford: Stanford University Press.

——. 2006. "Colonialism, Inequality, and Long-Run Paths of Development." *Understanding Poverty*, ed. A. Banerjee, R. Benabou, and D. Mookerjee, 37–62. Oxford: Oxford University Press.

Escobal, Javier, Jaime Saavedra, and Máximo Torero. 1998. "Los activos de los pobres." Working Paper no. 29. Lima: GRADE.

Escobar, Arturo. 1995. *Encountering Development: The Making and Unmaking of the Third World.* Princeton: Princeton University Press.

Esping-Anderson, Gøsta. 1990. *The Three Worlds of Welfare Capitalism.* Princeton: Princeton University Press.

Ewig, Christina. 2006a. "Global Processes, Local Consequences: Gender Equity and Health Sector Reform in Peru." *Social Politics* 13, no. 3: 427–55.

——. 2006b. "Hijacking Global Feminisms: Feminists, the Catholic Church and the Family Planning Debacle in Peru." *Feminist Studies* 32, no. 3: 632–59.

Fernandes, Sujatha. 2006. *Cuba Represent! Cuban Arts, State Power, and the Making of New Revolutionary Cultures.* Durham: Duke University Press.

Ferrer, Ada. 1999. *Insurgent Cuba: Race, Nation and Revolution, 1868–1898.* Chapel Hill: University of North Carolina Press.

Figueroa, Adolfo. 2001. *Reformas en sociedades desiguales: La experiencia peruana.* Lima: Fondo Editorial de la Pontificia Universidad Católica del Perú.

Figueroa, Adolfo, Teófilo Altamirano, and Denis Sulmont. 1996. *Exclusión social y desigualdad en el Perú.* Lima: OIT Oficina Regional para América Latina y el Caribe.

Firebaugh, Glenn. 2003. *The New Geography of Global Income Inequality.* Cambridge: Harvard University Press.

Folbre, Nancy. 2001. *The Invisible Heart: Economics and Family Values.* New York: New Press.

Fox, Jonathan. 1997. "The Difficult Transition from Clientelism to Citizenship: Lessons from Mexico." *The New Politics of Inequality in Latin America: Rethinking Participation and Representation*, ed. Douglas Chalmers, Carlos M. Vilas, Katherine Hite, Scott B. Martin, Kerianne Piester, and Monique Segarra, 391–420. Oxford: Oxford University Press.

Frank, André Gunder. 1967. *Capitalism and Underdevelopment in Latin America.* New York: Monthly Review Press.

Fraser, Nancy, and Axel Honneth. 2003. *Recognition or Redistribution? A Philosophical Exchange*. New York: Verso.

Frazer, Elizabeth, and Kenneth MacDonald. 2003. "Sex Difference in Political Knowledge in Britain." *Political Studies* 51: 67–83.

Friedland, William H., and Dorothy Nelkin. 1971. *Migrant: Agricultural Workers in America's Northeast*. New York: Holt, Rinehart and Winston.

Fuente, Alejandro de la. 2001. *A Nation for All: Race, Inequality, and Politics in Twentieth-Century Cuba*. Chapel Hill: University of North Carolina Press.

Furtado, Celso. 1970. *Economic Development of Latin America: A Survey from Colonial Times to the Cuban Revolution*. Cambridge: Cambridge University Press.

Galbraith, John Kenneth. 1979. *The Nature of Mass Poverty*. Cambridge: Harvard University Press.

Gallart, María Antonieta. 1999. "Restructuración productiva, educación y formación profesional." *Pobreza y desigualdad en América latina: Temas y nuevos desafíos*, comp. Víctor Tokman and Guillermo O'Donnell, 115–44. Buenos Aires: Paídos.

Gárate U., Werner, and Rosa Ana Ferrer G. 1994. *¿En qué trabajan las mujeres? Compendio estadístico 1980–1993*. Lima: ADEC-ATC.

García Canclini, Néstor. [1989] 1991. *Culturas híbridas: Estrategías para entrar y salir de la modernidad*. Mexico City: Grijalba.

García, Uriel. 1998. Former Minister of Health. Interview by author, 16 April 1998. Lima.

Gay, Robert. 1994. *Popular Organization and Democracy in Rio de Janeiro: A Tale of Two Favelas*. Philadelphia: Temple University Press.

George, Vic, and Paul Wilding. 2002. *Globalization and Human Welfare*. New York: Palgrave.

Gibson, Charles. 1964. *The Aztecs under Spanish Rule*. Stanford: Stanford University Press.

Glade, William. 1969. *The Latin American Economies: A Study of Their Institutional Evolution*. New York: Van Nostrand.

Goldberg, David Theo. 2002. *The Racial State*. Malden, Mass.: Blackwell.

Goldstein, Daniel M. 2004. *The Spectacular City: Violence and Performance in Urban Bolivia*. Durham: Duke University Press.

Gölte, Jurgen, and Norma Adams. 1990. *Los caballos de Troya de los invasores: Estrategías campesinas en la conquista de la Gran Lima*. Lima: Instituto de Estudios Peruanos.

González Casanova, Pablo. 1999. "La explotación global." *Globalidad: Una mirada alternativa*, coord. Ricardo Valero, 69–96. Mexico City: Porrúa.

———. 1964. *La Democracia en México*. Mexico City: Era.

González de la Rocha, Mercedes, and Alejandro Grinspun. 2001. "Private Adjustments: Households, Crisis and Work." *Choices for the Poor: Lessons from National Poverty Strategies*, ed. Alejandro Grinspun, 55–87. New York: United Nations Development Programme.

Goode, Judith, and Jeff Maskovsky, eds. 2001. *The New Poverty Studies: The Ethnography of Power, Politics, and Impoverished People in the United States*. New York: New York University Press.

Gootenberg, Paul. 2004. "Between a Rock and a Softer Place: Reflections on Some Recent Economic History of Latin America." *Latin American Research Review* 39, no. 2: 239–57.

Gordon, Linda, ed. 1990. *Women, the State and Welfare*. Madison: University of Wisconsin Press.

———. 1994. *Pitied but Not Entitled: Single Mothers and the History of Welfare, 1890–1935*. New York: Free Press.

Gray, Margaret. 2007. "Reproducing Inequality on the Farm: Race, Power, and Hiring." Paper presented at the American Political Science Association Meeting, Chicago, Illinois. August 2007.

Greenwood, Michael J. 1975. "Research on Internal Migration in the United States: A Survey." *Economic Literature* 13, no. 2: 397–433.

Griffin, Keith. 1969. *Underdevelopment in Spanish America*. London: Allen and Unwin.

Grindle, Merilee. 1977. "Patrons and Clients in the Bureaucracy: Career Networks in Mexico." *Latin American Research Review* 12, no. 1: 37–66.

Grossardt, Ted. 1996. "Harvest(ing) Hoboes: The Production of Labor Organization through the Wheat Harvest." *Agricultural History* 70, no. 2: 283–301.

Gudeman, Stephen, and Alberto Rivera. 1990. *Conversations in Colombia*. Cambridge: Cambridge University Press.

Guillén, Nicolas. 2002. "Prólogo a Sóngoro Cosongo." *Obra poética* 1, 1922–1958, 91–92. Havana: Letras Cubanas.

Guzmán, Alfredo. 2002. "Para mejorar la salud reproductiva." *La salud peruana en el siglo 21*, ed. Juan Arroyo, 185–238. Lima: Consorcio de Investigación Económica y Social, DFID, and the Policy Project.

Haber, Stephen. 2002. "Introduction: The New Institutional Economics and Latin American History." *The Mexican Economy, 1870–1930*, ed. Jeffery Bortz and Stephen Haber, 1–20. Stanford: Stanford University Press.

Haber, Stephen, Armando Razo, and Noel Maurer. 2003. *The Politics of Property Rights: Political Instability, Credible Commitments and Economic Growth in Mexico, 1876–1929*. Cambridge: Cambridge University Press.

Haber, Stephen, and William Summerhill, eds. 1997. *How Latin America Fell Behind: Essays on Economic Histories of Brazil and Mexico, 1800–1914*. Stanford: Stanford University Press.

Haggard, Stephen, and Robert R. Kaufman. 2008. *Development, Democracy, and Welfare States: Latin America, East Asia, and Eastern Europe*. Princeton: Princeton University Press.

Hahamovitch, Cindy. 1997. *The Fruits of Their Labor: Atlantic Coast Farmworkers and the Making of Migrant Poverty, 1870–1945*. Chapel Hill: University of North Carolina Press.

Hale Jr., Charles. 2006. *Más que un Indio: Racial Ambivalence and Neoliberal Multiculturalism in Guatemala*. Santa Fe: School of American Research.

Harris, Scott. 2000. "The Social Construction of Equality in Everyday Life." *Human Studies* 23: 371–93.

———. 2006. "Social Constructionism and Social Inequality." *Contemporary Ethnography* 35, no. 3: 223–35.

Harrison, Lawrence. 2000. *Underdevelopment Is a State of Mind: The Latin American Case*. Lanham, Md.: Center for International Affairs, Harvard University / University Press of America.

Harriss-White, Barbara. 2003. *India Working: Essays on Society and Economy*. Cambridge: Cambridge University Press.

Hartmann, Betsy. 1995. *Reproductive Rights and Wrongs: The Global Politics of Population Control*. Boston: South End.

Harvey, David. 1989. *The Condition of Postmodernity*. Oxford: Basil Blackwell.

Hasenbalg, Carlos, and Nelson do Valle. 1991. "Raça e oportunidades educacionais no Brasil." *Desigualdade racial no Brasil contemporáneo*, coord. Peggy Novell, 241–62. Belo Horizonte: CEDEPLAR/FACE.

Hayes, Bernadette. 2001. "Gender, Scientific Knowledge, and Attitudes toward the Environment: A Cross-National Analysis." *Political Research Quarterly* 54: 657–71.

Hernández Laos, José, and Jorge Velásquez. 2003. *Globalización, desigualdad y pobreza: Lecciones de la experiencia mexicana*. Mexico City: UAM/Plaza y Valdéz.

Hershberg, Eric, and Fred Rosen, eds. 2006. *Latin America after Neoliberalism: Turning the Tide in the Twenty-First Century*. New York: New Press.

Hirschman, Albert O. 1972. "Problem-Solving and Policy-Making: A Latin American Style?" *Journeys toward Progress: Studies of Economic Policy-Making in Latin America*, 227–50. New York: W. W. Norton.

———. 1981. "The Changing Tolerance for Inequality in the Course of Economic Growth." *Essays in Trespassing*, 39–58. Cambridge: Cambridge University Press.

———. 1987. "The Political Economy of Latin American Development: Seven Exercises in Retrospection." *Latin American Research Review* 22, no. 3: 7–36.

Hoffman, Kelly, and Miguel A. Centeno. 2003. "The Lopsided Continent: Inequality in Latin America." *Annual Review of Sociology* 29: 363–90.

Huber, Evelyne, and John D. Stephens. 2005. "Successful Policy Regimes? Political Economy, Politics and the Structure of Social Policy in Argentina, Chile, Uruguay, and Costa Rica." Paper delivered at the Conference "Democratic Governability," Kellogg Institute, Notre Dame, Indiana. 5–7 October 2005.

Huckfeldt, Robert, and John Sprague. 1995. *Citizens, Politics, and Social Communication*. Cambridge: Cambridge University Press.

Iglesias, Enrique. 1992. *Reflections on Economic Development*. Baltimore: John Hopkins University Press / Inter-American Development Bank.

Inter-American Development Bank. 1999. *Facing up to Inequality in Latin America: Report on Economic Progress in Latin America, 1998–1999*. Washington: Inter-American Development Bank.

Jacard, James, and Robert Turrisi. 2003. *Interaction Effects in Multiple Regression*. Thousand Oaks, Calif.: Sage.

Jaccoud, Luciana, and Nathalie Beghin. 2002. *Desigualdades raciais no Brasil: Um balanço de intervenção governamental*. Brasilia: Instituto da Pesquisa Econômica Aplicada.

Jacobs, Jane. 2000. *The Nature of Economics*. New York: Modern Library.

Jacobs, Lawrence R., and Theda Skocpol, eds. 2005. *Inequality and American Democracy: What We Know and What We Need to Learn*. New York: Russell Sage Foundation.

Jacobsen, Nils, and Cristóbal Aljovín de Losada, eds. 2005. *Political Cultures in the Andes, 1750–1950*. Durham: Duke University Press.

Jameson, Fredric. 1991. *Postmodernism, or, The Cultural Logic of Late Capitalism*. Durham: Duke University Press.

Johnson, John J. 1958. *Political Change in Latin America: The Emergence of Middle Sectors*. Stanford: Stanford University Press.

Joseph, Gilbert M., and Daniel Nugent, eds. 1994. *Everyday Forms of State Formation: Revolution and the Negotiation of Rule in Modern Mexico*. Durham: Duke University Press.

Karl, Terry. 2002. *The Vicious Circle of Inequality in Latin America*. Madrid: Instituto Juan March, Estudio 177.

Katz, Friedrich. 1972. *The Ancient American Empires*. New York: W. W. Norton.

Keller, Bill. 2006. *Class Matters*. New York: Times Books.

Kelley, Jonathan, and M. D. R. Evans. 1993. "The Legitimation of Inequality: Occupational Earnings in Nine Nations." *American Journal of Sociology* 99, no. 1: 75–125.

Kenski, Kate, and Kathleen Jamieson. 2000. "The Gender Gap in Political Knowledge: Are Women Less Knowledgeable Than Men about Politics?" *Everything You Think You Know about Politics . . . and Why You're Wrong*, ed. Kathleen Jamieson, 83–89. New York: Basic.

Klarén, Peter F. 2000. *Peru: Society and Nationhood in the Andes*. New York: Oxford University Press.

Korzeniewicz, Roberto P., and William Smith. 2000. "Poverty, Inequality and Growth in Latin America: Searching for the High Road to Globalization." *Latin American Research Review* 35, no. 3: 7–54.

Koven, Seth, and Sonya Michel. 1993. *Mothers of the New World: Maternalist Politics and the Origins of the Welfare State*. New York: Routledge.

Krosnick, Jon, and Michael Milburn. 1990. "Psychological Determinants of Political Opinionation." *Social Cognition* 8: 49–72.

Lamont, Michèle, and Marcel Fournier, eds. 1992. *Cultivating Differences. Symbolic Boundaries and the Making of Inequality*. Chicago: University of Chicago Press.

Laplantine, François, and Alexis Nouss. 1997. *Le métissage*. Paris: Flammarion.

Lardner, James, and David Smith. 2006. *Inequality Matters: The Growing Economic Divide in America and Its Poisonous Consequences*. New York: New Press.

Larson, Brooke. 2005. "Capturing Indian Bodies, Hearths and Minds: The Gendered

Politics of Rural School Reform in Bolivia 1920s–1940s." *Natives Making Nation: Gender, Indigeneity and the State in the Andes*, ed. Andrew Canessa, 32–59. Tucson: University of Arizona Press.

Lau, Richard, and David Redlawsk. 2001. "Advantages and Disadvantages of Cognitive Heuristics in Political Decision Making." *American Journal of Political Science* 45, no. 4: 951–71.

Lazarsfeld, Paul, Bernard Berelson, and Hazel Gaudet. 1944. *The People's Choice*. New York: Columbia University Press.

Lewis, Oscar. 1961. *The Children of Sanchez*. New York: Vintage.

Lewis-Beck, Michael, and Richard Nadeau. 2004. "Split-Ticket Voting: The Effects of Cognitive Madisonianism." *Politics* 66, no. 1: 97–112.

Lima, Venicio A. de. 1993. "Brazilian Television in the 1989 Presidential Campaign: Constructing a President." *Television, Politics, and the Transition to Democracy in Latin America*, ed. Thomas Skidmore, 97–117. Washington: Woodrow Wilson Center Press.

Linder, Marc. 1992. *Migrant Workers and Minimum Wages: Regulating the Exploitation of Agricultural Labor in the United States*. Boulder: Westview.

Locay, Luis. 1988. "Medical Doctors: Determinants of Location." *Health Care in Peru: Resources and Policy*, ed. Dieter K. Zschock, 133–63. Boulder: Westview.

Lomnitz, Claudio. 2001a. *Deep Mexico, Silent Mexico: An Anthropology of Nationalism*. Minneapolis: University of Minnesota Press.

———. 2001b. "Nationalism as a Practical System: Benedict Anderson's Theory of Nationalism from the Vantage of Spanish America." *The Other Mirror*, ed. M. Centeno and F. López-Alvez, 329–60. Princeton: Princeton University Press.

Love, Joseph. 1996. *Crafting the Third World: Theorizing Underdevelopment in Rumania and Brazil*. Stanford: Stanford University Press.

———. 2005. "The Rise and Decline of Economic Structuralism: New Dimensions." *Latin American Research Review* 40, no. 3: 100–25.

Lovell, Peggy, coord. 1991. *Desigualdade racial no Brasil contemporâneo*. Belo Horizonte: CEDEPLAR/FACE.

———. 2000a. "Race, Gender, and Regional Labor Market Inequalities in Brazil." *Review of Social Economy* 58, no. 3: 277–93.

———. 2000b. "Gender, Race and the Struggle for Social Justice in Brazil." *Latin American Perspectives* 115, no. 27: 85–113.

Lupia, Arthur, and Mathew McCubbins. 1998. *The Democratic Dilemma: Can Citizens Learn What They Need to Know?* Cambridge: Cambridge University Press.

———. 2000. "The Institutional Foundations of Political Competence: How Citizens Learn What They Need to Know." *Elements of Reason: Cognition, Choice, and the Bounds of Rationality*, ed. Arthur Lupia, Mathew D. McCubbins, and Samuel L. Popkin, 47–66. Cambridge: Cambridge University Press.

Lupia, Arthur, Mathew McCubbins, and Samuel Popkin, eds. 2000. *Elements of Reason:*

Cognition, Choice, and the Bounds of Rationality. Cambridge: Cambridge University Press.

Luskin, Robert. 2002. "From Denial to Extenuation (and Finally Beyond): Political Sophistication and Citizen Performance." *Thinking about Political Psychology,* ed. James Kuklinski, 217–52. Cambridge: Cambridge University Press.

Luskin, Robert, James Fishkin, and Roger Jowell. 2002. "Considered Opinions: Deliberative Polling in Britain." *British Journal of Political Science* 32: 455–87.

Madrid, Raul L. 2003. *Retiring the State: The Politics of Pension Privatization in Latin America and Beyond.* Stanford: Stanford University Press.

Mahler, Sarah J. 1995. *American Dreaming: Immigrant Life on the Margins.* Princeton: Princeton University Press.

Mainwaring, Scott. 1995. "Brazil: Weak Parties, Feckless Democracy." *Building Democratic Institutions: Party Systems in Latin America* ed. Scott Mainwaring and Timothy Scully, 354–98. Stanford: Stanford University Press.

Majka, Linda C., and Theo J. Majka. 1982. *Farm Workers, Agribusiness, and the State.* Philadelphia: Temple University Press.

Mallon, Florencia. 1995. *Peasant and Nation: The Making of Postcolonial Mexico and Peru.* Berkeley: University of California Press.

Malloy, James M. 1979. *The Politics of Social Security in Brazil.* Pittsburgh: University of Pittsburgh Press.

Mannarelli, María Emma. 1999. *Limpias y modernas: Género, higiene y cultura en Lima del novecientos.* Lima: Centro Flora Tristán.

Martí, José. 1963. "El plato de lentejas." *Política y revolución,* 26–30. Vol. 3 of *Obras completas.* Havana: Editorial Nacional de Cuba.

Martin, Scott. 1997. "Beyond Corporatism: New Patterns of Representation in the Brazilian Auto Industry." *The New Politics of Inequality in Latin America: Rethinking Participation and Representation,* ed. Douglas Chalmers, Carlos M. Vilas, Katherine Hite, Scott B. Martin, Kerianne Piester, and Monique Segarra, 45–71. Oxford: Oxford University Press.

Marzal, Manuel, Catalina Romero, and José Sánchez, eds. 2004. *Para entender la religión en el Perú.* Lima: Fondo Editorial de la Pontificia Universidad Católica del Perú.

Massey, Douglas S., Rafael Alarcón, Jorge Durand, and Humberto González. 1987. *Return to Aztlán: The Social Process of International Migration from Western Mexico.* Berkeley: University of California Press.

Massey, Douglas S., Jorge Durand, and Nolan J. Malone. 2002. *Beyond Smoke and Mirrors: Mexican Immigration in an Era of Economic Integration.* New York: Russell Sage Foundation.

Mateo, D. 2003. "Todos los negros no tomamos café: Conversación con Roberto Diago." *La Gaceta de Cuba* (May–June): 22–26.

Mauro Machuca, Raúl. 2002. *Cambios de la pobreza en el Perú: 1991–1998.* Lima: CIES/DESCO.

Mayer, Enrique. 2005. *Casa, chacra y dinero: Economías domésticas y ecología en los Andes*. Lima: Instituto de Estudios Peruanos.

McAdam, Doug. 1982. *Political Process and the Development of Black Insurgency, 1930–1970*. Chicago: University of Chicago Press.

McClintock, Cynthia. 1999. "Peru: Precarious Regimes, Authoritarian and Democratic." *Democracy in Developing Countries: Latin America*, ed. Larry Diamond, Jonathan Hartlyn, Juan Linz, and Seymour Martin Lipset, 309–65. Boulder: Lynne Rienner.

McWilliams, Carey. 1939. *Factories in the Field: The Story of Migratory Farm Labor in California*. Boston: Little, Brown.

Melo da Silva, Lea. 1991. "Todos somos iguais?" *Desigualdade racial no Brasil contemporáneo*, Peggy Lovell, coord., 161–75. Belo Horizonte: CEDEPLAR/FACE.

Meneley, Annette. 1996. *Tournaments of Value: Sociability and Hierarchy in a Yemen Town*. Toronto: University of Toronto Press.

Mesa-Lago, Carmelo. 1978. *Social Security in Latin America: Pressure Groups, Stratification, and Inequality*. Pittsburgh: University of Pittsburgh Press.

——. 1989. *Ascent to Bankruptcy: Financing Social Security in Latin America*. Pittsburgh: University of Pittsburgh Press.

Mettler, Suzanne. 1998. *Dividing Citizens: Gender and Federalism in New Deal Public Policy*. Ithaca: Cornell University Press.

Miguel, Luis Felipe. 1999. "Mídia e eleições: A campanha de 1998 na Rede Globo." *Dados* 42, no. 2: 253–76.

Milanovic, Branko. 2005. *Worlds Apart: Measuring International and Global Inequality*. Princeton: Princeton University Press.

Milkman, Ruth. 2006. *L.A. Story: Immigrant Workers and the Future of the U.S. Labor Movement*. New York: Russell Sage Foundation.

Mink, Gwendolyn. 1995. *The Wages of Motherhood: Inequality in the Welfare State, 1917–1942*. Ithaca: Cornell University Press.

Mitchell, Timothy. 2002. *Rule of Experts: Egypt, Techno-Politics, and Modernity*. Berkeley: University of California Press.

Mondak, Jeffery, and Mary Anderson. 2004. "The Knowledge Gap: A Reexamination of Gender-Based Differences in Political Knowledge." *Politics* 66, no. 2: 492–512.

Monge, Álvaro and Renato Ravina. 2003. "Más allá del componente objetivo en la medición de la pobreza: Análisis geográfico de las dimensiones objetiva y subjetiva de la pobreza en el Perú." *Buscando el bienestar de los pobres: ¿Cuán lejos estamos?*, ed. Enrique Vásquez and Diego Winkelried, 61–100. Lima: Centro de Investigación, Universidad del Pacífico.

Mooney, Patrick H., and Theo J. Majka. 1995. *Farmers' and Farmworkers' Movements: Social Protest in American Agriculture*. New York: Twayne.

Moreiras, Alberto. 2001. *The Exhaustion of Difference: The Politics of Latin American Cultural Studies*. Durham: Duke University Press.

Morgenstern, Scott, and Elizabeth Zechmeister. 2001. "Better the Devil you Know than the Saint you Don't? Risk Propensity and Vote Choice in Mexico," *Journal of Politics* 63, no. 1: 93–119.

Murillo, M. Victoria. 1997. "Union Politics, Market-Oriented Reforms, and the Reshaping of Argentine Corporatism." *The New Politics of Inequality in Latin America: Rethinking Participation and Representation,* ed. Douglas Chalmers, Carlos M. Vilas, Katherine Hite, Scott B. Martin, Kerianne Piester, and Monique Segarra, 72–94. Oxford: Oxford University Press.

Murphy, Arthur, and Alex Stepick. 1991. *Social Inequality in Oaxaca: A History of Resistance and Change.* Philadelphia: Temple University Press.

Murphy, Arthur D., Colleen Blanchard, and Jennifer A. Hill, eds. 2001. *Latino Workers in the Contemporary South.* Athens: University of Georgia Press.

Nelkin, Dorothy. 1970. *On the Season: Aspects of the Migrant Labor System.* Ithaca: New York State School of Industrial and Labor Relations, Cornell University.

Nepantla: Views from the South 1, no. 1. 2000. Durham: Duke University Press.

Niemi, Richard, and Herbert Weisberg, eds. 2001. *Controversies in Voting Behavior.* Washington: Congressional Quarterly Press.

Núñez, Javier, and Roberto Gutiérrez. 2004. "Classism, Discrimination and Meritocracy in the Labor Market: The Case of Chile." Working Paper no. 208. Santiago: Universidad de Chile, Department of Economía.

Nussbaum, Martha. 1993. "Non-Relative Virtues: An Aristotelian Approach." *The Quality of Life,* ed. Martha C. Nussbaum and Amartya Sen, 242–69. Oxford: Clarendon.

O'Connor, Julia S. 1996. "From Women in the Welfare State to Gendering Welfare State Regimes." *Current Sociology* 44, no. 2: 1–124.

O'Connor, Julia S., Ann Shola Orloff, and Sheila Shaver. 1999. *States, Markets, Families: Gender, Liberalism and Social Policy in Australia, Canada, Great Britain and the United States.* Cambridge: Cambridge University Press.

O'Donnell, Guillermo. 1999. "Pobreza y desigualdad en América Latina: Algunas reflexiones políticas." *Pobreza y desigualdad en América latina: Temas y nuevos desafíos,* comp. Víctor Tokman and Guillermo O'Donnell, 69–93. Buenos Aires: Paidós.

Oliveira, Clovis L. P. 1999. "Struggling for a Place: Race, Gender and Class in Political Elections in Brazil." *Race in Contemporary Brazil: From Indifference to Inequality,* ed. Rebecca Reichmann, 167–77. University Park: Pennsylvania State University Press.

Orihuela Paredes, Víctor. 1980. "Diagnóstico general de salud." *La salud en el Perú,* 1–15. Cuaderno no. 28. Lima: Centro Latinoamericano de Trabajo Social.

Ortiz, Fernando. 1983. *Contrapunteo cubano del tabaco y el azúcar.* Havana: Ciencias Sociales.

Ortner, Sherry B. 1996. *Making Gender: The Politics and Erotics of Culture.* Boston: Beacon.

Oxfam America. 2004. *Like Machines in the Fields: Workers without Rights in American Agriculture.* Boston: Oxfam America.

Papademetriou, Demetrios G., and Gerald W. Hopple. 1982. "Causal Modeling in

International Migration Research: A Methodological Prolegomenon." *Quality and Quantity* 16, no. 5: 369–402.

Parker, David S. 1998. *The Idea of the Middle Class: White-Collar Workers and Peruvian Society, 1900–1950.* University Park: Pennsylvania State University Press.

Patai, Daphne. 1988. *Brazilian Women Speak: Contemporary Life Stories.* New Brunswick: Rutgers University Press.

Peralva, Angelina. 2000. "Égalité et nouvelles figures du conflit urbain au Brésil." *Cahiers des Amériques Latines* 35, no. 3: 75–90.

Pérez Saínz, Juan Pablo, and Minor Mora. 2007. "Las desigualdades estructurales en América Latina: Una propuesta analítica y metodológica alternativa." Paper presented at Congreso Latinoamericano y Caribeño de Ciencias Sociales, Quito, October 2007.

Perlman, Janice. 1976. *The Myth of Marginality: Urban Poverty and Politics in Rio de Janeiro.* Berkeley: University of California Press.

———. 2004. "The Metamorphosis of Marginality in Rio de Janeiro." *Latin American Research Review* 39, no. 1: 183–204.

———. 2010. *Four Decades of Living on the Edge in Rio de Janeiro.* Oxford: Oxford University Press.

Pfeffer, Max J., and Pilar A. Parra. 2004. "Immigrants and the Community." Report no. 1, November. Ithaca: Cornell University.

Piore, Michael J. 1979. *Birds of Passage: Migrant Labor and Industrial Societies.* Cambridge: Cambridge University Press.

Piven, Frances Fox, and Richard A. Cloward. 1979. *Poor People's Movements: Why They Succeed, How They Fail.* New York: Pantheon.

Pogge, Thomas. 2005. "The First UN Millennium Goal: A Cause for Celebration?" *Real World Justice: Grounds, Principles, Human Rights, and Social Institutions,* ed. Andreas Follesdal and Thomas Pogge, 317–38. Dordrecht, Netherlands: Springer.

Poole, Deborah. 1997. *Vision, Race and Modernity: A Visual Economy of the Andes.* Princeton: Princeton University Press.

Popkin, Samuel. 1991. *The Reasoning Voter.* Chicago: University of Chicago Press.

Portes, Alejandro. 1985. "Latin American Class Structures: Their Composition and Change during the Last Decade." *Latin American Research Review* 20, no. 1: 7–39.

Portes, Alejandro, and Robert L. Bach. 1985. *Latin Journey: Cuban and Mexican Immigrants in the United States.* Berkeley: University of California Press.

Portes, Alejandro, and Kelly Hoffman. 2003. "Latin American Class Structures: Their Composition and Change during the Neoliberal Era." *Latin American Research Review* 38, no. 1: 41–82.

Portes, Alejandro, and John Walton. 1981. *Labor, Class and the International System.* New York: Academic.

Potter, Russel A. 1995. *Spectacular Vernaculars: Hip-Hop and the Politics of Postmodernism.* Albany: State University of New York Press.

Pribble, Jennifer. 2006. "The Politics of Women's Welfare in Chile and Uruguay." *Latin American Research Review* 41, no. 2: 4–111.

Puerto Rican/Hispanic Task Force. 1995. *Separate and Unequal: New York's Farmworkers.* Albany: New York State Senate-Assembly Puerto Rican/Hispanic Task Force, Joint Temporary Task Force on Farmworker Issues.

Quadagno, Jill. 1996. *The Color of Welfare: How Racism Undermined the War on Poverty.* New York: Oxford University Press.

Rahn, Wendy. 1993. "The Role of Partisan Stereotypes in Information Processing about Political Candidates." *American Journal of Political Science* 37: 472–96.

Reich, Michael, David M. Gordon, and Richard C. Edwards. 1973. "A Theory of Labor Market Segmentation." *American Economic Review* 63: 359–65.

Reichmann, Rebecca, ed. 1999. *Race in Contemporary Brazil: From Indifference to Inequality.* University Park: Pennsylvania State University Press.

Reygadas, Luis. 2008. *La apropiación: Destejiendo las redes de la desigualdad.* Barcelona: Anthropos.

Riofrío, Gustavo, and J. C. Driant. 1987. *¿Qué vivienda han construido? Nuevos problemas en viejas barriadas.* Lima: CIDAP/TAREA/IFEA.

Robinson, William. 2006. "Promoting Polyarchy in Latin America: The Oxymoron of 'Market Democracy,'" *Latin America After Neoliberalism: Turning the Tide in the 21st Century?* ed. Eric Hershberg and Fred Rosen, 96–119. New York: New Press.

Roemer, Milton I. 1964. *La atención médica en America Latina.* Secretaría General de la OEA. Washington: Unión Panamericana

——. 1969. *The Organization of Medical Care under Social Security: A Study Based upon the Experience of Eight Countries.* Geneva: International Labour Office.

Rose, Tricia. 1994. *Black Noise.* Hanover, N.H.: Wesleyan University Press.

Rosemblatt, Karin. 2000. *Gendered Compromises: Political Cultures and the State in Chile, 1920–1950.* Chapel Hill: University of North Carolina Press.

Rothenberg, Daniel. 2000. *With These Hands: The Hidden World of Migrant Farmworkers Today.* Berkeley: University of California Press.

Roxborough, Ian. 1992. "Neo-Liberalism: Limits and Alternatives." *Third World Quarterly* 13, no. 3: 421–40.

——. 1994. "The Urban Working Class and Labor Movement in Latin America since 1930." *The Cambridge History of Latin America*, Vol. 6, ed. L. Bethell, 307–78. Cambridge: Cambridge University Press.

Rubin, Jeffrey W. 1997. *Decentering the Regime: Ethnicity, Radicalism, and Democracy in Juchitán, Mexico.* Durham: Duke University Press.

Rueschemeyer, Dietrich, Evelyne Huber Stephens, and John D. Stephens. 1992. *Capitalist Development and Democracy.* Chicago: University of Chicago Press.

Saavedra, Jaime, and Juan Chacaltana. 2001. *Exclusión y oportunidad: Jóvenes urbanos y su inserción en el mercado de trabajo y en el mercado de capacitación.* Lima: GRADE.

Sassen, Saskia. 1991. *Global Cities: New York, London, Tokyo.* Princeton: Princeton University Press.

Sautu, Ruth, ed. 2004. *Catálogo de prácticas corruptas: Corrupción, confianza y democracia.* Buenos Aires: Lumiere.

Sawyer, Mark Q. 2006. *Racial Politics in Post-Revolutionary Cuba.* New York: Cambridge University Press.

Sayad, Abdelmalek. 2004. *The Suffering of the Immigrant.* Malden, Mass.: Polity.

Schmitter, Phillippe. 1974. "Still the Century of Corporatism?" *Review of Politics* 36: 85–131.

Schoultz, Lars. 1998. *Beneath the United States: A History of U.S. Policy toward Latin America.* Cambridge: Harvard University Press.

Secretaría Técnica de la Comisión Interministerial de Asuntos Sociales. 2005. *Perú: Políticas para superar la pobreza.* Lima: Gobierno del Perú, Comisión Interministerial de Asuntos Sociales.

Sen, Amartya. 1999. *Development as Freedom.* New York: Alfred A. Knopf

Sheahan, John. 1999. *Searching for a Better Society: The Peruvian Economy from 1950.* University Park: Pennsylvania State University Press.

Shugart, Matthew, Melody Valdini, and Kati Suominen. 2005. "Looking for Locals: Voter Information Demands and Personal Vote-Earning Attributes of Legislators under Proportional Representation." *American Journal of Political Science* 49, no. 2: 437–49.

Shumway, Nicholas. 1991. *The Invention of Argentina.* Berkeley: University of California Press.

Sieder, Rachel, ed. 2002. *Multiculturalism in Latin America: Indigenous Rights, Diversity and Democracy.* Houndmills, England: Palgrave Macmillan.

Singer, Judith. 1998. "Using SAS PROC MIXED to Fit Multilevel Models, Hierarchical Models, and Individual Growth Curve Models." *Educational and Behavioral Statistics* 24, no. 4: 323–55.

Sjaastad, Larry A. 1962. "The Costs and Returns of Human Migration." *Political Economy* 70, no. 5: 80–93.

Skidmore, Thomas W. [1974] 1993. *Black into White: Race and Nationality in Brazilian Thought.* Durham: Duke University Press.

Skocpol, Theda. 1992. *Protecting Soldiers and Mothers: The Political Origins of Social Policy in the United States.* Cambridge: Belknap / Harvard University Press.

Smith, Peter H. 2005. *Democracy in Latin America: Political Change in Comparative Perspective.* New York: Oxford University Press.

Sniderman, Paul. 2000. "Taking Sides: A Fixed Choice Theory of Political Reasoning." *Elements of Reason: Cognition, Choice, and the Bounds of Rationality,* ed. Arthur Lupia, Mathew D. McCubbins, and Samuel L. Popkin, 67–84. Cambridge: Cambridge University Press.

Sokoloff, Kenneth, and Stanley Engerman. 2000. "History Lessons: Institutions, Factors Endowments, and Paths of Development in the New World." *Economic Perspectives* 14, no. 3: 217–32.

Sommers, Doris. 1991. *Fictional Foundations: The National Romances of Latin America.* Berkeley: University of California Press.

Stein, Stanley, and Barbara Stein. 1970. *The Colonial Heritage of Latin America*. New York: Oxford University Press.

Stepan, Nancy. 1991. *The Hour of Eugenics: Race, Gender and Nation in Latin America*. Ithaca: Cornell University Press.

Stevens, Willy. 1999. *Desafíos para América Latina*. Mexico City: Taurus.

Stiglitz, Joseph E. 2002. *Globalization and Its Discontents*. New York: W. W. Norton.

Szekely, Miguel, and Marianne Hilgert. 1999. "What's Behind the Inequality We Measure? An Investigation Using Latin American Data." Luxembourg Income Study, Working Paper no. 234. Syracuse: Luxembourg Income Study.

Task Force Report: Farmworker Collective Bargaining. 1991. *Agricultural Labor Markets in New York State and Implications for Labor Policy*. Ithaca: Cornell University.

Thomas, Robert J. 1985. *Citizenship, Gender, and Work: The Social Organization of Industrial Agriculture*. Berkeley: University of California Press.

Thorp, Rosemary. 1996. "A Long-Run Perspective on Short-Run Stabilization: The Experience of Peru." *The Peruvian Economy and Structural Adjustment: Past, Present and Future*, ed. Efraín Gonzáles de Olarte, 59–75. Miami: University of Miami, North-South Center Press.

——. 1998. *Progress, Poverty and Exclusion: An Economic History of Latin America*. Washington: Inter-American Development Bank.

Thurner, Mark. 1997. *From Two Republics to One Divided: Contradictions of Postcolonial Nationmaking in Andean Peru*. Durham: Duke University Press.

Tilly, Charles. 1998. *Durable Inequality*. Berkeley: University of California Press.

——. 2007. *Democracy*. Cambridge: Cambridge University Press.

Todaro, Michael. 1976. *International Migration in Developing Countries: A Review of Theory, Evidence, Methodology and Research Priorities*. Geneva: International Labor Office.

Tokman, Víctor, and Guillermo O'Donnell, eds. 1998. *Poverty and Inequality in Latin America: Issues and New Challenges*. Terra Haute, Ind.: University of Notre Dame Press.

Tulchin, Joseph, ed. 2001. *Democratic Governance and Social Inequality*. Boulder: Lynne Rienner.

Tutino, John. 1989. *From Insurrection to Revolution in Mexico, 1750–1940*. Princeton: Princeton University Press.

United Nations Development Programme (UNDP). 2003. *Human Development Report 2003*. New York: United Nations Development Programme / Oxford University Press.

van den Berghe, Pierre, and George Primov. 1977. *Inequality in the Peruvian Andes: Class and Ethnicity in Cuzco*. Columbia: University of Missouri Press.

Varillas, Alberto, and Patricia Mostajo. 1990. *La situación poblacional peruana: Balance y perspectivas*. Lima: INANDEP.

Vásquez, Enrique, Carlos E. Aramburú, Carlos Figueroa, and Carlos Parodi. 2001. *Los desafíos de la lucha contra la pobreza extrema en el Perú*. Lima: Centro de Investigación, Universidad del Pacífico.

Vásquez, Enrique, and Enrique Mendizábal, eds. 2002. ¿Los niños . . . primero? El gasto público social focalizado en niños y niñas en el Perú 1990–2000. Lima: Centro de Investigación, Universidad del Pacífico.

Vásquez, Enrique, and Gustavo Riesco. 2000. "Los programas sociales que 'alimentan' a medio Perú." Políticas sociales en el Perú: Nuevos aportes, ed. Felipe Portocarrero S., 89–151. Lima: RDCSP.

Verba, Sidney, Nancy Burns, and Kay Schlozman. 1997. "Knowing and Caring about Politics: Gender and Political Engagement." Politics 59: 1051–57.

Verba, Sidney, Steven Kelman, Gary Orren, Ichiro Miyake, Joji Watanuki, Ikuo Kabashima, and G. Donald Ferree. 1987. Elites and the Idea of Equality: A Comparison of Japan, Sweden, and the United States. Cambridge: Harvard University Press.

Verdera V., Francisco. 1997. "Seguridad social y pobreza en el Perú: Una aproximación." Working Paper no. 84. Lima: Instituto de Estudios Peruanos.

Vuskovic, Pedro. 1996. Pobreza y desigualdad en América Latina. Mexico City: Universidad Nacional Autónoma de México.

Wade, Peter. 1997. Race and Ethnicity in Latin America. London: Pluto.

Waitzkin, Howard. 1998. "Is Our Work Dangerous? Should It Be?" Health and Social Behavior 39, no. 1: 7–17.

Waitzkin, Howard, Celia Iriart, Alfredo Estrada, and Silvia Lamadrid. 2001. "Social Medicine Then and Now: Lessons from Latin America." American Journal of Public Health 91, no. 10: 1592–1601.

Wallerstein, Immanuel. 1998. Utopistics: Or, Historical Choices for the Twenty-First Century. New York: New Press.

Walzer, Michael. 1983. Spheres of Justice. New York: Basic.

Weinstein, Barbara S. 2008. "Developing Inequality." American Historical Association Presidential Address. American Historical Review 113, no. 1, 1–18.

Weismantel, Mary. 2001. Cholas and Pishtacos: Stories of Race and Sex in the Andes. Chicago: University of Chicago Press.

Wolf, Eric R. 1999. Envisioning Power: Ideologies of Dominance and Crisis. Berkeley: University of California Press.

Wolf, Martin. 2004. Why Globalization Works: The Case for the Global Market Economy. New Haven: Yale University Press.

Wolff, Edwin N. [1995] 2001. Top Heavy: A Study of Increasing Inequality of Wealth in America. New York: Twentieth Century Fund.

World Bank. 2003. Inequality in Latin America and the Caribbean: Breaking with History? Washington: International Bank for Reconstruction and Development / World Bank.

Yamada, Gustavo. 2005. Horas de trabajo: Determinantes y dinámica en el Perú urbano. Lima: Consorcio de Investigaciones Económicas y Sociales.

Yashar, Deborah. 2005. Contesting Citizenship in Latin America: The Rise of Indigenous Movements and the Postliberal Challenge. Cambridge: Cambridge University Press.

Ypeij, Annelou. 2000. *Producing against Poverty: Female and Male Micro-Entrepreneurs in Lima, Peru*. Amsterdam: Amsterdam University Press.

Zabin, Carol, Michael Kearney, Anna García, David Runsten, and Carole Nagengast. 1993. *Mixtec Migrants in California Agriculture: A New Cycle of Poverty*. Davis: California Institute for Rural Studies.

Zárate, Patricia, ed. 2005. *¿Hay lugar para los pobres en el Perú? Las relaciones Estado-sociedad y el rol de la cooperación internacional*. Lima: DFID.

Zulawski, Ann. 2000. "Hygiene and 'The Indian Problem': Ethnicity and Medicine in Bolivia, 1910–1920." *Latin American Research Review* 35, no. 2: 107–29.

Zúñiga, Victor, and Rubén Hernández-León, eds. 2005. *New Destinations of Mexican Immigration in the United States: Community Formation, Local Responses and Inter-Group Relations*. New York: Russell Sage Foundation.

Zurbano-Torres, Roberto. 2008. "'¡Mami, no quiero más reggaetón!' o el Nuevo perre(te)o intelectual." *Movimiento: Revista Cubana de hip-hop* 6: 4–12.

JEANINE ANDERSON, a dual U.S.-Peruvian national, earned her doctorate in Anthropology from Cornell University in 1978. She studied Peru at the end of the 1960s for a dissertation project on middle-class women. Her research and applied work, supported by various nongovernmental organizations, has centered on urban and rural poverty, as understood within complex social, political, economic, and cultural systems. She is a professor of anthropology at the Catholic University of Peru (PUPC, Lima).

JAVIER AUYERO, Joe R. and Teresa Lozano Long Professor of Latin American Sociology at the University of Texas, Austin, taught at Stony Brook University until 2008. He is a political ethnographer from Argentina who studied with Charles Tilly at the New School. His books include *Poor People's Politics* (Duke, 2001), *Contentious Lives* (Duke, 2003), and *Routine Politics and Collective Violence in Argentina* (2007). He is currently editor of *Qualitative Sociology*.

ODETTE CASAMAYOR, an assistant professor at the University of Connecticut, Storrs, was raised in Cuba. She received her doctorate in Language Arts and Literature from the School of Advanced Studies in Social Sciences (EHESS), in Paris, concentrating on contemporary Latin American culture. In 2005, she was a Rockefeller Fellow at the Latin American and Caribbean Studies Center at Stony Brook University. In 2003, her essay "Negros de papel: Algunas apariciones del negro en la narrativa cubana después de 1959" received the Juan Rulfo literary award from Radio France Internationale.

CHRISTINA EWIG is an associate professor of women's studies and political science at the University of Wisconsin, Madison. Her book *Second-Wave Neoliberalism: Gender, Race, and Health Sector Reforms in Peru* (2010) was supported by a Fulbright New Century Scholars fellowship. As a Rockefeller Fellow at Stony Brook University, she worked on a comparative history project analyzing the role of gender and race in the development of Latin American health and pension policies. Her publications have appeared in the *Latin American Research Review*, *Social Politics*, and *Feminist Studies*.

PAUL GOOTENBERG, with a doctorate from the University of Chicago, is a professor of history and sociology at Stony Brook University and a specialist on modern Peruvian history. As director of Stony Brook's Latin American and Caribbean Studies

Center (2000–2005), he initiated the Rockefeller-supported program "Durable Inequalities in Latin America." Gootenberg's books include *Between Silver and Guano* (1989), *Imagining Development* (1993), and the edited volume *Cocaine: Global Histories* (1999). His latest book, *Andean Cocaine: The Making of a Global Drug* (2008), is a commodity history of cocaine between 1850 and 1980.

MARGARET GRAY, who received her doctorate from the City University of New York, is an assistant professor of political science at Adelphi University. In 2005–2006, she was a Rockefeller Fellow at the Latin American and Caribbean Studies Center at Stony Brook University. Her work on Latino and labor politics focuses on immigration, transnationalism, race, and ethnicity and will appear as a monograph with Cornell University Press. Along with Carlos Decena, she guest-edited an issue for *Social Text* (88, fall 2006), "The Border Next Door: New Latinos in New York State." Gray has also long worked for nonprofits on economic-justice issues.

ERIC HERSHBERG, former president (2008–2009) of the Latin American Studies Association (LASA), is a professor of government and director of the Center for Latin American and Latino Studies at American University. He has also taught at Simon Fraser University, Princeton, Columbia, New York University, and the New School, and worked for many years at the Social Science Research Council, in New York. He currently chairs the Board of Directors of the North American Congress on Latin America (NACLA). He is coeditor, with Paul Drake, of *State and Society in Conflict: Comparative Perspectives on Andean Crises* (2006) and, with Fred Rosen, of *Latin America after Neoliberalism: Turning the Tide in the 21st Century?* (2006).

LUCIO RENNO, an associate professor in the research center and graduate program on the Americas at the University of Brasilia, received a doctorate in political science from the University of Pittsburgh. He was a Rockefeller Fellow at Stony Brook University in 2004–2005 and in 2009–2010 held a Humboldt Foundation Research Fellowship at the Institute for Global and Area Studies in Hamburg, Germany. He has published on elections and legislation in the *American Journal of Political Science*, *Journal of Politics*, *Electoral Studies*, *Journal of Latin American Studies*, *Latin America Politics and Society*, *Journal of Legislative Studies*, and in various Brazilian journals. He is the author of three recent books in Portuguese on political reform in Brazil.

LUIS REYGADAS is a professor and recent coordinator of the graduate anthropology program at Universidad Autónoma Metropolitana, Iztapalapa, Mexico. His recent areas of research include social movements, exclusion, and inequalities, and he has published books on the mining industry, maquiladoras, work cultures, and local development. Among his recent publications are *Ensamblando culturas: Diversidad y conflicto en la globalización de la industria* (2002) and *La apropiación: Destejiendo las redes de la desigualdad* (2008).

PAUL GOOTENBERG is a professor of history and
sociology at Stony Brook University.

LUIS REYGADAS is a professor in the graduate
anthropology program at the Universidad Autónoma
Metropolitana, in Mexico.

Library of Congress Cataloging-in-Publication Data
Indelible inequalities in Latin America : insights from
history, politics, and culture / edited by Paul
Gootenberg and Luis Reygadas; foreword by Eric
Hershberg.
p. cm.
Includes bibliographical references and index.
ISBN 978-0-8223-4719-4 (cloth : alk. paper)
ISBN 978-0-8223-4734-7 (pbk. : alk. paper)
1. Equality—Latin America. 2. Social classes—Latin
America. I. Gootenberg, Paul, 1954– II. Reygadas,
Luis.
HN110.5.Z9S6458 2010
305.098—dc22
2010016646